The Embroidered Tent: Five Gentlewomen in Early Canada (1982)
Redney: A Life of Sara Jeannette Duncan (1983)
Below the Peacock Fan: First Ladies of the Raj (1987)
Blenheim: Biography of a Palace (1989)

IN A GILDED CAGE

IN A GILDED CAGE

From Heiress to Duchess

Marian Fowler

VINTAGE BOOKS
A Division of Random House of Canada, Toronto

Canadian Cataloguing in Publication Data
Fowler, Marian, 1929-
In a gilded cage: from heiress to duchess

ISBN 0-394-22389-6

1. Nobility – Great Britain – Biography. 2. Upper classes – New York (N.Y.) – Biography.
3. Wives – Great Britain – Biography. 4. Marriage – England – History – 19th century.
I. Title.

DA562.F68 1993   941.081′092′2   C93-094043-1

Printed and bound in the United States of America
10 9 8 7 6 5 4 3 2 1

Toronto, New York, London, Sydney, Auckland

THIS BOOK IS DEDICATED
WITH LOVE
TO ROBERT CRAMER
("POPPET")
WHO APPRECIATES LIFE'S GILDING

CONTENTS

She's only a bird in a gilded cage,
A beautiful sight to see.
You may think she's happy and free from care,
She's not tho' she seems to be.

—POPULAR SONG OF 1899
Words by Arthur J. Lamb
Music by Harry von Tilzer

INTRODUCTION

"The almighty dollar will buy, you bet, / A superior class of coronet," sings the heroine of the Edwardian musical comedy *The American Girl*, winking broadly at her audience. "That's why I've come from over the way / From New York City in U.S.A.," she trills, with a saucy flip of her bustle. In Gertrude Atherton's novel *His Fortunate Grace* (1897), Augusta Forbes, an American girl with a dowry of five million almighty dollars, buys herself a British husband who is mean-spirited, undersized, oversexed, utterly penniless — but a Duke, and Augusta is thrilled to be his bride.

Such transatlantic unions were the fashion of the time. Between 1870 and 1914, 454 American girls captured titled Europeans, or their sons, in the highly competitive scramble. One American social historian, E. Digby Baltzell, estimates that more than $220 million crossed the Atlantic in the wake of these so-called dollar princesses.

For an outlay of only $1, American girls could go peer-shopping comfortably at home through the pages of *Titled Americans*, issued quarterly in New York, revised annually, illustrated with enticing "armorial bearings." It not only listed "American Ladies Who Have Married Foreigners of Rank" but at the back gave a carefully compiled list of eligible nobles still on the loose. Girls who preferred to inspect peers in their natural habitat crowded onto the steamships that, once the Civil War was over, began to offer frequent, comfortable transatlantic travel. The girls set sail with high-flying hopes, and low-necked ballgowns carefully folded into huge steamer trunks between tissue-paper dreams. Mama usually accompanied her American daughter, but not Papa; he was much too busy in New York or points west earning the necessary dollars to pay, first of all, for all the fans, feather boas and lace parasols considered essential peer bait and, second, for the peer himself once he was caught.

Of those 454 girls who succeeded in their quest, 354 had to be content with nobles from Continental Europe. They were less desirable than British ones, not only because they spoke a different language but also because of their debased status. European monarchies had crumbled; moreover, unlike British custom, every son of a European noble, not just the eldest, got a title and a piece of the ancestral pie, if any still remained.

One hundred lucky girls found husbands in the British peerage, forty making do with younger sons, sixty marrying the titled article himself. The British peerage, unlike deposed and dime-a-dozen European nobility, was powerful and properly discriminating. Peers sat in the House of Lords and, in their wakeful moments there, helped rule the country; laws of primogeniture gave title, land, castles, heirlooms, everything, to the eldest son, and laws of entail made sure that all the family treasures and land got passed on intact. At the bottom of peerage pecking order came knights (lifetime peers) and wives; baronets (hereditary) and wives, both addressed as Sir and Lady. Above them in ascending rank were Baron and Baroness; Viscount and Viscountess; Earl and Countess; Marquess and Marchioness, all referred to in everyday parlance as Lord and Lady. Next came Duke and Duchess, both addressed in person as Your Grace, right below the Princes and Princesses who were offspring of King and Queen. The heir to the throne was Prince of Wales; other sons were plain Prince or, if the King so willed, the more exalted Duke.

Apart from the Royal Dukes, there were only twenty-seven others in Britain, whose ancestors somewhere, sometime, had stood tall and brave enough to be rewarded in perpetuity with highest title and richest gifts of land and jewels by a grateful monarch. The eldest son used one of the Duke's secondary titles — Dukes had a long string of them — usually Viscount or

Marquess, until he succeeded to the Dukedom. Other offspring of a Duke and Duchess were Lords and Ladies.

In the forty-four years from 1870 to 1914, among those hundred American girls who married into the British peerage, only six secured Dukes. The Southern belle, Consuelo Yznaga, married the future 8th Duke of Manchester in 1876; in 1888 Lily Hammersley reeled in the 8th Duke of Marlborough; in 1895 Consuelo Vanderbilt, godchild of the first Consuelo, secured the 9th Duke of Marlborough. Five years later, Helena Zimmerman from Cincinnati caught Consuelo Yznaga's son, the 9th Duke of Manchester. And in 1903 May Goelet landed the greatest catch of all: the handsome 8th Duke of Roxburghe. (A sixth American girl, an actress called Mary Yohe, wed the 8th Duke of Newcastle, but since she used only beauty, not bullion, as lure, for she wasn't an heiress, she doesn't fit the norm and won't appear in this study. The Duke married her in 1894, and in spite of the fact that she danced for him with the Hope diamond flashing in her navel, he divorced her in 1902; perhaps he decided, after an eight-year assessment, that beauty just wasn't enough.)

The number of dollars bartered for a life with His Grace, the Duke, escalated from first-wed bride to last, thus proving the law of supply and demand. The number of eligible Dukes at any one time remained constant at two or three — the rest of the twenty-seven being minors or married or moribund. Since the mania for marrying Dukes steadily increased in America between 1876 and 1903, up went the price. Like so many other customs in colonial America, that of the dowry, whereby a father gives a lump sum of money to his daughter's bridegroom, originated in Europe, where it had been entrenched since early Greek and Roman civilizations. Consuelo Yznaga's Duke was content with a dowry of $1 million, a mere bagatelle; the Duke of Roxburghe considered himself fully worthy of May Goelet's $20 million.

But dollars were the least of it. In other ways all five American women paid a high price for the title of Duchess. Challenges and changes and culture shocks were many and profound. Raised in a freewheeling, young, open society, they found themselves after marriage locked into a rigid, time-worn, closed one.

Both American and British societies of the time, however, were equally patriarchal, so that pressures on these women to conform to the selfless roles of daughter, wife and mother were strong. The ideal of female behavior endorsed in the United States from about 1820 until 1865, when Consuelo Yznaga and Lily Hammersley were growing up, was that of the "True Woman," so named in conduct books of the period, which young ladies were given as birthday gifts and required to read and heed. Most of the books were British in origin, reprinted in America in numerous editions throughout the century. As Helen Papashvily points out in *All the Happy Endings* (1956), American domestic novels of mid-century reinforced the stereotype with heroines drawn from a single pattern: hair and brow smooth, eyes and head drooping, rosebud mouth pursed, the best-known being Elsie Dinsmore, the saccharine creation of Martha Finley, who churned out almost one Elsie book a year from 1867 to 1909. Elsie is a sweet, prudish, long-suffering prig of a Southern girl, but her contemporaries loved her. When her father barks out an order, Elsie obeys, even if it means playing the piano until she faints, falls off the stool and cracks her head open.

True Women like Elsie, before all else, were pious, their lives being one long act of devotion: to God, husband, children, servants, the poor, humanity. Second, they were passive, without any desire to strive or achieve for themselves. Third, they were "pure." Marriage was their career — spinsters were pitied and regarded as failures — and virginity and total sexual ignorance were crucial counters in the marriage mart:

> *Her eye of light is the diamond bright,*
> *Her innocence the pearl,*
> *And those are ever the bridal gems*
> *That are worn by the American girl.*

So begins the poem "The American Girl" in *The Young Lady's Offerings*. As Dr. William Acton notes in *The Functions and*

Disorders of the Reproductive Organs, published in England and re-printed throughout the nineteenth century in America, True Women had no erotic urges whatsoever: "The majority of women (happily for society)," he writes, "are not very much troubled with sexual feeling of any kind." Women were never to think about "impure subjects nor to allow men to discuss them in their presence." Alexis de Tocqueville remarks in *Democracy in America* (1835) that American men "always show by their conduct that they consider women virtuous and refined, and that in their presence everyone is guarded in his remarks, to avoid obliging them to hear language which might offend them."

In addition to her piety, passivity and purity, the True Woman, as an 1850 article in *Putnam's* magazine puts it, knew that "domesticity is her honor and glory." Once she was married, her sphere of activity was the home front, not the wider world beyond.

After the Civil War, sparked in part by the publication in England of John Stuart Mill's *On the Subjection of Women* (1869), a different role model called the New Woman appeared in the United States, and steadily gained converts while Consuelo Vanderbilt, Helena Zimmerman and May Goelet were growing up. Mill objected strenuously to the fact that "all the moralities" and "all current sentimentalities" told women that "it is their nature to live for others; to make complete abnegation of themselves." The New Woman demanded the right to have a proper career outside the home, to remain unwed from choice, not because no man had asked her, to vote and smoke and ride a bicycle — this last being a crucial advance, as we shall see in Consuelo Vanderbilt's story. The proportion of American women who never married, which from 1770 to 1970 varied from 11 to 4 percent, was highest in the years 1860 to 1900. The New Woman jettisoned piety, submissiveness and domesticity but hung on to her moral purity. Charles Dana Gibson sketched her in *Life* magazine in boater hat, tailored no-nonsense skirt that cleared the ground and high-necked shirtwaist whose leg-o'-mutton sleeves clearly advertised her new muscular aggression.

The New Woman, or "American Girl," as she was often called, became in the 1880s and 1890s the revered symbol for a fast-growing, industrial nation that, like her, embodied confidence, enthusiasm, initiative, "snap" and "go." The American Girl *was* America, not only to her own countrymen but to the rest of the world. When Lily Hammersley arrived in London in 1888 as bride of the 8th Duke of Marlborough, his English friends called her "Hail, Columbia." (Lily was tall and well built; perhaps she brought to mind the two-year-old Statue of Liberty.) In Henry James's novel *The Portrait of a Lady* (1881), Ralph Touchett sketches Isabel Archer, that exemplary American girl, draped in the American flag and calls her "Columbia." In his book *The Land of Contrasts: A Briton's View of His American Kin* (1908), James Fullerton Muirhead describes the American girl as far bolder and freer than her English cousin, admiring "her candour, her frankness...her spontaneity, her vivacity, her fearlessness." He was charmed by her "fearless individuality" and "the absence of undue deference to masculine dignity." "In no country are women, and especially young women," agreed James, Lord Bryce in *The American Commonwealth* (1912), "so much made of. The world is at their feet. Society seems organized for the purpose of providing enjoyment for them."

Why would 454 of these splendid, freewheeling young creatures give up their American citizenship, as they were required to do when they married foreigners, and eagerly turn their backs on family, friends and a homeland that adored and indulged them? What could possibly have propelled them across the cold Atlantic to ancient heraldic arms?

The transatlantic marriage trend was sparked, first of all, by social ambition, both the bride's and her parents'. To understand it, we need to take a quick look back along the path American society had followed. In colonial days, settlers, many of them British, almost without exception were middle or lower class. As the old adage puts it, "Dukes don't emigrate." Because they came from Europe, American colonists sought status through the ownership of land. As the eighteenth century waned, most of the fertile, accessible land had been claimed, and cities where the mercantile class was beginning its rise to dominance grew bigger. Culture came from Europe; almost all books published in America were reprints from England and France. Then came the American Revolution of 1776.

A young nation with strong political, cultural and racial ties to parent Britain found them suddenly, brutally, severed. Americans felt rejected, angry, full of wounded pride. Relations with Britain for the next few years were frosty and strained, and the Canadian-American skirmish of 1812 exacerbated them further. By the time the Civil War came, anger and animosity to Britain had cooled, and two types of aristocracy were struggling for dominance: the rural Southern aristocracy securely tied to land and the urban Northern plutocracy tied to industry: a group of bankers, mill owners, shipping magnates, speculators in real estate, who were getting richer every day and who ultimately prevailed. By 1865, as Frances Hodgson Burnett explains it in *The Shuttle*, old grievances against Britain "having had time to fade away" were replaced by "something akin to homesickness." "Americans in increasing numbers," she writes, discovered that "it was the simplest thing in the world to drive down to the wharves" and take a steamer headed for England. "We were children put out to nurse and breathe new air in the country," declares Bettina Vanderpoel, *The Shuttle's* American heroine who weds a British lord. "Now we are coming home, vigorous and full-grown."

And extremely class-conscious. Ever since Thomas Jefferson and the other founding fathers declared that "all men are created equal," Americans had been quietly creating their class divisions and hierarchy. As the novelist William Dean Howells realized, "inequality is as dear to the American heart as liberty itself." It may well be that an American can move more freely than a European from one class to another, but the class strata are definitely there, and once America had finished the Civil War, left its sleepy, rural agricultural past behind it and headed in a great rush toward an urban, industrial future of great economic prosperity, the basis of America's class structure was a very simple one: money. Three main classes, upper, middle and lower, possessed a great deal of money, less money and no money, respectively. John Adams had spotted this simple class determinant as early as 1808: "We have one material which actually constitutes an aristocracy that governs the nation," he noted. "That material is wealth. Talents, birth, virtues, services, sacrifices, are of little consideration with us." America's upper class came to be subdivided, as capitalism flourished and wealth piled up, into Old Money and New, depending on how long a family had had it, and whether it was inherited or earned. Old Money kept its frock coat on; New Money was still in shirtsleeves.

Old Money tended to marry at home one of their own kind, but the New Rich, believing, in their new consumer society, that money could buy anything, set about legitimizing and improving their social status by buying up everything from the Old World that the American collective unconscious still hungered for, including castles and coronets, Counts and Dukes. America's plutocracy saw a way to recover what their raw republic lacked: class distinctions more finely discriminated, more subtle than economic ones; the inherited gentility of a land-based elite, such as the South had once had; the panoply and pomp of ermine and glass coaches and heraldic banners. In short, the New Rich longed, lusted for the *poetry* of class. The brave gunfire and bright rhetoric of the Revolution had been too sudden, too precipitate. Only Reason could assent; Imagination dragged its feet like a small child, pulled, protesting, toward a practical future, looking back over its shoulder to a romantic European past.

Two recent books examine this ongoing American hunger for aristocracy: *The Wish for Kings: Democracy at Bay* (1993), by the editor of *Harper's* magazine, Lewis H. Lapham, and *The Refinement of America: Persons, Houses, Cities* (1992), by the historian Richard L. Bushman. Bushman demonstrates that the desire for refinement, respectability and gentility has always been as powerful a force in American life as the belief in work and equality.

In the last two decades of the nineteenth century, it was Britain, not the United States, that was the foremost world power.

In 1895, the year Anglo-American marriages peaked, the British Empire comprised one-quarter of the land surface of the globe and one-quarter of the world's population: eleven million square miles, 372 million people. It was a cliché that "the sun never sets on the British Empire," but it was true.

Beginning in the 1870s, when the first wave of American girls boarded steamships, Anglomania in American society became a positive fever, particularly in New York, where most of the New Rich congregated, home to half of those 454 brides, and to all but one American Duchess. In the 1880s Tiffany and Company felt compelled to open a special heraldry department to attend to "blazoning, marshalling and designing of arms," almost all of them bogus. In 1886 Mrs. Burton Harrison, a smart New York hostess, satirized the rage for all things English in *The Anglomaniacs*, a novel appearing in *Century* magazine, illustrated by Charles Dana Gibson. The refrain of an American comic song of the 1880s declared: "O the things that we say, the queer things we do / Are English, you know! Quite English, you know!"

In addition to social ambition, each bride married for the sake of her imagination, fed since childhood on fairy tales of moats and castles and sentimental novels of swashbuckling knights. Since young ladies were programmed not to acknowledge to themselves any erotic urges toward the opposite sex, all such sexual feelings got channeled into the romantic projections of overheated imaginations.

Motives for marrying, if we turn to the Dukes, were a simpler matter altogether. They had to marry, for Dukes had to sire the next Duke, and while they were often very good at siring, the next Duke had to be born within the legal institution of marriage. For begetting a son, however, an English bride would serve. Dukes and lesser nobles chose American ones because, not to put too fine a point on it, they were hard-pressed for cash. "The plain truth is," an Englishwoman told George Smalley, London correspondent for the *New York Times* in 1889, that "every Englishman who has married an American has married money." Beginning in the 1870s, English Dukes found themselves losing income and prestige; American dollars could recoup both. Late-nineteenth-century Britain, like America, moved from an agrarian, rural nation to an industrial, urban one. Its population, which doubled during Queen Victoria's reign, deserted the countryside and went to work in city factories. Dukes and other great landowners lost their tenants — and their rent rolls. Apart from the tenant drain, they were hit by a severe agricultural depression lasting until World War I — most of it America's fault. The opening of the American prairies to wheat growing led to the lowering of British grain prices; the innovation of refrigeration on ever-faster ships meant that American meat took more trade away from Britain. Peers were further impoverished by income taxes and death duties, imposed in 1894 and increased in 1909. One couldn't go into trade or sell ancestral acres; it simply wasn't done. Americans had caused these woes; let them make amends. Let them make an offer of dollars-cum-daughters.

It wasn't as if marrying for money was anything new. Peers had been doing that for three hundred years, so it was a tradition, which made it quite all right. Heretofore, with few heiresses in their own circle, peers had pumped new pounds into sagging fortunes by marrying the well-dowered daughters of the British trading class. Any quick dip into eighteenth-century memoirs and letters will yield examples of this ongoing barter of pounds for peers. Lord Fermanagh's son married a banker's daughter in 1740 and had £40,000 transferred to his account. In 1793 the Earl of Pomfret got a wine merchant's daughter worth £90,000, not to mention a lot of free wine, and when, in 1787, the Earl of Pembroke's son married his penniless first cousin, his father sighed mightily: "It would have been lucky for us, had ye found a thirty-thousand pounder as agreeable to ye." By the time Anthony Trollope wrote *The Way We Live Now* (1875), bolstering noble purses with mercantile pounds had "become an institution, like primogeniture, and is almost as serviceable for maintaining the proper order of things. Rank squanders money; trade makes it — and then trade purchases rank by regilding its splendor."

Now if a Duke should opt for precise precedent and choose a rich English merchant's daughter, he would feel the class degradation every time she got her tongue around a vowel, and her vulgar relatives would be always on his marble doorstep. An American girl was outside the tight hierarchy of British class, and with any luck, her relatives would stay on their own side of the Atlantic.

There was one other reason for choosing an American heiress. Britain was fast acquiring its own plutocracy — men like Cecil Rhodes, who'd made his fortune in South African diamond and gold mines, and Thomas Lipton, who'd got rich from Indian tea plantations. These new members of Society were not so much the nouveaux riches as the real rich — and they liked to fling their wealth about in ostentatious ways, by building enormous Park Lane mansions and racing thoroughbreds. If Dukes wanted to keep abreast and not lose prestige, they needed new money, too. And they certainly weren't going to get it by dirtying their hands in the Empire's outposts, for to actually *work* meant loss of status. An American bride was a capital solution.

What about love, one might well ask indignantly, taking a twentieth-century stance. Surely love was a motivation? In eighteenth-century Britain and America, love was not an expected prelude to marriage. Choosing a life partner was a practical, rational affair based on mutual "esteem" — the key word. One widely circulated anonymous treatise, *Reflections on Courtship and Marriage* (1779), sees the ideal match as "a union of mind, and a sympathy of mutual esteem and friendship for each other." Middle and upper classes shared this view.

In the nineteenth century, inspired by the Romantic movement, which emphasized emotion over reason, the idea of love in courtship gained some currency among Britain's middle class and became strongly institutionalized among America's. Basing their view on Plato's concept, reintroduced by the Romantic movement, that for every passive, emotional female there existed somewhere her ideal missing half, an active, rational male, middle-class Americans believed that all the two halves had to do was meet and marry and live happily ever after in perfect, blissful union.

The British upper class, in the nineteenth and early twentieth century, continued to discount love as a reason for marrying. Lady Dolly in *Moths* (1908), by the English novelist Ouida (Marie Louise de la Ramée), sums up the typical attitude: "Love and marriage are two totally different things; they ought never to be named together; they are cat and dog; one kills the other." When, in *The Making of a Marchioness* (1901), by Frances Hodgson Burnett, the Marquess of Walderhurst proposes to Englishwoman Emily Fox-Seton he tells her bluntly, "I am not a marrying man, but I must marry, and I like you better than any woman I have ever known," with no mention of love. Emily is thrilled to accept him, for she "had not lived in a world where marriage was a thing of romance."

Unlike the British, the American upper class, if rather grudgingly, made room for love. Sir Nigel Anstruthers, in *The Shuttle* (1907), by Burnett, is amazed to discover, while courting an American heiress, Rosalie Vanderpoel, that "in the matter of marriage, Americans had an ingenuous tendency to believe in the sentimental feelings of the parties concerned." Upper-class parents, nonetheless, realizing that large amounts of money and property were at stake, took steps to keep sentiments of love between marriageable offspring on a tight rein. Young ladies were strictly chaperoned by mothers or elders at all social events; a single male was never allowed to be alone with a single girl unless they were engaged, and then only in a carriage; the services of matchmakers were sometimes used; and finally, if a daughter did fall in love and choose a spouse on her own initiative, parents still had the right to veto her choice.

In light of all this, a British Duke and his American bride entered matrimony with very different attitudes and expectations. He liked her money; she longed for love. Cynicism and romanticism met head-on: this was one painful culture clash for each bride; two very different sexual codes produced another. American brides were conditioned to their country's Puritan attitude to adultery as a Scarlet Letter sin. Puritan sexual ideals came over on the *Mayflower* and remained strong because settlers in any colony tend to keep the manners and mores of their parent nation long after the heart of empire has modified or discarded them. British Dukes were not only unsentimental and mercenary, but liked to freely indulge their bed-hopping inclinations. All this perplexed and pained their True Woman, American brides.

In the lives of these five American duchesses were dark places where irony and pathos gathered, under the veneer. There was also a central paradox: at a time when most women were kept dependent on men because they themselves had no money, these American heiresses, each with an independent fortune, became, in many ways, the most oppressed group of all. All that talk of the American girl's freedom of self-expression was, in the final analysis, only for middle-class girls who, needing to earn money, were just beginning to attend college and have professional careers. Heiresses were idle clotheshorses and status symbols inside an extremely patriarchal group. Class works in reverse for women, so that poor ones live in a matriarchy, going out to work and controlling family pay packets. Rich men's wives and daughters, on the other hand, don't have careers or power bases, and this hasn't changed in the past hundred years.

Amid the exuberance and optimism and new freedoms of America's Gilded Age (1880–1914) when, as Mark Twain puts it, there was "invitation in the air and success in all the wide horizon," these five brides were the Age's martyrs, victims of both their own social-climbing version of the American dream and that of a greedy nation on the make. American Duchesses were raised to the level of myth and icon by a populace hungry for wealth and prestige. They were the celebrities of the time in the same way that film stars and pop singers are now. Before radio, movies and television appeared, American newspapers were powerful instruments of social and moral influence, and American Duchesses got front-page coverage of their social appearances, their wedding gifts and, in the case of Consuelo Vanderbilt, her underclothes. America's working-class women — there were over four million of them in 1890, almost all unmarried, comprising one-sixth of the labor force — hadn't much time or energy to spare for a Duchess's doings, but middle-class women read and marveled and did their best to emulate, the single ones dreaming that someday their Duke would come, the married ones noting Her Grace's dress and manners. For middle-class women, such newspaper spreads were part conduct book, part real-life romance.

As for the five American brides themselves, they walked up the aisle into confinement. "You're going to be put in a cage," Ralph Touchett warns American heroine Isabel Archer in Henry James's *The Portrait of a Lady*, as she contemplates a European marriage. Maggie Verver, having married an Italian Prince in James's *The Golden Bowl* (1904), had "flapped her little wings as a symbol of desired flight, not merely as a plea for a more gilded cage and an extra allowance of lumps of sugar."

Yet inside that prison, five American Duchesses struggled, survived and — each in her own way — triumphed on a personal level and left an indelible mark on British society as well. Confronted with a strange man and stranger land, two Duchesses leaned heavily on tried-and-true American patterns of behavior; the other three used their British milieu as a springboard to a new persona. All five lives are worth recording for two reasons beyond mere entertainment. First of all, a picture of a whole period, filled in almost to the last brush stroke, emerges as we paint the individual portraits of these five heiresses. Second, some interesting differences can be detected between British and American societies in their attitudes to wealth, women and marriage.

Beginning in the 1960s, American feminist historians have been busy detailing the lives of American middle-class and working-class women that earlier historians, mostly male, failed to record. Rich upper-class women, to date, have been either totally ignored or mentioned in passing in a way that trivializes them, reducing their lives to the minutiae of glove buttons and calling cards, denying them any real historic relevance. It is high time to give these women their dignity and their due.

CONSUELO YZNAGA

1 Consuelo Yznaga, 8th Duchess of Manchester

England is all right for splendor but dead slow for fun.

—CONSUELO,
Duchess of Manchester

IN HER GROWING-UP YEARS, Consuelo Yznaga went recklessly, rapidly, from one state to another, in both a geographical and psychological sense. She paddled from Louisiana to Mississippi and back again, often two or three times a day; she seesawed from conformist to rebel, from good girl to bad just as often. But when she married, she chose once and for all a domain and role that fitted her like a glove; after that there would be no more drift or swing.

On the Louisiana state side of the great, rushing Mississippi River, which occasionally rose up and spread over her father's cotton fields, stood Ravenswood, the plantation home where Consuelo was born in 1858. The family's two-story wooden house was painted not traditional white but a crazy canary yellow, and its second floor bulged out beyond the walls of the first, so the house looked like a big yellow mushroom that had puffed up overnight in the wake of flooding. Relaxed figures snoozed on the veranda that encircled the house; chickens and turkeys scratched lazily in sunbaked earth; undergrowth ran wild beyond. Everything at Ravenswood encouraged a wayward, lax originality.

2 Ravenswood, Consuelo's plantation home

On the Mississippi state side of the river stood the town of Natchez, named for the Indian tribe which once lived there. Civil War battles passed Natchez by, so that the pillars of its mansions remained erect, upholding past proprieties. On a spring evening in 1875, seventeen-year-old Consuelo, with a young escort and her mother as chaperone, crossed the river from Ravenswood to Natchez by boat, as they always did — there was no bridge — to attend a ball. They walked up the wide steps of an imposing house, its portico scrubbed as white as wedding-cake icing, its adjacent lawns velvet smooth. Consuelo and her mother, Ellen, shed their wraps in the cloakroom, then made their way to the ballroom where the young man waited impatiently for his pretty, vivacious partner to appear.

As Consuelo entered, everyone gasped; the young man's face blanched, his mouth hanging open. The other young ladies standing about giggled nervously in the sudden hush, all of them wearing "the usual costume of the day — tight-fitting waists and bodices," as one spectator, Edith Ogden (afterward Mrs. Carter Harrison), writes in her memoir, *Strange to Say*, where she records the details of that shocking event. The matrons present frowned, then shrugged. What could one expect of an Yznaga? Mrs. Yznaga

4

could be seen often enough smoking a cigarette, or with skirts hiked up, bare legs and feet in plain view, puddling about in some stream; her son, Fernando, at twenty-three, hardly ever wore socks.

For several minutes, no one moved or spoke; all eyes were on Consuelo. Her face was angelic, her strawberry blond hair like spun sugar, her big, clear eyes like topazes, but her figure showed no waist at all, not the slightest indentation. She ballooned and billowed in a "sort of Mother Hubbard or big white nightgown." The young man rushed up to her and begged her to go to the cloakroom and tie a sash, a ribbon, a string — anything — around her waist to confine that inadmissible free flow. Consuelo resisted. It was a warm evening. She'd put on the first comfortable garment that had come to hand and left off her corset for two reasons: she hated its rigid whalebone pinching her into the requisite eighteen inches so that she couldn't breathe, couldn't dance as wildly as a Gypsy, and she wanted to create a sensation, to stand out from other girls, to have all eyes on her.

The young man pleaded, and when Consuelo sensed his very real anxiety, she capitulated. Men were the superior sex, and women's role was to keep them happy and amused. At seventeen, Consuelo was still more Southern belle than her own fey self. She went meekly to the cloakroom, found a ribbon and returned properly cinched and confined. The young man smiled broadly and whirled her onto the dance floor while Mrs. Yznaga seemed not at all nonplussed by the event.

Ellen Yznaga was a free spirit: cultured, animated, "full of fine scorn and humor," as one Natchez resident described her. Almost six feet tall, she had olive skin, dark hair and eyes and beautiful, small hands. She had produced four children: Fernando, Natica, Consuelo and Emily, in that order. Mrs. Yznaga was the daughter of Capt. Samuel Clement who had come from Dutchess County, New York, to New Orleans to initiate steamboating on the Mississippi. He had married late, a Miss Little, from a New England family, and retired to Ravenswood when his steamboating days were over. He died there in 1833, at fifty-two, of cholera. Ellen, his only child, inherited Ravenswood and married Don

Antonio Yznaga, born near the little town of Maria Spirita in the interior of Cuba, where his family had large sugar plantations. He was related to several aristocratic houses in Spain, his mother having been a Del Valle. Ellen managed the Ravenswood plantation with its three hundred slaves and three thousand acres, while Antonio acted as Spanish Consul in New Orleans and ran a business in New York City, importing produce from Cuba. His fortune, like the Mississippi, ebbed and flowed alarmingly, and his family's Northern base shifted from Thirty-seventh Street near Fifth Avenue to the Westminster Hotel and then to Orange, New Jersey. As it did for most Southerners, the Civil War brought hard times for the Yznagas, and in 1866 Antonio had to give up his New York business and retrench at Ravenswood.

There "Miz Consuelo" ran wildly about, spoiled and indulged by black servants. On hot, humid afternoons, she lay dreaming under the orchard's peach and fig trees where tiger lilies rioted in rich earth and overhead parakeets screeched and gorged and preened their yellow-green feathers. There was no railroad anywhere near Ravenswood; its many visitors had to come across the river from Natchez. The unpretentious ten-room home was two miles inland along a mud road; it had no bathroom and was furnished simply in old-fashioned mahogany, with a rocking chair in every room. Upstairs, wooden bedsteads had their feet in glasses of oil, but somehow bugs still found their way into the tumble of sheets and quilts. The house pulsated with music, loud laughter, songs, toe-tapping. Ellen had a fine mezzo-soprano voice; Consuelo rattled away on the piano and could play any tune by ear; sister Emily was wonderfully proficient on the banjo. Like most cultured Southerners, the Yznagas prided themselves, as one British visitor to the South noted, on being "perfectly *au fait* with the literary, dramatic and personal gossip of London and Paris."

If Ravenswood formed Consuelo, Paris in the Second Empire "finished" her. Sometime after 1866, Ellen flitted off with her three daughters to the glamorous city where living was cheap, culture plentiful and where all but one of our five American brides were partly educated, acquiring a European polish and worldliness that

6

would later serve them well. In Paris Consuelo learned a new language, a new flirtatiousness and, before she left in 1870 at age twelve, a new sexual code that she was mature enough to grasp. Her witty mother was warmly welcomed into the circle of Napoléon III and Empress Eugénie and invited often to the Tuileries palace for Monday musicales and balls for five thousand guests. Consuelo was enchanted by Paris: its wide boulevards planned by Baron Haussmann, where ladies in gowns with lace-edged, ruffled skirts passed in open carriages on their way to the Bois de Boulogne; its gleaming white buildings topped with golden eagles spread against blue sky; couturier Worth's Salon de Lumière, where her mother ordered gowns and ladies primped before mirrored walls in wide crinolines. Whereas a corset constrained and diminished the female form, a crinoline, Consuelo noted, freed and amplified it. One's legs could scissor at will inside a light, steel-banded cage as one moved about, taking up plenty of space in the world's scheme of things. It was hard to ignore a bell shape three feet wide, dipping and swaying like a storm-tossed ship. Consuelo could hardly wait to grow up enough to wear a crinoline.

Paris gave Consuelo two important role models. The first was Empress Eugénie herself, who would become a lifelong friend. A beautiful Spanish adventuress with sapphire eyes and coiled auburn hair, Eugénie knew, when she came to Paris, exactly what she wanted: the Empress's crown. Emperor Louis-Napoléon lusted for a woman one minute, bedded her the next, but Eugénie resolved to win him with charm and flattery alone. He proposed to her at a Tuileries ball; he was forty-four, she twenty-six. After their marriage in 1853, he went back to his philandering and Eugénie became style-setter for a court and a country.

Consuelo was invited into the Empress's boudoir, with its white satin curtains, its crystal sea of bottles and bowls for perfume and powder. As Eugénie chattered while her hairdresser, clad in knee breeches and sword, arranged her chignon over cotton pads, Consuelo could see that a True Woman dressed with care and artifice and often used a bit of fakery.

Observing Eugénie's captivating manners, Consuelo picked up the fine art of charming and a taste for conspicuous show, for the Empress realized that a sparkling Court was not possible if one received only the out-at-elbows *ancienne noblesse* and that "money," as one French journalist put it, "is always chic." Eugénie never permitted a woman to appear twice in her presence in the same gown. Dress and decor had to be wonderfully *luxe*. The two American girls whom Consuelo met in Paris and who became lifelong friends, Jennie Jerome (later Churchill) and Alva Smith (later Vanderbilt), would help Consuelo spread the gospel of conspicuous show to England and America.

In addition to Empress Eugénie, Consuelo took as role model Princess Pauline Metternich, wife of the Austrian Ambassador. She was only twenty-two when she arrived in Paris in 1860, but very soon became its acknowledged social leader with her quick repartee, her amusing stories, her theatrical flair. From Pauline, Consuelo learned that wit was as useful a feminine lure as a fan and that Society gave a woman both a fine stage and an audience.

Consuelo was dazzled by Second Empire gloss and theatricality. She went, with her mother and sisters, to matinees at the Bouffes Parisiennes, the Comédie Française, the Opéra. She played Offenbach on the piano, and sang the songs from the revue *Paris s'amuse* (Paris at Play). "*Sans la toilette / Et le plaisir / Faut en convenir / La vie est bête*" ran the words of one song. (Without finery and pleasure, one must agree, life is just stupidity.) She would make that her life's theme song.

Consuelo also glimpsed the Second Empire's lax morality and sexual excesses, so different from still-Puritan America's, and took them in her stride. The Emperor's mistresses were legion, including a circus rider and a *Comtesse* who slept in black satin sheets to flatter her white skin. At every Tuileries party, Louis-Napoléon would sidle up to some woman who caught his fancy and whisper, "Tonight," in her ear. One *Marquise* has left an account of "tonight." At 1:30 a.m., through a secret door, into a silk-swagged, gilt-corniced room, strode Louis-Napoléon in mauve silk nightshirt with golden bees embroidered on its collar;

at 2:00 a.m., without having spoken a single word, out strode Louis-Napoléon through the same door.

Consuelo overheard her mother's friends gossiping and whispering, saw how rouged demimondaines were revered and copied for their style. Then suddenly, in 1870, Paris's music and flirting stopped, its sparkle vanished as grim Prussian soldiers marched in and took the city. All foreigners, including the Yznagas, fled, and Consuelo reluctantly returned to sleepy, backwater Ravenswood. But she had glimpsed, in crystal and looking glass, her natural milieu: a world of carefully staged make-believe. Somehow, somewhere, she would find another.

3 Consuelo (right) with her parents, Ellen and Don Antonio Yznaga

Her chance came five years later, in the summer of 1875, several months after she had disgraced herself at the Natchez ball. The Yznagas decided to take their daughters for a holiday to Saratoga Springs in New York State. Consuelo was wild with excitement as Aunt Debby, the cook and maid, stuffed Consuelo's sprigged-muslin gowns with tissue paper and stacked them in a Saratoga trunk, its iron-banded lid curved high to accommodate them. Aunt Debby also packed Consuelo's corsets and, mindful of her naughty puffery at the Natchez ball, made a firm resolve to keep Miz Consuelo properly laced at all times.

The Yznagas went first to New York, where they had a house at 262 Third Avenue. From New York, the family journeyed north by train to Saratoga Springs, where a mixed society of Yankee entrepreneurs and Southern planters showed its finery and stalked husbands for its daughters. No one came for their health any more. Saratoga, as the *New York Times* noted on July 4 that year, was "famous for its flirtations for, after all, people do not come to Saratoga to drink the waters. Miss Nellie, Miss Abbie, and Miss Fannie are here to find someone with whom they may fall in love, and who may fall in love with them, who may be acceptable to ma, and be considered eligible by pa, and who may lead them to the nuptial altar sometime next spring." Saratoga had plenty of Lovers' Walks and Lovers' Rests and Courtship Mazes and weekly dances at its grand hotel, the United States, guaranteed to prime the mating process. There was one other deluxe hotel, the Grand Union; it offered stiff competition to the United States that year because its owner, A. T. Stewart, had completely rebuilt its northeast wing to the tune of $400,000. But with three eligible daughters, the Yznagas surely chose to stay at the United States on account of its dances.

The United States Hotel had been completed only the year before, after two years' construction, the original hotel of the same name having burned down in 1865. The new one was built of brick, with 232 feet of frontage on Broadway and 655 on Division Street. It had 768 sleeping rooms and sixty-five suites. Its drawing room was superbly furnished with Axminster carpets, carved walnut and marble furniture, frescoed ceilings, lace curtains, chandeliers, mirrors. Not quite the Tuileries palace, but there was still plenty of glitter. The entire south wing, 566 feet long, called the Cottage Wing, contained suites with parlor, bathroom, water closet and from one to seven bedrooms. In one of the larger suites, Aunt Debby unpacked all the alluring lace-and-ribbon furbelows of three contenders in the matrimonial stakes, while beyond the windows waiters raced across emerald lawns, from kitchen to Cottage Wing, with huge, snowy-covered trays balanced on their heads.

In the mornings, Consuelo paraded arm in arm with Natica, up and down the hotel's "piazza" (far too elegant to be called a veranda), talking and giggling, her flounces still crisp, her little hands in kid gloves holding a lace parasol. Other girls in tandem strutted too, conscious of male eyes upon them. Young men lounged against the railings; parents sat about in rocking chairs. Mothers fanned themselves and clinked the ice in their glasses of lemonade; fathers in frock coats savored their Havana cigars; Southern and Northern accents answered each other indolently while a haze of golden dust hung below the green elms along the street as carriages passed. As the temperature went up to ninety, the fans accelerated, the curled mustaches drooped, the sideburns grew moist, but still the young ladies passed and repassed, still the young men ogled, and only Consuelo peeled off her hot kid gloves and crumpled them into a ball.

On the night of the weekly dance, she waltzed merrily into her future. The splendid setting was apt: a ballroom more than a hundred feet long, a parquet floor smooth as glass from constant rubbings with cornmeal, sparkling chandeliers suspended from a twenty-six-foot ceiling, orchestra playing Strauss waltzes from behind banked palms and ferns. It was a champagne ball, where ice cream and blancmange were served in addition to ices, and tickets cost $5 rather than the usual $2.

A slight young man with beaked nose, low forehead and sandy hair that stuck up in all the wrong places asked Consuelo to dance, held her extremely tightly, kept her hand in his when the waltz ended so that through two layers of glacé kid, his and hers, she could feel the warmth, the pressure. He'd drunk quite a lot of champagne, even though it was new brût rather than ten years old, which was what he drank in England. Talking in little spurts, running all the words together, with long pauses between, he told her he'd had rather a run of luck that day, don't you know, at the racetrack and the gaming tables. He was Viscount Mandeville, twenty-three-year-old son and heir of the 7th Duke of Manchester, as Consuelo and her mother had already ascertained. Consuelo listened, flattered him in all the pauses, flirted with eyes and fan, flaunted her innocence like a pearl drop on her forehead. This young man could lead her into a social world as shimmering with promise as the Second Empire's. He didn't look like much, but he was heir to a dukedom, and every girl in the room wanted him.

4 *Kim, the future 8th Duke of Manchester*

George Victor Drogo Montagu, always called Kim, born June 17, 1853, in London's Cavendish Square, Earl of Manchester, Viscount Mandeville and Baron Kimbolton in the peerage of England, had never met any girl at all like Consuelo. His full, sensual lips curved into a slow smile, his eyes under sandy lashes softened. She certainly wasn't like the English peers' daughters, from among whom his parents expected him to choose a wife. The typical English girl, as the American journalist George Smalley described her, was "still the bread-and-butter miss, even after she 'came out,' still the nonentity, still the shy, silent, unformed creature" she'd been in the nursery. "She is not sure of herself, or of anybody else. She has no conversation. She is what her mother and governess have made her. Her notions are purely conventional." English girls stood about in their dowdy frocks, arms stiff, eyes looking down — in consternation? — at their large feet. Consuelo wasn't at all like that. In her soft Southern drawl, she talked in a ceaseless silver-bubble stream, her eyes as round as a cat's. She was candid, familiar, perfectly natural, and she asked him disconcerting questions, and in the course of the evening told him funny stories, promising to dance for him with a Spanish shawl and sing him minstrel songs or French ones or whatever he liked best. Her innermost thoughts and feelings came gushing forth so easily; he himself couldn't possibly reciprocate. She was mercurial, different every minute, and Kim, being himself quite unoriginal and unreflective, craved novelty above all, as he always would, in women, in sport, in places.

In the days that followed, Kim was often at Consuelo's side, while Ellen made sure all the pushy mamas on the piazza knew who he was. The young couple went for walks in the Deer Park. When he and Consuelo rested in the shade of a giant oak, she changed moods again, grew indolent and dreamy, slowed the fluttering of her fan. Like other Saratoga couples, she and Kim probably rented a phaeton from the livery stable, raced out to Saratoga's lake, dismounted at Moon's for cherry cobbler and ices and reined in their horse to a walk while they detoured, and dallied, in some dead-end green lane.

Kim felt relaxed at Saratoga, almost happy. He'd been in the United States for several months, found it too Puritan and staid by half, but Saratoga was a bit wicked, like Brighton, with the same jostling, gaudy, riotous mix and mood. Kim played faro and roulette in the smoky main-floor rooms of the Club House, where no women were allowed, while John Morrissey, "Old Smoke," the owner, immensely fat and wheezing, with a new cigar always sprouting from his mouth, stood outside waving a green umbrella and directing carriages. Kim placed his bets at the racetrack, and doffed his gray top hat to the painted prostitutes who circled in open carriages, advertising themselves as best they could, since they weren't allowed to promenade in hotel lobbies. Kim enjoyed his gambling and Consuelo, in that order.

Whether Kim returned to England for the intervening months or remained in America is not known, but the early spring of 1876 found him accepting an invitation from the Yznagas to visit them at Ravenswood. There he smelled the scent of cape-jasmine hedges, listened to the mockingbirds, felt the South's sybaritic spell wrap him round with Consuelo at its seductive center. Old South families conveniently forgot the Yznagas' eccentricities, came to meet a real live Duke-to-be, stayed to dine on mock-turtle soup, stuffed shad, escalloped oysters, prawn pie. Kim felt suspended in a dream, but one evening the dream grew fevered, rooms spun round, Consuelo's face ballooned and thinned. He had contracted typhoid and was prostrate in bed for many days.

Ellen was all smiles. A captive peer, in a weakened state; dear Consuelo must nurse him. When the neighboring matrons heard the news, their lips tightened. Those wild Yznagas had cornered a Viscount; normal courtship conventions, extremely strict in Southern families, could be completely bypassed! The usual pattern was for a young man to dispatch a friend to ask the chosen one's father if he might call. All very slow and tedious. Couples were never left alone. The young man played endless games of dominoes with the girl's father, while her mother asked him searching questions about his intentions, for no girl wanted to waste her wiles on a man who had "a heart like an artichoke" with a leaf for every girl he met. Southern girls were, of course, all bent on marriage; if they hadn't found husbands by the age of twenty-five, they might as well throw their corsets to the back of the armoire and sink down, ruefully, into the swamp of spinster-hood. It was harder now for Southern belles to find mates; the fabulous balls and parties of antebellum Louisiana had never resumed after the Civil War. Everyone envied the Yznagas.

Don Antonio stopped fishing in Lake St. John long enough to visit the sickroom and tell the lackluster Viscount that he would give Consuelo a dowry of £200,000 (by that day's reckoning, the equivalent of $1 million). Kim had gone through a good deal of money in the United States, what with his dedication to gambling, and, in any case, he was always short of funds. He came from a long line of spendthrifts, culminating, but not ending, with the 7th Duke, his father. Kim proposed to Consuelo and was accepted.

She was ecstatic, caught up in a whirl of congratulations and elder sister Natica's envious eyes and herself center stage and so much to decide on, all the trousseau gowns to be ordered and twelve dozen of everything hand embroidered. When she looked in the mirror she saw her springy curls topped by the heirloom Manchester tiara, with its heart-shaped scrollwork four inches high, all diamonds, huge ones, or the Duchess's coronet, eight strawberry leaves above a rim of gold. She was eighteen; it was all an impetuous lark, a thrilling adventure, a way to keep the spot-light trained on *her*, someday soon to be Duchess of Manchester, pet and darling of British Society.

Kim, meanwhile, in trepidation, put off announcing his engage-ment to his parents. The bombshell, however, found its own way to Kimbolton Castle, the ducal seat in Huntingdonshire. On Monday, March 13, William Drogo Montagu, 7th Duke of Manchester, made a terse entry in his diary where, in cryptic comments over the next fortnight, we can read his anger and grim consternation that his harebrained son would, even for a minute, contemplate marriage with a vulgar American. His pen scored the paper deeply:

Monday, March 13.
Louise [his wife] heard from Augusta I.W. of Kim's intended marriage to Miss Yznaga.

Saturday, March 18.
At dinner telegram from Dufferin [then Governor-General of Canada, resident in Ottawa]. Kim to be married on 8 April. Answer: "Try to prevent it."

Sunday, March 19.
Wrote Mrs. Yznaga. Kim extravagant and weak.

Monday, March 27.
Telegram from Kim: "Mind made up. Telegraph consent."

Tuesday, March 28.
Letter from Kim affectionate and dutiful. Louise wrote and telegraphed to him. Self wrote to Mrs. Yznaga.

Tuesday, April 4.
Telegram from Mrs. Yznaga. No answer.

Ellen Yznaga could feel that cold wind of ducal displeasure and disdain blowing across the Atlantic, but she ignored it and sailed blithely on, scheduling the wedding for Monday, May 22, in New York.

Edith "Pussy" Wharton, born Edith Newbold Jones in New York in 1862, into an Old Money family, records in her novel *The Buccaneers* the "indecent haste" of the marriage of Miss Conchita Closson, a Southern belle closely modeled on Consuelo Yznaga, to the rakish Lord Richard Marable, clearly modeled on Viscount Mandeville. Edith Wharton's biographer, R. W. B. Lewis, affirms that Edith knew Consuelo "as a young girl"; they would renew their friendship later in London. Ellen Yznaga knew, as Wharton notes in *The Buccaneers*, that "in good society it was usual for a betrothal to last at least a year," but Ellen paid little heed to convention. She did, however, follow Southern custom, which decreed that Mondays and Tuesdays were the best days for weddings. Wednesdays and Thursdays would do in a pinch, but Friday never, being Hangman's Day, and Saturday and Sunday were "common."

The Yznagas left Ravenswood for their Third Avenue brownstone and secured Grace Episcopalian Church for the wedding. Southern society, beginning with the tidewater planters of Virginia, had always allied itself with the Church of England, which in America was renamed the Protestant Episcopal Church.

Ellen and Antonio Yznaga were pleased that through Consuelo's marriage they were forging closer ties to Europe, where they felt most at home. Antonio's roots were in Spain; Ellen had lived in France; like all Southerners, their cultural ties to Britain were strong. With land holdings of their own in Louisiana and Cuba, the Yznagas were gratified to form bonds with Britain's landowning elite, and to recapture, at one remove, what the South had lost in the Civil War: an aristocratic, hierarchical society with all its usual traditions of gentility, cultural refinement and hereditary preoccupations, for in its colonial days the South, like Britain, had espoused the laws of primogeniture and entail.

Ellen Yznaga carefully compiled her invitation list, a mix of Old Money names with plenty of New. New York's Old Money families had inherited, not earned, wealth, and had mainly Dutch forebears. They were the "Knickerbockers," or as they later became known, the "nobs," who lived in plain brownstones near Washington Square and formed a tight little clique. Like the social elites of Boston and Philadelphia, Knickerbockers could trace their ancestors back to America's colonial beginnings; they valued lineage, privacy and culture.

In the 1870s, these Old Money families of New York, the Schermerhorns, Rhinelanders, Goelets and Livingstons, felt their preeminence threatened by the New Rich, those with earned, mostly first-generation wealth, the so-called swells or goldfish who were trying to elbow their way in and who were building vulgar, ostentatious mansions along Fifth Avenue. In *The Buccaneers* and *The Age of Innocence*, Edith Wharton cleverly, catching all the nuances, details the changes taking place in the 1870s inside the "great gilt cage" that was Society, as New Money pushed against the bars, replacing Knickerbocker values of lineage, privacy and culture with new ones of money, publicity and costly material goods.

Ellen and Antonio Yznaga were far too bohemian and worldly for most narrow, straitlaced Knickerbockers, but a few fingered their invitations, conceded Mr. and Mrs. Yznaga's cultural savvy and decided to grace the wedding with their presence.

Gifts in beribboned boxes, many from Black, Starr and Frost, New York's fashionable jeweler, were delivered to the Yznaga house by a steady stream of liveried footmen. Custom decreed that wedding gifts be personal items for the bride — grooms were ignored — rather than household goods. Consuelo tore off the tissue, crumpled the ribbons, exclaimed in wonder at jewels, laces, fans, adornments fit for Empress Eugénie — or a spectacular Duchess destined for a long run.

As one might expect, New Rich wedding guests sent the showiest presents: priceless point lace from Consuelo's friends Minnie Stevens and Alva Smith Vanderbilt; a jeweled locket and sleeve buttons from James Gordon Bennett, Jr.; heavy gold bracelets from Leonard Jerome, father of her dear friend Jennie. The most stunning gift of all was a diamond-and-ruby bracelet splendid enough for the wrist of a Queen — which, as we shall see, was exactly where it ended up. The bracelet was from the Edward Luckmeyers. He was a rich importer who stormed Society by giving the costliest dinner ever at Delmonico's, New York's most fashionable restaurant, on February 17, 1873, for seventy-two carefully chosen guests. Luckmeyer did what one might expect of a goldfish: he had a thirty-foot oval pool built down the length of the table, with gold-wire netting reaching to the ceiling, four real swans, drugged for the occasion, gliding up and down, and gold cages of songbirds suspended above. Society gasped, smiled and inched open its doors.

For Consuelo, the wedding ceremony itself on May 22 was glimpsed through a white-lace mist with the groom a mere shadow figure. It was the cheering crowds, the push and melee, that she would remember. Only one American girl before her had captured a British peer: on April 15, 1874, Jennie Jerome had married a younger son of the 7th Duke of Marlborough, Lord Randolph Churchill, but the marriage had taken place at the British Embassy in Paris, so New York had no chance to gape, and the *New York Times* accorded it only one line of type. The Yznaga-Mandeville nuptials were mobbed by sightseers and received full coverage in the *Times* and *Tribune*, for in 1876 Anglomania in America, particularly in New York, was in its first fine frenzy.

The wedding at Grace Church on Broadway near Tenth was scheduled for three-thirty in the afternoon, but hours before, Broadway was packed all the way to Fourteenth Street with carriages and sightseers as fourteen hundred people hurried to the church. "Fully an hour previous to the beginning of the ceremony," the *New York Times* noted, "all the seats in the church were filled, and around the chancel were gathered in great confusion a large crowd of ladies who watched with eager and anxious faces the coming of the bridal party." The few Knickerbockers present squirmed and whispered in their pews as the procession started up the aisle. Ellen Yznaga had flouted Form again!

The bride on her father's arm came first, as she should, looking like an angel in white satin damask trimmed with point lace, her face — was it *powdered?* — obscured by a white point-lace veil. But behind her, not stationed unobtrusively at the altar, as he should have been, slouched the groom himself, in full, plain, public view, the Yznagas' great plum, the nobbiest nob of all, Earl of Manchester, Viscount Mandeville, Baron Kimbolton, disappointingly small, with sandy hair neatly parted on the left side but sticking up like pigs' bristles on the crown. In hot pursuit behind him, dreaming of peer spouses for themselves, came five attendants, all in white, clutching white lilacs, including Consuelo's sisters Natica and Emily, and friend Minnie Stevens, already four years on the trail but with no peer in sight.

Dark-haired, twenty-three-year-old Minnie, who would play a key role in Consuelo's English life, had hard green eyes, a sharp little nose and a determined chin. From a front pew, her mother, Mrs. Paran Stevens, dreamed and schemed as darling Minnie walked up the aisle to the wedding march. Marietta Reed, daughter of a grocer from Lowell, Massachusetts, had married Paran Stevens in 1850 when she was nineteen and he was a widower in his forties, owner of a chain of hotels. The hotel business prospered, but when the New Rich Stevenses moved into 244 Fifth Avenue, no Knickerbockers came to call, for they had heard that Marietta had once been a chambermaid in one of her husband's hotels. When the Prince of Wales came to town in 1860 and booked into the Fifth Avenue Hotel, built by Paran two years before, Marietta saw her chance. Minnie was fetched from the nursery to meet the Prince. When Paran died in 1872, Marietta and Minnie set sail for England, and two years later Minnie was dancing as Ace of Hearts in the Card Quadrille at Marlborough House, the Prince's London home, but that was, thus far, her only coup. Minnie had promised to take enough time off husband-hunting to launch Consuelo into the Prince's set.

At the rear of the bridal procession walked the best man, Col. William Jay, lawyer and hard-playing sportsman, and the six ushers, including Fernando Yznaga, properly dressed right down to his socks, and Kim's crony, Englishman Sir Bache Cunard, twenty-four-year-old grandson of the founder of Cunard Steamship Lines. In 1895 Sir Bache would wed *his* rich American, Maud Burke of San Francisco, heiress to an uncle's millions. Maud wanted to marry Polish Prince André Poniatowski, but he jilted her, so she settled for Sir Bache, second Baronet, a fox-hunting, horse-racing Leicestershire squire with whom she had nothing in common. Maud consoled herself for a bad marriage with emeralds ("Call me Emerald," she instructed her friends) and with the Anglo-Irish novelist George Moore as longtime lover. Maud and Consuelo would become good friends in London.

The bridal party reached the altar and the Reverend Morgan Dix began the marriage service while New Rich women, awash in bugle beads and pearls, counted Old Money ladies in faded brocades smelling of camphor. There was Ward McAllister, Society's self-appointed ringmaster, in his Savile Row suit. Ward was a pompous little man with large mustache and larger pretensions, the biggest snob and Anglomaniac in New York. Born in Savannah, Georgia, in 1827, he'd made an easy fortune in San Francisco in its Gold Rush days, an even easier one by marrying the well-dowered daughter of a rich Georgian. Ward had come to New York in 1852 and begun his task of trying to define and limit and contain Society in a kind of invisible netting whose size he would determine. In 1872 he'd set up the twenty-five Patriarchs to sponsor balls; in 1892 he would list in the *New York Times* "the 400" who regularly found themselves in Caroline Astor's ballroom. But goldfish, more and more of them, just kept finding their way inside Ward's circle. He dearly loved a lord, so when Lord Hartington, heir to the Duke of Devonshire, visited New York in 1863, Ward had invited him to dinner one night, noted on another that Lord Hartington was Ellen Yznaga's escort at August Belmont's masked ball. Ellen was boldly campaigning that year on Yankee turf for support for the South in the Civil War. As Ellen and Hartington shook hands with General McLellan (commander in chief of the U.S. Army), Ward saw with amazement that Hartington sported a Confederate flag in his buttonhole.

Now, taking in every detail of the nuptials of Ellen's daughter, as Reverend Mr. Dix droned on, Ward approved the cut of the groom's coat and curled his lip at the flashy getup of James Gordon Bennett, Jr., seated just where the groom's family was so conspicuously absent.

With his unerring instinct for the seamy and sordid, Kim had managed to find, even in straitlaced America, compatible friends, one of them being Bennett. His father, a properly moral Scot, had founded the *New York Herald* in 1835, and five years later had smuggled the very first Society reporter into a fancy-dress ball, thereby initiating press coverage in America of Society events. James Gordon Bennett, Jr., had picked up his wicked ways in Paris, where he'd been educated; he liked to drive stark naked through Central Park at night on the box of his four-in-hand. He became engaged to Caroline May, a New York doctor's daughter, but when, on New Year's Day, rather too full of punch, James relieved himself into the May fireplace, Caroline called off the wedding, returned his letters and sent her brother next day to horsewhip James on the steps of the Union Club. He retreated to France where, late in life, he would marry Baroness de Ruyter and become increasingly eccentric. Several months before the Yznaga wedding, catching the fever of Anglomania then spreading in New York, he had brought polo mallets and balls from England and with the help of his polo-playing friend, Kim, Viscount Mandeville, arranged the very first games played in America, in Jerome Park, the New York racecourse founded by Leonard Jerome, who sat nearby, debonair and dapper, his mustache, like everything else about Leonard, wildly exaggerated.

Leonard Jerome had made his fortune selling short in the stock-market panic of 1857; married Clara Hall; fathered three daughters, Jennie, Clara and Leonie, who would all marry Englishmen; built a red-brick mansion at Madison and Twenty-sixth Street; celebrated with an extravagant ball where one fountain gushed champagne and another eau de cologne. (Could tipsy guests, one wonders, still distinguish?) When Jennie got engaged to Lord Randolph Churchill, Leonard wrote to her: "You are no heiress and it must have taken heaps of love to overcome an Englishman's prejudice against 'those horrid Americans.'" Randolph had felt a *coup de foudre* when he first saw Jennie at a ball. She was brown eyed and olive skinned, with the pent-up energy of a panther. Leonard settled £3,000 ($15,000) a year on the couple, but stipulated that £1,000 ($5,000) of it was for Jennie's own use, rather than, as was the British custom, all for her husband's.

As Kim and Consuelo, now joined in holy wedlock, knelt for prayers, twenty-three-year-old Alva Vanderbilt felt a stab of envy. Friend Consuelo had snared a future Duke; she herself had

5 Jennie Churchill (née Jerome) about 1895

ignored social status and settled for mere money. Like Consuelo, Alva was from the South, which had given them an instant bond when they'd first met during schooling in Paris following the Civil War. It was Consuelo who, when they were both back in New York, had introduced Alva to William Kissam Vanderbilt, at a party at the home of his grandfather, uncouth old Commodore Cornelius, founder of the Vanderbilt fortune. Willie K. and Alva had married in April 1875, with Consuelo as pretty bridesmaid, so that they had just celebrated their first anniversary. Alva was strong willed, plump, pugnacious; her snub-nosed face had the look of a scrappy Pekinese. The Vanderbilts had no social standing at all in New York; no Knickerbocker could be expected to countenance the cursing Commodore, but Alva was determined to change all that.

Toward Grace Church's fake stone vaulting rose the organ peals of Mendelssohn as Viscount and Lady Mandeville hurried down the aisle. Then everyone rushed to the Yznaga residence for the four o'clock "wedding breakfast," viewed the presents, computed, most accurately, their cost, and waited eagerly to read all about this novel, milestone event of an American girl's wedding to a future British Duke in next day's papers.

The *New York Times*' headline "Lord Mandeville's Wedding" showed its bias by ignoring the bride. "Lord Mandeville is an English nobleman. His father is the seventh Duke of Manchester, and his lineage is that of a brilliant family," gushed the *Times*, although "brilliant" was a word no one in England would use to describe the Manchesters. In 1876 the attitude of the American press to transatlantic marriages was still starry-eyed and wildly enthusiastic. The American heiress Bettina Vanderpoel in *The Shuttle* (1907) by Burnett sums up the typical attitude: "She saw her country, its people, its newspapers, its literature, innocently rejoiced by the alliances its charming young women contracted with foreign rank. She saw it affectionately, gleefully, rubbing its hands over its duchesses, its countesses, its miladies. The American Eagle spread its wings and flapped them sometimes a trifle, over this new but so natural and inevitable triumph of its virgins."

On May 11, 1877, the *New York Times* ran a long editorial, "Noble Husbands and Republican Wives," deciding that "an English title generally eclipses all others" because "it is much rarer; Barons and Counts are common on the Continent" and because it "almost always rests on a foundation of English acres." Then the editorial applied the spur to the American girl's ambition: "Marriage into an English noble or even county family is very rarely the fortune of an American woman. In the few cases in which it does happen, and in which the husband is a man of intrinsic worth of character, the lady's lines fall in pleasant places."

The very first novel to show an American heiress marrying a British peer, *A Transplanted Rose*, by the etiquette writer Mrs. M. E. W. Sherwood, would appear in 1882. Rose Chadwick is a rough, tough heiress from the Wild West who once shot a grizzly. She comes to New York, learns how to talk, walk and manage a train, then marries Sir Lytton Leycester and lives happily ever after in his ivy-draped English mansion. American maidens read, dreamed and learned proper English etiquette from *A Transplanted Rose*.

Viscount and Viscountess Mandeville defied it by not going off on at least a month's sequestered honeymoon. The newlyweds stayed in New York through June, and Marietta Stevens gave a tea in their honor.

Meanwhile, at Kimbolton Castle, Kim's parents, the august Duke and Duchess of Manchester, were still in shock. "Louise [the Duchess] brought two letters from Mrs. Yznaga," the Duke scratched in his diary on June 3, "the later one announcing Kim was married and a newspaper describing it." In July, Kim and Consuelo finally sailed for England and their arrival on July 22 was duly noted. "Kim and wife arrived from U.S.A.," wrote the Duke laconically.

Next day, Consuelo suffered through the icy ordeal of dinner with the Duke and Duchess at their London house in Great Stanhope Street. As she laughed and chattered in her charming, ingenuous way, their Graces began to thaw. Seated at the head of the table was Kim's father, the fifty-three-year-old 7th Duke of Manchester. He was "silly but not dull," as one acquaintance put it, with an extreme Tory bias in keeping with the family motto, which was *Disponendo me non mutando me* (You can use me, but you cannot change me). The Duke had a strong antipathy to all things republican, including Americans. Once at a dinner hosted by the Prince of Wales, he spluttered to an American guest that "the most outrageous thing in all history was your rebellion and separation from the best government on earth." The Montagu family tree — they had come to England at the time of the Norman Conquest — contained, like that of most noble English families, its share of spendthrifts, womanizers and hard-nosed opportunists. The 1st Earl of Manchester (1563–1642), a man of "more application than capacity," became Lord Chief Justice and pronounced the death sentence on Sir Walter Raleigh, who had established America's very first colony. The 1st Duke (1660–1721), elevated from Earl to Duke in 1719, had served George I as Lord of the Bedchamber, and cannily married an English heiress to replenish ever-diminishing family coffers. The 4th Duke of Manchester (1737–1788), whom gossipy diarist Nathaniel Wraxall called "a man of very dissipated habits," actually sided with the colonies in America's struggle for independence. His son, the 5th Duke, married, in 1793, Lady Susan Gordon, daughter of the 4th Duke of Gordon, but the marriage was unhappy, so he escaped to Jamaica, where he served as Governor for nineteen years, and passed a reform law exempting women from flogging. The 6th Duke (1768–1843), a naval commander, was remarkably pious for a Montagu, and wrote religious tracts, including one entitled *Things Hoped For*. The 7th Duke, Kim's father, born at Kimbolton Castle in 1823, succeeded to the title in 1855 after having served Albert, Prince Consort, as Lord of the Bedchamber for nine months in 1852. The Duke had commercial interests in Canada and Australia, but true to his respect for tradition, he managed to be as careless with money as his forebears, so that his estates were all heavily mortgaged and his debts enormous.

Part of the drain on his purse came from his wife's love of gambling. Sitting very erect at the foot of the mahogany dinner table was the intimidating Duchess. Born Countess Louise Fredericke von Alten, daughter of a Hanoverian Count, forty-two-year-old "Lottie," as her friends called her, had come to England as the Duke's bride in 1852. She bore her profligate spouse the requisite "heir and spare," Kim and Charles, added three daughters for good measure, Louisa, Alice and Mary, and then went her own way, devoting her days to horse racing, gambling and a lifelong love affair with Lord Hartington, who had once worn Ellen Yznaga's Confederate favor in his buttonhole. Lottie was the fastest lady in London's "fast" set, which revolved around naughty Edward, Prince of Wales. Queen Victoria strongly disapproved of her, refused to invite her to the 1863 wedding of Prince Edward to Danish Princess Alexandra and urged the latter, unsuccessfully, to drop her at once. "She may not, and I believe, *does not* do anything positively wrong," wrote Queen Victoria, but she had "done more harm to Society from her tone, her love of admiration and 'fast' style than almost anyone." Lottie was a woman of iron who would have a marked moral influence on her innocent new daughter-in-law.

Consuelo gazed at her across the dinner table, fascinated and awed. Her mother-in-law had frizzed brown hair, very blue eyes, a short, thick neck, the beginnings of a double chin and a face, once considered beautiful, painted with makeup, which, to maintain the illusion, would be ever more thickly applied. The Duchess of Manchester had "an almost grim personality," according to the Countess of Warwick. "She never relaxed, never revealed any emotion. She appeared neither angry nor pleased nor vexed, though at times she would be strident, emphatic and persistent." Lottie was a stickler for correct posture, and as the dinner conversation limped ahead, and silver forks scraped against the Meissen, Lottie looked at Kim lounging in his chair and declared, in her guttural German accent, "Sit up, Kimbolton! Sit up immediately!" Consuelo could hear in her tone of voice all her mother-in-law's pent-up anger at her son's choice of bride.

Consuelo would have been even more intimidated had she known that Lottie's repressed emotion could, on occasion, erupt in violent ways. Once, when she took two companions for a drive, all three had dismounted to admire the scenery. As Lottie climbed back into the waggonette, one of the horses moved. The coachman checked it at once, but Lottie was thrown onto her knees in the carriage. She hit the coachman sharply across the back with her stick and then, without the flicker of an eye, seated herself and resumed her conversation: "As I was saying..."

The fact that the formidable Duchess would come to grudging admiration of Consuelo was partly due to the latter's charm, and partly to the fact that Lottie always listened to Lord Hartington, who would speak warmly of the Yznagas, remembering Ellen's wit and winning ways thirteen years before. "Harty-Tarty" as he was called, in contrast to Lottie's own impoverished Duke, would, when he succeeded as 8th Duke of Devonshire, be an immensely rich one. He was tall, bearded, with heavy-lidded eyes and a thin, aquiline nose. Like Lottie, he was extremely reserved and proud. Once, discussing the best way of replying to the odd American greeting "Pleased to meet you," Harty-Tarty exclaimed: "If the fellow addressed me like that I would say, 'So you damn well ought to be!'" About everything except his love affairs, Harty had a terrible indolence. He slept continually in the House of Lords and when roused and asked for his opinion, always replied, "Far better not." His summer visits to Lottie's bed at Great Stanhope Street and winter ones to Kimbolton Castle ostensibly for the hunting came to a sudden stop in the early 1860s when he fell passionately in love with a famous courtesan, Catherine Walters, called "Skittles" since the day she scolded a group of drunken Guards officers with the threat that she'd knock them down "like a row of bloody skittles [ninepins]." Skittles had come from Liverpool to London, learned to ride there at a livery stable whose enterprising owner sent her off to Hyde Park's Rotten Row, where Society rode in season, mounted on his best horses and wearing a riding habit so tight that she had to be naked underneath. Demimondaines were usually given little houses in the suburbs, but Harty installed Skittles in Mayfair and appeared openly with her at such Society functions as the Derby horse race while Lottie flushed beneath her rouge and turned her very straight back. It was when gossip about his affair with Skittles flamed too high — the *Times* and *Telegraph* were full of it — that Harty-Tarty retreated to America and amused himself with Ellen Yznaga, and Skittles went in search of new conquests to France. After his return, Harty turned up one day in Great Stanhope Street in time for tea. "One lump, as always, Lord Hartington?" Lottie asked simply, and their love affair resumed.

Consuelo arrived in London when "the Season," begun in May and lasting through August, was in full swing. She entered Society with a fine, eye-catching pirouette to much applause, and never looked back. On Hyde Park gallops, at luncheon parties, teas, balls, evening receptions, Ascot Week for the races, Consuelo whirled and twirled, tiptoe with excitement. The London Season had all the pace and polish of Second Empire days, but now Consuelo was at the center, not banished to the sidelines. Lottie took note that in whatever part of a room her daughter-in-law stood, the group was denser and the laughter louder. If she could amuse, presumed Lottie, she would succeed. According to the Duke of Portland, Consuelo did just that, for he writes that she "took Society completely by storm by her beauty, wit and vivacity and it was soon at her very pretty feet."

To be sure, her dear friends Jennie and Minnie had already paved the way. Jennie records in her *Reminiscences* that when she entered Society in 1874, it couldn't distinguish a cultured American girl from a crass one, so that "the daughters of the newly-enriched California miner" were lumped together with the "aristocratic Virginian" and the "refined Bostonian," all of them "tarred with the same brush." "The American woman," writes Jennie, "was looked upon as a strange and abnormal creature, with habits and manners something between a Red Indian and a Gaiety Girl. Anything of an outlandish nature might be expected of her." The cartoons of the day zeroed in on her supposedly vulgar speech. "I'm pretty crowded just now," says one American girl in *Punch*, when offered a plate of food, and another explains that "Papa don't voyage; he's too fleshy."

Consuelo and Minnie and Jennie changed all that, and made their mark. "It was in the seventies," remembers Lady Dorothy Nevill, that "a new and powerful force began to make its influence felt in society," referring to the American invasion. "Society was languishing," comments Lord Dunraven. "It received a charming tonic in the arrival of Americans of the gentler sex." The fact that Consuelo, Minnie and Jennie were all attractive, witty and well-read young ladies augured well for the American girls who would follow them. They not only replaced a negative image with a very positive one, but changed the tone and appearance of English Society. Minnie and Jennie, both of whom were fanatically concerned with dress and decor, spurred Englishwomen to compete, to throw off their moth-eaten, dowdy draperies and learn the American lesson of conspicuous show.

Consuelo was pregnant that first summer, and was learning quickly what to expect in her new life. She realized that whereas American Society was ruled by its women — the men being much too busy making money to take an active part — English Society revolved around the men. As Price Collier notes in *England and the English from the American Point of View*, "Society is so patently, even impertinently, for the women in America, that to the American it is with some awe that he sees even social matters dominated by and adjusted to, the convenience and even to the whims of the men here." In England, Consuelo realized, wives had to fit themselves in as best they could around their husbands' pleasures as they single-mindedly pursued women in the spring and summer, grouse and pheasants in the fall and foxes in the winter.

Consuelo was also learning the true nature of the man she'd married. Like his mother, Kim couldn't show emotion. "The English heart," as E. M. Forster would observe years later, "is not so much cold as undeveloped." So it was with Kim. Consuelo knew that an American husband, to a wife expecting their first child, would have been full of hugs and reassurances and thoughtful little gifts. But Kim was a peer of the realm, used to deference from all inferiors, including his wife. From the day they landed in England, Kim more or less ignored her and went back to his pleasures: gambling, shooting, drinking — and womanizing.

By the Season's end in August, Kim had gone through an astonishing amount of money, and his father laid down the law. "Kim will take Consuelo to Tandragee and stay alone for a year's trial," the Duke wrote in his diary on September 15, "expenses too great in England." Tandragee Castle was the Manchester country seat in County Armagh, northern Ireland. After London's whirl, and a brief visit to historic Kimbolton Castle, a Tudor stronghold splendidly rebuilt by Vanbrugh and Adam in the eighteenth century, Tandragee was a shock for Consuelo. Kimbolton had beautiful gilded rooms with murals by the Venetian artist Pellegrini, and paintings by Titian, Rubens and Van Dyck. Tandragee Castle, in contrast, was cold, echoing, run-down, with cobwebbed rooms filled with relics of furniture and fireplaces that smoked. To Consuelo, it felt like a prison she'd been unfairly condemned to. She was homesick, pregnant, unappreciated, in limbo. Like the American Duchess of Tintagel just after her marriage in Wharton's *Buccaneers*, Consuelo was "no longer able to reach back to her past" and hadn't yet "learned how to communicate with her present."

Moreover, there was an underlying harsh teasing to life at Tandragee that frightened Consuelo. Kim and his bachelor friends Peter and Derry Westenra, the latter 5th Earl of Rossmore, who lived nearby at Rossmore Park, liked to discommode Tandragee's few guests. They filled a visiting curate's water tumbler with gin, got him so drunk that it was three days before he could face his shocked rector. They poured icy water from a room above onto a visiting General as he stood naked in his bathroom, and laughed to see him blue and shivering. "Lady Mandeville, I cannot say that I have thoroughly enjoyed my visit here," he told the embarrassed Consuelo as he took his leave. Kim's constant companion as he shot pheasants and grouse in Tandragee's Bull Park cover was hard-drinking, hard-hitting Ned, 24th Baron de Clifford. In 1879, the twenty-four-year-old Baron would marry a beauty called Hilda Balfour. At a men's dinner that he subsequently hosted, he boasted that she was the world's most beautiful bride. To prove it, he "went upstairs to his wife's bedroom, dragged the terrified girl from her bed, and forced her, clad as she was in her nightdress, to go downstairs and face his guests. The poor girl was absolutely terrified, but her protests were disregarded." Several years later, Hilda followed her husband's example, and took to drink.

Consuelo's only recourse to Tandragee's isolation and heartless sport was to invite her own friends to stay. During 1877, two of them were with her: Minnie Stevens and Cornelia Adair (née Wadsworth) from Genesco, New York. Cornelia's first husband, Montgomery Ritchie, had died of Civil War wounds; in 1869, with a dowry of $300,000, she married Englishman John Adair, who owned vast tracts of land in England, Ireland and Texas. Mrs. Adair wrote to her English friend Lady Waldegrave: "We have just been staying up at Tandragee with Lord and Lady Mandeville — poor little thing, she is so delicate — so utterly helpless — and *most* charming. She cannot endure a country life and is quite miserable at Tandragee, although she has Miss Stevens with her who is the brightest, cheeriest companion. The more I see of her the more I like her. I hope she will marry an Englishman; she is suited to life in this country which poor little Consuelo Mandeville is not."

Consuelo was back in London and had her mother with her when on March 3, 1877, she gave birth to a son, christened William Angus Drogo, but, like his father, always called Kim. Willie K. Vanderbilt stood as godfather; his wife, Alva, across the ocean in New York, one day before, on March 2, had produced a daughter, christened Consuelo after her titled godmother.

In May, just as the London Season began, Consuelo was banished again to Tandragee with her two-month-old son and her scapegrace spouse. The New York gossip sheet *Town Topics* printed an accurate summary of the Mandevilles' marriage thus far:

Lady Mandeville has Spanish blood in her veins; she shows Bohemianism in her character and the style of dress she chooses. She is married to the elder son of the celebrated Duchess of

Manchester, Viscount Mandeville, whose taste for gallant adventures marriage does not seem to have cured.

Occasionally he leaves London to give himself up all the more freely to his pranks and betakes himself to Ireland, where he loves to stay and where his society is loved in turn. Viscount Mandeville has a seat in Parliament as a Conservative, but the stenographers have never noticed his presence there as far as I can learn. I do not believe he is intelligent, notwithstanding his evident efforts to play smart. He is fond of politics, but he was intended rather for manual than intellectual labour.

Kim had earlier in 1877 been elected M.P. for Huntingdonshire, the seat usually claimed by a Montagu of Kimbolton, and would remain so until April 1880, when his dissatisfied constituents would throw him out in favor of a more responsible and attentive member.

Married to a man whose only talent was for spending money, Consuelo had an unhappy lot. "Look at poor Conchita," says an American mother in *The Buccaneers*. "Her husband drinks, and behaves dreadfully with other women, and she never seems to have enough money." In England a woman's dowry normally became part of her husband's estate. Kim thus controlled, and was rapidly squandering, the £200,000 capital that Antonio Yznaga had settled on his daughter; according to English custom, Kim doled out only a meager allowance, or "pin money," to Consuelo. There was always a worrisome pile of unpaid bills at Tandragee and unpaid servants threatening to leave. As Edith Wharton notes of her fictional counterpart, Conchita "had lost her lovely indolence and detachment, and was now perpetually preoccupied about money."

It was in February 1878 that a typical incident, one of many, brought Consuelo face-to-face with husband Kim's sordid life-style. They went to Ross-Trevor to stay with his friend Lord Newry. A "painted lady" with vulgar manners, acting as hostess, received them and at dinner exclaimed to the whole table, "Newry has laced me too tight!" As Lady Waldegrave reported in a letter to a friend, Consuelo suspected that her hostess was *not* Lady Newry, but, fearing his displeasure, said nothing to Kim. At a ball next evening, a gentleman advised Consuelo that she shouldn't stay another day at Ross-Trevor, that her hostess was currently, after many such liaisons, Newry's mistress. Only aristocrats far gone in debauchery and well outside Society's pale paraded their mistresses so publicly.

Through that long night, Consuelo looked hard at the facts of her marriage, realizing how degenerate Kim was, how disgraced in polite British Society. That night, like Henry James's heroine Maggie Verver in *The Golden Bowl* (1904), also transplanted from America to Britain, Consuelo became aware of "what's called Evil — with a very big E." Her passage from innocence to experience had begun and would accelerate but would be less traumatic and shocking than it was for very innocent Jamesian heroines. Consuelo was well prepared for it by her bohemian upbringing and her Second Empire days.

Next morning at Ross-Trevor, Consuelo pleaded illness and persuaded Kim to leave with her, revealing nothing of her real motive and anxieties — which tells us much of the distance and lack of candor between them.

Like many British upper-class men who, in their formative years, had been hugged and cuddled only by working-class maids and nannies, Kim had developed a taste for lower-class women. He formed a liaison with a music-hall singer named Bessie Bellwood whose speciality before the footlights was singing saucy coster songs, she herself having once skinned and sold rabbits from an East End street barrow. She became, as one journalist noted, "the chosen domestic companion" of Lord Mandeville, and this became public knowledge when Kim was called as police witness after Bessie punched the nose of a hansom-cab driver who was merely trying to collect an old debt from Kim. All the London newspapers carried a full report. According to one account, "everybody's attention was directed to his [Mandeville's] disgraceful position. Many similar and no less shameful incidents occurred."

Consuelo grew to womanhood overnight, and a brave little letter that she sent to Lady Waldegrave at this time shows how well she was coping:

Dear Lady Waldegrave,

Mandeville is yachting with the Gosfords and his movements are so erratic that I think I had better say he won't come
with me on Sunday, nor on the 13th either. He so often disappoints me that I generally make up my mind to go without
him. Au revoir till Sunday.

Affectionately yours,
Consuelo Mandeville

"He so often disappoints me"; it was as much as she could say; the
rest was silence. Part of Consuelo's galling constraint was that no
wife could talk about her husband's philandering. "Any public
recognition of it was unthinkable," writes E. F. Benson in his
memoir *As We Were*, "and even more unthinkable was it that she
should talk about it, or seek to protect herself against a domestic
situation even if it threatened to ruin her life or render it intolerable. It was correct to be blind, and dumb, and to see or speak was
an offence against the laws that governed the behaviour of her
class." There was no hope of reforming Kim. Consuelo was by
nature too easygoing in her relationships with people even to try.

Nor could she escape from her situation with a divorce;
divorce was almost unheard of at that time and would bring
instant and permanent social ostracism. She had no choice but to
stay married, and to learn to stand alone. As Barbara Welter
points out in *Dimity Convictions*, the American girl was supposed
"to attach herself to some sturdy oak of a man, whose goodness
and strength would protect her from the winds of adversity." To
realize that there was no husband to shield and protect her, that
her husband was, in fact, the problem, and the whole of it, was a
bitter pill for a Southern girl like Consuelo to swallow.

In April 1878 she went off to Paris with Minnie Stevens, where
Minnie bought Worth gowns by the dozen for her trousseau, for at
twenty-five, after seven years in the marriage mart, to the immense
relief of her mother, Marietta, Minnie had found a husband:
twenty-seven-year-old, tall, taciturn Capt. Arthur Paget, grandson

6   Minnie, Lady Paget, about 1900,
in a tea gown designed by Worth

of the 1st Marquess of Anglesey and the Prince of Wales's close
friend and aide.

While Minnie debated over plumes and laces and chattered
about dear Arthur, Consuelo, in the city of light where her dreams
had sparked, realistically planned her future life. Her husband had
more or less deserted her, disgraced her publicly, dragged her
name through gossip columns, made her the subject of barroom

jokes. But she was plucky, vibrant, optimistic, ambitious — and a born survivor. She might have been raised a magnolia-soft Southern belle, but she had her own kind of steely resources. Using her considerable talents of worldly charm, magnetism and intelligence, she determined to make a name for herself that English Society and the general public would respect and admire. She would lead and manipulate, change and challenge; Society would dance to her tune.

She had already had a close enough exposure to have taken the measure of British Society. American Society was young, open, in flux, with Old Money retreating and New Rich people gaining ground, in the grip of Puritan morals and work ethic, looking to its future. British Society was old, closed, static, in the grip of aristocratic privilege and leisure, looking to its past. But British Society was also far more stimulating, more sexually permissive, more male oriented, more focused on politics and the arts than America's. Consuelo liked everything about it, including its hint of decadence. The sentiments of her fictional double, Conchita Marable in *The Buccaneers*, probably coincided with Consuelo's: "I'd rather starve and freeze here than go back to all the warm houses and the hot baths and the emptiness of everything, people and places." American wives hung on "at any price because London's London and London life was the most exciting and interesting in the world."

After Minnie and Arthur were duly married on July 26 in London's fashionable St. Peter's Church in Eaton Square, they set up house in Belgrave Square, and Consuelo, who was often a guest there, initiated the first step in her plan, which was to become a close friend of the Prince of Wales. It was the thirty-seven-year-old Prince Edward who ruled Society, not its staid, sequestered monarch. Since the death from typhoid of her husband, Prince Albert, in 1861, Queen Victoria had closeted herself as much as possible at Windsor Castle or Buckingham Palace or Balmoral

Castle in Scotland. She still mourned and refused to socialize, but she would, most exclusively, rule. She gave Prince Edward nothing at all to do in the way of statecraft, so he got very good at amusing himself — with horse racing, cards, gourmet feasts and pretty women, preferably married or American or, best of all, both. Consuelo, like Jennie and Minnie before her, was soon part of the Marlborough House set whom Edward and his wife, Alexandra, gathered around them. J. F. C. Sewell, the editor of *Personal Letters of King Edward VII*, asserts, as do others, that by the late 1870s "His Royal Highness was very friendly with Lady Mandeville." The youthful Consuelo observed Edward and Alexandra at parties, listened to the gossip, and began to understand how blue-blooded marriages worked.

Edward and Alexandra's marriage had initially been a love match. "I frankly avow to you," he had written beforehand to his mother, "that I did not think it possible to love a person as I do her. She is so kind and good, and I feel sure will make my life a happy one." Alexandra, who was slender and beautiful, with brown poodle-curls and an oval face, declared, for her part, that if Edward "were a cowboy I would love him just the same." They married on March 10, 1863, and in the next seven years "dear sweet Alix," as the Queen called her approvingly, produced five children. Alexandra was a child who never grew up; she loved dancing and high jinks and Hans Christian Andersen. But she was good-natured, loving and remarkably tolerant of her husband's womanizing, treating it as an engrossing kind of hobby. Occasionally her pique showed: once when he bedded a vulgar American, Jeannie Naylor-Leyland (née Chamberlain), whom Alix called "Chamberpots" and again when he passed on to Alix a gonorrheal infection that gave her a stiff knee for life.

As for her "naughty little man," as Alix called her husband, he had a gargantuan appetite for women as well as for food. Over the years Lily Langtry, Sarah Bernhardt, Daisy, Countess of Warwick, and Alice Keppel served as habitual fare, along with actresses, courtesans, his friends' wives, Parisian demimondaines and fresh Americans added for variety.

Ever since American girls had mobbed him in New York in 1860, Edward had admired their snap and sparkle, and was always eager to meet what he calls in a letter "a few fair Stars and Stripes." "The secret of American popularity in royal circles," George Smalley decided in *London Letters*, "lay in this American freedom from the purely conventional notion about royalty which prevails in England. A girl from New York talked to the Prince of Wales as if royalty had no more rights than republicanism. She spoke her mind, as she expected the Prince to speak his; he was delighted by the girl's frankness." Edward told Jennie Churchill that he liked American women "because they are original and bring a little fresh air into Society. They are livelier, better educated and less hampered by etiquette. They are not as squeamish as their English sisters and they are better able to take care of themselves." Before Consuelo was added to the list, Minnie and Jennie were the Prince's closest American friends — and possibly lovers. The novelist George Moore claimed that Jennie had a total of two hundred lovers, including, briefly, the Prince. His Royal Highness would surely, given his record, make advances to pert, blond Lady Mandeville.

Could one say no to a Royal, one's future King? Edward had a habit of writing to his lady loves in French, and there is one such undated billet-doux to Consuelo. In any case, she became a regular at evening parties at Marlborough House; at week-long gatherings either at Sandringham, the Prince's mansion in Norfolk, or at other country houses where the Prince liked the shooting, and where the host was expected to invite whomever His Royal Highness desired, a list of his chosen ones having been sent on ahead.

Having secured the Prince's friendship, Consuelo proceeded to the second step in her plan. She set herself up as social mentor and marriage broker for the steady flow of rich Americans who were coming to England in search of elevated status or titled spouses. For a hefty fee, an American girl would be groomed and schooled by Consuelo, taught how to curtsy and comport herself in English Society, presented at Court and — if she measured up — invited to a select party where the Prince would be a guest. After that it was up to her to charm him. If the Prince liked her, all Society would be instantly at her feet. If she was looking for a peer, Consuelo would cast about for suitable ones and introduce her. One of the girls whom Consuelo launched into the matrimonial sea was Elizabeth Livingston, who had been a guest at Consuelo's wedding. Elizabeth married George Cavendish-Bentinck, grandson of the 3rd Duke of Portland, on August 12, 1880. Consuelo also helped Adele Grant, pretty daughter of David Beach Grant of New York, hook the 7th Earl of Essex. She married him on December 14, 1890, and thereafter, having a literary turn of mind, Adele invited Henry James and Edith Wharton often to her country seat, Cassiobury.

In her chosen career, Consuelo was trailblazer and trendsetter; others soon followed her lead. Minnie dabbled for a while, but she and Arthur had their hands full acting as the Prince's bookmaker and stockbroker, placing bets and buying stocks for him in their name, rather than his. By 1905, as the novelist Marie Corelli writes in *Free Opinions...of Modern Social Life*, there were "at least a dozen well-known Society women" who accepted "huge payments in exchange for their recommendation or introduction to Royal personages, and who add considerably to their incomes by such means." If others got in on the act, it was Consuelo, Viscountess Mandeville and future Duchess of Manchester, who ran the most select and sought-after introduction-and-marriage bureau in the land. She pocketed the handsome fees for her own use, for since the passing of the Married Women's Property Act in Britain in 1870, wives were allowed to keep their own earnings.

Kim returned to his wife's bed long enough to do his duty as a good peer should and sire a spare to follow the heir. In 1879 Consuelo gave birth to twin girls, christened Mary and Alice, the latter always called Nell.

In the following year, on May 30, we glimpse Consuelo at a dinner party that shows, perhaps with Kim and the Prince as catalysts, how far she'd progressed along that road from wide-eyed innocence to world-weary sophistication. Jennie Churchill wrote to her sister Leonie: "Consuelo proposed herself to dinner the other night. We had old Chancellor Ball and Lord Portarlington and she being *enivrée* [inebriated] insisted on telling 'roguey poguey' stories, which I think astonished them, they did me; quite between ourselves I think it *du plus mauvais goût* [in the worst taste] to talk like that before men."

Society agreed. E. F. Benson in *As We Were* notes that the social code banned naughty stories except in all-male company. From then on, whenever it suited her, Consuelo would fling correct form aside and let her true playfulness and impulse find free expression. An English friend was shocked, visiting Consuelo one day when she was ill in bed, to find little Kim rolling about on the floor, playing with the chamberpot. Consuelo merely shrugged: "It seems to be the only thing that amuses him," she said with a laugh, and her son played on.

One hot, oppressive summer evening, Consuelo sat perspiring in a carriage on her way to a Court ball. As an English friend watched in amazement, Consuelo wiggled and twisted, pulled her corset out from the top of her low-cut gown and threw it, hard, into a corner. It was her declaration of independence; the flung corset was her rebel's flag. Henceforth there would be no more vacillation from one state to another, from propriety to passion, from nice girl to naughty one. On the evening when she jettisoned her corset, Consuelo threw off American True Woman ideals of strict public decorum and chastity after marriage once and for all. She would live the rest of her life without even an inch of Puritan whalebone, a true European sophisticate, an English version of James's Mme de Vionnet in *The Ambassadors*.

Part of the American True Woman ideal was sexual purity, and in America, husbands were expected to be as faithful after marriage as wives. As Auguste Carlier points out in *Marriage in the United States* (1867), the American husband "recognizes the sanctity of the conjugal tie." Edith Wharton records in *The Age of Innocence* that "a certain measure of contempt was attached to men who continued their philandering after marriage."

In English Society, however, standards were very different. As in America, unmarried girls stayed virgins, while young men sowed their wild oats. After marriage, both sexes could opt for sexual freedom. Wives of aristocrats stayed faithful to their spouses long enough to produce several sons to ensure that title and estate could be passed on directly; after that married women were free to take a series of lovers and let the pregnancies come where they might. No one cared who sired the tail end of a family. Lady Louisa Moncreiffe advised her debutante daughter: "Never comment on a likeness," and Lady Louisa herself produced eight sons and eight daughters; adultery was allowed; birth control wasn't. When the last child was due, someone asked Lady Louisa whether she wanted a boy or girl. "I don't care if it's a parrot," she snapped.

A husband was a convenience or a curse, as the case might be, but a lover was a divine ("deevie" was their word), delicious, self-indulgent pleasure. Society wives weren't promiscuous. It took months for an affair to progress from chairs to bed, and one often kept the same lover for years. At week-long country house parties, there was much traffic up and down bedroom corridors each night as male lovers tiptoed eagerly to the beds of their chosen ones.

Since women were encouraged to ignore sexual impulses, according to the prescribed feminine ideal, they tended to emphasize romance and play down passion. And to notions of romance, English lovers played up wonderfully in a way that husbands never did. They wooed with letters and verses, flowers and daily visits, usually during the tea hour, because then spouses were conveniently absent and women appeared without inhibiting corsets in fetching tea gowns — "teagies," they called them — loose garments with fichu front and slight train in muslin, silk or satin well frothed with lace. Tea gowns were for married ladies only; young girls never wore them.

Adultery was permitted, but one had to be discreet about it with no disclosure to public or press. This makes it hard going for future biographers, but private letters sometimes slip into candor, and one from Consuelo's friend Gladys, Lady de Grey, to her sister-in-law, who was told to burn it but didn't, reveals Consuelo's first lover. Although much diligent but fruitless digging was undertaken, it seems that Consuelo was the only one of our five heiresses who indulged herself with lovers à la mode, probably because in both temperament and conditioning she was the one best suited to do so.

Consuelo's lover was a fitting choice, for he too was something of a rebel. Joseph Chamberlain, born July 8, 1836, came from a middle-class family and left school at sixteen to enter the family business, making Spanish-leather boots and shoes. Two years later, he went to Birmingham to help establish a metal-screw factory owned by his father and uncle. For eighteen years, Joe stuck to screws, and when he retired from active business in 1872, his factory produced two-thirds of all metal screws manufactured in England, and Joe was a very wealthy man. He became Mayor of Birmingham, and at age forty, in the summer of 1876, just after Consuelo was married, Joe was elected to Parliament as a Radical Liberal. He had once flirted with the idea of republicanism for Britain, and made a speech denouncing peers as a class who "toil not, neither do they spin." By 1880 he was a member of Gladstone's Cabinet and in 1895 would become Colonial Secretary, consistently supporting the concerns of the middle class, the shopkeeper, the Nonconformist. The public named him Radical Joe and took him to their hearts.

Chamberlain was of medium height, pale, clean-shaven, immensely handsome, his black hair brushed back smoothly on his small head. He favored elegant cutaway coats, a red cravat drawn through a gold ring, a gold-rimmed monocle hung on a black ribbon and always in his buttonhole a fresh orchid plucked from the vast greenhouses at Highbury, his country seat near Birmingham, where he grew and hybridized exotic orchids.

Joe had a cool smile, a fascinating voice. He was what one friend called "a man of obvious mystery with rather frightening qualities held in leash." When he and Consuelo became lovers sometime in the 1880s he'd already buried two wives. He'd married at twenty-five, only to have his wife die producing a son, Austen. At thirty, Joe had married a cousin of his first wife, but she too

7 *Joseph Chamberlain, suave and elegant,*
with monocle and orchid

died giving birth, to Neville, who would become Britain's Prime Minister from 1937 to 1940.

In 1889, when he was fifty-three, Joe would marry an American, twenty-five-year-old Mary Endicott, daughter of Grover Cleveland's Secretary of War. Joe met her at a Washington reception in his honor and married her in Washington's St. John's Church, opposite the White House. Queen Victoria described Mary in her journal as "very pretty and very lady-like, with a nice, frank, open manner," but Joe's third marriage only made a short hiatus, not an end, to his affair with Consuelo. When he and Mary held a house party at Highbury shortly after their marriage, Consuelo was one of the guests, and Gladys de Grey comments in a letter that another guest, observing Joe and his bride, "does not seem impressed by their great mutual love."

Consuelo conspired to be in London as much as possible, staying with friends, or at the town house of sister Natica, who, on December 5, 1881, had married Sir John Lister-Kaye, a Baronet with a large estate, Denby Grange, in Yorkshire, and a reputation almost as rakish as Kim's. Later, when she had her own town house, Consuelo gave political dinners for Joe. At one dinner party on November 6, 1903, she tried to heal the political acrimony that had arisen over the Free Trade versus Imperial Preference (tariffs outside the Empire) debate. She courageously invited the Prime Minister, Arthur Balfour, Lord Rosebery, Winston Churchill and the Duke of Devonshire, who espoused free trade, to join Joe Chamberlain, who didn't, and who had recently resigned from Parliament in protest.

Having helped herself to a lover, Consuelo next set about changing Society to suit her own tastes. She gathered about her a group of writers and musicians and artists, including the opera singer Madame Nordica, Sir Arthur Sullivan and such visiting Americans as Edith Wharton, Stephen Crane and Mark Twain. Consuelo, who was extremely well read, once astounded friend Thomas Hardy by reciting the whole of Thomas Gray's "Elegy in a Country Churchyard" without forgetting a single line. A mix of artists enlivened Society, but it was still far too stiff and self-conscious. At dinner parties, people talked in well-modulated voices, rarely waved their hands about, never roared with laughter. The women's faces were expressionless, fingernails buffed to shell-sheen, hair brushed to high gloss. They should all be placed, Consuelo may have thought, feeling another tendril of hair unwinding on her neck, inside a museum case or bell jar.

"England is all right for splendor," she told a friend, "but dead slow for fun." What was needed was some good old American pie-in-the-face slapstick. At country-house parties, Consuelo got guests to toboggan down the stairs on large silver trays, a sport she had first seen Kim and the Westenra boys indulging in at Tandragee. She made everyone play charades, dressing up in draped curtains and cushion crowns. She thought up elaborate practical jokes: apple-pie beds, shaving soap where one expected meringue, ordinary soap where one expected cheese. Consuelo's friend Gladys de Grey had the footman drop a full tray of cheap china bought for the purpose behind her husband's chair at dinner so that he would think the priceless family Sèvres was crashing to the floor. Daisy, Princess of Pless, a blond beauty whose brother would be Jennie Churchill's second husband, was witness to so many of these pranks that she mistook a very real earthquake for a joker under her bed. *It Was Such Fun*, Society matron Mrs. Hwfa Williams would call her memoirs, remembering it all, and it was Lady Mandeville, with some help from her lively American friends, who got Society rolling.

More and more, her social set looked to Consuelo, their mascot and clown, for comic relief, and she obliged by rattling away on the piano singing minstrel songs, or telling funny stories, many of them about Mark Twain.

"Did you hear Consuelo's latest?" they would ask one another, enameled faces and agate eyes lighting up. There was, for instance, the story of "the fixed bath," recorded by the Duke of Portland, host of many an oh-so-merry house party at Welbeck Abbey. "We never considered any party complete without her dear and witty presence," he writes of Consuelo:

Looking back, I can still see everyone crowded round her at tea-time, all happily laughing at her continual flow of witty and amusing stories delivered in a charming, soft Southern voice. One of these stories occurs to me. When in an hotel, she was in what she called "a fixed bath," when, to her horror, the door suddenly opened, and in walked a man. "How awful! What *did* you do?" everyone asked. "My dear, I just covered myself with soap-suds, and sat down in the water as deep as I could." Such, however, was the good feeling of the man that he turned round, opened the door and, as he went out, said "I beg your pardon SIR, for my intrusion!" Everyone loved this story and our guests often said: "Now, Consuelo, tell us about the *fixed bath*."

Then there was the hilarious tale of Consuelo's visit to Queen Victoria, with her twins, aged three. That one kept Society laughing for a whole Season. Her Majesty received the three visitors sitting impossibly erect in a high-backed chair in her black widow's weeds. Little Mary and Nell, lifted onto two chairs opposite her, immediately stuck their thumbs into their mouths, looked down shyly and observed her from beneath their lashes. Suddenly they jumped down, ran to the Queen, climbed onto her lap, hugged her and kissed her, lisping "Nice Queen! Nice Queen!" Her Majesty was so amused that she invited her three guests to stay for lunch, where chicken was served. The Queen picked her bones up in her fingers, whereupon the twins, whose strict nanny, Miss Ellis, had impressed on them the importance of proper table manners, each pointed a finger at the Queen and shrieked, "Oh, Piggy-Wiggy!"

Consuelo had even tried to inject some fun into Scotland's Balmoral Castle, which the Queen, brooding on her lost love, Prince Albert, taken from her so suddenly, had turned into a life-less shrine. Hot water was still provided for dead Albert each evening in his dressing room; sheets and towels were changed; his chamber pot was scalded and placed beneath his bed. The Queen, who, contrary to her public image, was a very sensual woman, slept hugging Albert's nightshirt, with his photo on the pillow. Society's word for the Castle's marmoreal mood, its ban of all laughter and loud voices, was "Balmorality." Not even Consuelo could work her magic there. "Lady Mandeville, who called blue with cold," reported the Queen's Private Secretary, Henry Ponsonby, in 1884, "was equally sour in her remarks on our Highland Palace."

But with everyone except the Queen, Consuelo was a great hit, slated for a long run. She was on her own socially; Kim pursued his own sports elsewhere. A Society poet, writing of its favorites, immortalized her in verse: "And next, with all her wealth of hair unrolled / Was Lady Mandeville, bright-eyed and witty." Actress Lily Langtry, the Prince's chosen flower, notes that Consuelo "was of so merry and witty a disposition that she was a general favourite, and was persona grata at Marlborough House." Other Society members in their memoirs recall Consuelo as "an amusing woman rarely guilty of saying a stupid thing"…"worth going miles to see"…"celebrated for her brilliance and beauty"…"beautiful, witty, gay and gifted."

Of course other American wives, such as Jennie and Minnie and Natica, did their star turns too. "One of the direct results of the presence of so many American wives in English society," wrote George Smalley in November 1888, "is to make it livelier. This may seem a bold thing for an American to say, but I am, in fact, only quoting what I have heard the English themselves say, and say often."

Even poker-stiff Lottie, Duchess of Manchester, watching the antics of her daughter-in-law, indulged in the fun and the limelight. At London's only nightclub, in 1887, where the Prince of Wales was giving a small party to unwind after all the stuffy ceremonies celebrating Mama's fifty years on the throne, at two in the morning, as the orchestra struck up "La Belle Hélène," Lottie got up and danced a cancan for the Prince. Perhaps, as he watched her stout legs going up and down like pistons, he remembered the night at her Paris house when Cora Pearl, one of his favorite demimondaines, had danced the cancan nude on a carpet of orchids.

Consuelo went to New York for the winter of 1883, taking her three children, but leaving Kim, with great relief, on the Atlantic's far side. She was anxious to get the children away from his influence. While she herself was an easygoing, sometimes careless parent, Kim was strict to the point of cruelty. He taught his son to swim by tossing him from a boat into a lake. "When my father thought me full enough of water," records the adult Kim, "he yanked me back into the boat and emptied me out." When Kim was four, his father taught him to ride by putting him on a pony, giving it a hard slap on the rump, and when it galloped off, throwing Kim to the ground, he was immediately put back on the pony, over and over, until he learned to cling.

In New York Consuelo stayed with her old friend Alva Vanderbilt, whose sister Jennie, on September 22, 1880, at Idlehour, Alva and Willie K.'s Long Island home, had married Consuelo's brother, Fernando, who then, with Willie K.'s help, got a job with the brokerage firm of H. R. Hollins and was on his way to easy riches. Consuelo set about the task of getting Alva to the pinnacle position in New York Society. She had to give the grandest party ever, Consuelo told her, ostensibly in honor of her titled guest, Lady Mandeville, but actually to show off her splendid new Fifth Avenue mansion. The party was to take place on the Monday after Easter. New York's Old Money still piously kept Lent; after six weeks of cloistered self-denial, they would be ready for some fun. Then too, Monday was the evening when Mrs. William Backhouse Astor (née Schermerhorn), Society's undisputed queen, helped onto her throne by Ward McAllister, held her "At Homes." Caroline Astor had never deigned to call on Mrs. Vanderbilt, but Consuelo saw a way to get her to the party. They would ask her to organize the star quadrille, in which the ladies dressed as stars, one of whom would be Mrs. Astor's daughter Carrie. Invitations to the ball would be issued in Consuelo's name; even Caroline Astor couldn't refuse to meet a future Duchess. Gleefully, Alva and Consuelo sent off twelve hundred invitations, including ones to

Schermerhorns, Rhinelanders and all the other cold-shouldering Knickerbockers. Mrs. William Schermerhorn had given New York's first costume ball in 1854, but twelve years later the nobs had suddenly stopped giving them. That was because at Henry Brevoort's 1869 fancy-dress ball, Matilda Barclay, still in costume, had run off with unsuitable, vulgar Captain Burgoyne at four in the morning, and married him before breakfast. Alva and Consuelo would bring the costume ball, with a great, brassy flourish, back into fashion.

Consuelo hadn't felt so happy in years as she planned the details. She loved being social fairy and impresario, creating costumes, backdrops, a whole world of make-believe, imagination swinging high. Alva caught her enthusiasm; they set to work like children before a birthday party, with no boredom or cynicism for Society's rituals, only anticipation and delight, remembering the glitter of Second Empire days. They would dazzle New York's drab old fusty-musty nobs with the same kind of conspicuous show that Empress Eugénie had masterminded so brilliantly for Paris Society.

They would, they promised each other, laughing delightedly, go the Empress one better. They would stage a party New York would never forget. And they succeeded; more than one social historian calls it the most famous party ever given in the United States.

Like Consuelo, Alva was unhappy in her marriage. "Why my parents ever married remains a mystery to me," her daughter would comment years later. Alva had the drive and discipline of a self-made man; she loved screaming matches and a good fight. Willie K. leaned back comfortably on the cushions of great wealth; he was quiet, gentle and hated strife. Both Consuelo and Alva were looking for escape routes from their marriages. Focusing on the spangled stardust of a costume ball was just the thing.

On Monday, March 26, hours before the ball was to begin, some five hundred people, mostly girls and women, gathered outside the new Vanderbilt mansion on Fifth Avenue at Fifty-second Street to watch sugarplum dreams materialize. As Thorstein Veblen points out in *The Theory of the Leisure Class* (1899), the masses needed a focus for their envy, a "radiant body" by which they could work out their "social salvation," and in the Gilded Age that "radiant body" was Society.

About eleven o'clock, the hour when fashionable balls began, carriages full of crowns and powdered curls drew up importantly before the mansion and their occupants "walked up to the canopy which was the entrance to fairyland," as the *New York Times* put it, the account of the ball taking up almost the whole front page of next day's paper. Guests were eager to see inside the new Vanderbilt house, its interior alone, so everyone said, having cost $3 million. With a little help from the architect, Richard Morris Hunt, Alva had created there at the corner of Fifty-second and Fifth a crazy pastiche of the European past. Inside an immense white stone edifice, turreted and gabled like a French Renaissance château, crowded furniture, tapestries, paintings, armor, carvings, stained-glass windows, wainscotings that were French, Italian, Dutch, English, medieval, Louis XV, eighteenth-century, quattrocento. Old Money cherished antiques because they'd come down in the family from father to son. New Rich like Alva amassed them because they screamed "Money!" with every creak of a drawer.

New York's first florist, Klunder, had decorated the huge ground-floor rooms with "gilded baskets filled with natural roses of extraordinary size," every one of which, as Alva pointedly informed press and public, had cost $2, twice as much as Mrs. Astor paid for hers. Six thousand roses at $2 each; guests did some quick arithmetic as they walked, conscious of trains and diamond-buckled shoes, up the grand staircase and into a vast gymnasium decorated with enough palms, giant ferns and orchids to make a good-sized jungle. Alva and Consuelo received them, standing side by side, together with Willie K., feeling silly as the Duc de Guise in yellow silk tights. Alva was a Venetian princess of the Renaissance in a variegated Worth gown with brocade overskirt shaded "from deepest orange to lightest canary," gold-embroidered bodice in blue and gold-embroidered train in red. On her brown ringlets, above the pug nose, the pugnacious

*8   The only on-the-spot drawing of Alva Vanderbilt's 1883 ball,
printed in* Leslie's Weekly

chin, was a half-moon cap emblazoned with a proud peacock in
many-colored, all-genuine gems. In contrast, Consuelo was taste-
fully dressed in black velvet, having copied a Van Dyck painting
of Princess de Croy.

At midnight, the hundred dancers, who had been practicing
their French Quadrilles for weeks, formed up in the gymnasium,
marched down the stairway, through the hall, through the parlor
and into the Louis XV salon with its Gobelin tapestries, carved-
walnut wainscoting ripped from a French château, ceiling
emblazoned by painter Paul Baudry with the ultimate irony, given
the incompatibility of the Vanderbilt union, namely, the idyllic

marriage of Cupid and Psyche. After a very long trek, the quadrille members reached the dining room and went through the paces of their six storybook quadrilles, after which general dancing began, but many guests were too encumbered to join in.

Watching wide-eyed high above the crowd were young Kim Mandeville and Consuelo Vanderbilt, both of whom had celebrated their sixth birthday earlier that month. The adult Kim remembers "sitting in my nightshirt looking down from a gallery upon the glittering assembly" with Consuelo beside him, brown eyes alight. Godmother Consuelo had indeed waved a fairy wand, for there were the rough, tough railroad magnates of New York, and their pouter-pigeon wives, transformed into suave kings and queens and courtiers. As they dragged their trains and clattered their swords, all of them were assuaging their New World hunger for romantic Old World hierarchies. There was, to be sure, one authentic noble in the crowd, the Duc de Morny, and one authentic hero, Gen. Ulysses S. Grant. But the rest were far gone in fantasy. Marietta Stevens came as Queen Elizabeth with a point-lace ruff and "superb diamonds." Ward McAllister was Count de la Mole, lover of Marguerite de Valois, in a suit of purple velvet slashed with scarlet silk. Doublet and hose were so complex and convoluted that Ward had spent an hour climbing into them from a stepladder, with the aid of two manservants. Mrs. Ogden Goelet, mother of heiress May, still at home in the nursery, was more modestly garbed in a "pretty Polish riding costume with short flying jacket," but then the Goelets were Old Rich and didn't go in for flash and show. Through it all Mrs. William Astor, whose actual costume no one seems to remember, perhaps because of the $200,000 worth of diamonds hung about her person, wore a grimly cordial, pasted-on smile.

Dancing continued till 6:00 a.m., when a flushed, triumphant Alva, with Consuelo close behind, led a Virginia reel as the signal that the revels were ended, but guests were reluctant to break the spell. The ball had cost the Vanderbilts in excess of $250,000, at 1883 prices, but undeniably Alva Smith Vanderbilt, with a little help from her friend, had made her dream of social eminence come true. After the ball, New York Society would never be the same; the nobs were out and the swells were in, and conspicuous show was the order of the day. "All Society in Costume," shouted the *New York Times* headline. Indeed it was, and so it would remain, there in its Gilded Age, until World War I rang down the curtain. In that era, there was no compunction, no shame, at displaying one's vast wealth in such blatant ways before the poor have-nots. Flaunting it elicited no moral overtones of disapproval, or aesthetic ones either, come to that. It was all just novel, rollicking *fun*.

Alva immortalized her coup by having her photo taken in her costume, posing in the company of six white doves — stuffed, of course. There she stands, Society's new self-anointed queen, in all her gold-embroidered puffery, with a peacock, age-old Moghul symbol of royalty, well anchored to her head. Three doves gaze enraptured — or astonished — at her princess getup; two more are grasped firmly in the iron grip of Alva's pudgy hands; the sixth dove is suspended above her head, seemingly in high, free flight, for the gilt wire supporting it is quite invisible.

Back in London in the spring of 1884, Consuelo took on a new challenge. She'd proved masterful at keeping Society in general entertained. Now she focused on its leader, the Prince of Wales. The Marlborough House Set had been hard at it for twenty years trying to amuse him, but His Royal Highness was growing increasingly petulant and "snappish."

Edward was forty-three; he'd already tasted every delicacy, bedded every pretty woman, shot everything that flew or hopped or ran. He suffered now, more and more, from acute fits of boredom. The pale blue codfish eyes would half close at dinner parties; the thick fingers would begin to drum, drum upon the table. The Prince had no inner resources; he hated to be alone, or to sit quietly reading. Someone had to be always at his elbow with new stories, new gossip, new songs, new practical jokes. Consuelo

*9 Alva Vanderbilt in her 1883 ball costume,
with attendant doves*

took on the daunting task, and the Prince was properly grateful. By the late 1880s, as their correspondence shows, Consuelo and the Prince were close friends. "My dear Lady Kim," he wrote to her from Hungary on September 26, 1888, where he'd gone after shooting elk with the King of Sweden, "many thanks for your long and amusing letter of 19th. Without the slightest flattery, I may say that nobody writes more amusing letters than you do." He ends this five-page, closely written letter with the words "My *love* to Emily." Consuelo's younger sister, Emily, had taught the Prince to play the banjo; she rejected all suitors and lived a happy single life as a prominent socialite in England and France. Consuelo's mother also became a favorite with Prince Edward. Ellen often rented a London house for extended stays and invited him to breakfast parties where Aunt Debby's buckwheat cakes and syrup were helping his chest and waist reach their forty-eight-inch girth. When one of London's smart hostesses thought it might be "amusing" to invite Aunt Debby to luncheon, she replied, "I ain't never eat with white folks at home, and I ain't going to begin now."

Consuelo needed her own family and princely friend, for Kim, now living apart, was far gone in debauchery. Every evening he set out with his disreputable chums for London's "night-houses" clustered in narrow, dark streets behind Leicester Square, full of prostitutes, pickpockets, cardsharks, then moved on to Mott's and the Cremorne for champagne, gambling and painted courtesans, called "soiled doves," who fawned and fondled. There is an incident, recorded by his son, that explains in part Kim's self-destructive downward swirl. He had a strong streak of masochism. Once when he was running for a train, the porter slammed the carriage door on Kim's finger. He rode to the next station with his finger still in the door, calmly reading his newspaper. The finger, finally extricated, was crushed for life.

Consuelo was mortified when the London *Times*, in three installments, reported the sordid facts of Kim's insolvency. On March 7, 1889, came notice that various creditors were suing Lord Mandeville for £118,179 worth of unpaid bills. Appearing in court, His Lordship attributed his poverty "to losses by betting and gambling and to his expenditure having been in excess of his income." The case ground on, and on March 29, at the final hearing, the creditors' lawyer revealed that "Lord Mandeville had signed various affidavits full of false information as to his prospects." A committee of inspection was appointed, and on April 2 Viscount Mandeville was declared bankrupt. He was then living in Charlotte Street, Bedford Square, in lodgings whose owner had first launched the suit against him for arrears of rent. Before that he had lived at the seedy Hotel Windsor in Victoria Street. Consuelo was conscious, as she tripped her light fantastic, her heart heavy, from party to party, of pitying eyes on her, of whispers behind her back.

Across the Atlantic, it was her brother, Fernando, who hit the headlines. On Tuesday, March 4, 1890, Fernando Yznaga, thirty-eight, "well-known man-about-town," according to the *New York Times*, having been divorced from wife Jennie five years before, married pretty, blond Mabel Wright, twenty-two, rather precipitately, with no attendants, in the Wrights' parlor with the bride's mother, very ill at the time, having to be carried hence. "It was said some years ago by a bright woman," the *Times* noted, "that the Yznaga family could be safely depended on for giving New York society more or less of a sensation at intervals of a year." (Fernando's second marriage would end in divorce in October 1895.)

Kim's father, the 7th Duke of Manchester, died of peritonitis and dysentery on Friday, March 21, 1890, at the Hotel Royal, Naples. His wife, Lottie, gambling at Monte Carlo, managed to get to Naples just as he expired. It was her younger son, Lord Charles Montagu, not Kim, who met Lottie at Turin and accompanied her and the Duke's remains home to England for burial in the family vault beneath the Lady Chapel of Kimbolton church.

After a fourteen-year wait, Consuelo found herself at long last Duchess of Manchester, entitled to wear the heavy diamond tiara that she had long imagined on her head. With a rueful little smile, she signed her letters "Consuelo Manchester" on her newly coroneted notepaper. The title of Duchess had come too late. She had already made Society her minion, and the name Manchester was not one to give her added luster. The spendthrift 7th Duke, in spite of the fact that the Kimbolton estate brought in £10,000 annually and Tandragee £12,000, had gone through every penny and left huge debts besides.

Consuelo's own father died at seventy-three on May 6, 1892, at New York's Hotel Lennox, where he'd gone to attend a wedding, "from complications ensuing from a severe cold and attack of grip." The *New York Times* called him "a man who attained prominence through his children," explaining that his daughter Consuelo was married "to what the British call a *mauvais sujet*," adding that "the Duke and Duchess of Manchester have not, it is said, been very happy since their marriage on account of the Duke's dissipated habits."

The long nightmare of her marriage ended for Consuelo at Tandragee, on August 18, 1892. She was beside Kim, with a terrible inner turmoil of mixed feelings, as he died, aged thirty-nine, after "lying ill and in great suffering for some time." None of the British newspapers revealed the cause of death; it may have been cirrhosis of the liver from excessive drinking, or syphilis, from excessive womanizing. "Unknown as a politician or a country gentleman" was the terse verdict on his life of the *Illustrated London News.*

Kim's mother, Lottie, was conspicuously absent from Tandragee at the time of Kim's death, for Lottie was on her honeymoon. Two days before, on August 16, after his thirty years of attachment, Harty-Tarty had finally made an honest woman of her. He had become the very rich 8th Duke of Devonshire on the death of his father in the previous December. So the proud Dowager Duchess of Manchester became the even prouder Duchess of Devonshire, and Society thereafter acknowledged her feat by calling her the Double Duchess.

Kim's funeral at Tandragee was pure farce. Consuelo invited everyone back to the castle for a proper wake, where food and liquor were plentiful. The Irish guests imbibed freely. One of them, a cub reporter on an Irish newspaper, came up to fifteen-year-old Kim, now 9th Duke of Manchester, to say goodbye. Kim waited for some gentle words of sympathy on his bereavement, but the swaying reporter bawled out, "It's a damned foine funeral, Your Grace, but your beer's rotten!"

True to the Manchester tradition, his father had left the new Duke, still an Eton schoolboy, no great inheritance. From an estate of £25,190, there were debts totaling £20,000 to be paid.

Young Kim seems to have set himself assiduously to follow his father's prodigal path. When he left Trinity College, Cambridge, in 1895, after one year there, he was £2,000 in debt. Consuelo banished him to Germany to learn the language and went herself that spring with her pretty twin daughters to Rome. Italy, with its golden light, rose and russet buildings, streets full of laughter and song, suited Consuelo's Latin temperament.

But tragedy, even in that sunny land, sought her out. On March 11, 1895, Consuelo's daughter Mary, sixteen, died suddenly of double pneumonia. Shocked and numb, Consuelo accompanied the body to Naples, and thence home on a friend's yacht to England, for burial in the Kimbolton family vault. She absented herself from the 1895 social Season to grieve and gather strength, but was back in harness for the 1896 whirl.

The London Season was particularly hectic in 1897 as Society celebrated Queen Victoria's sixty years on the throne. In July Consuelo helped Lottie organize the most spectacular costume ball London had ever seen, at splendid Devonshire House. Consuelo dressed as Anne of Austria, in white satin swagged with gold, with a diamond diadem whose single pearl was centered on her forehead. As always at a party, Consuelo was in her element, and hated it all to end. "On the Saturday following the great entertainment," Jennie Churchill wrote, "I went to Kimbolton to stay with the Duchess of Manchester, where most of the company were persuaded to don their fancy dress once more." Like Consuelo, Jennie had become a widow; Randolph, aged forty-five, had died of syphilis two years before, on January 22, 1895, after harrowing months of mental and physical decline.

In August, and for every August but one thereafter, Consuelo rented Egypt House at Cowes on the Isle of Wight, to better entertain the Prince, who always came there for Regatta week. Anchored before the Royal Yacht Squadron Esplanade were yachts from around the world, come to compete in the races, looking like giant white butterflies. On the sloping green turf beside them, English gentlemen in navy blazers and white flannels chatted with Consuelo and other Duchesses, seated in wicker chairs, nibbling ices, while the Squadron's Commodore, the portly Prince of Wales, strolled about, always with white yachting cap, cigar and ebony cane. When Consuelo tired of fine clothes and formality, she could saunter incognito on streets packed with clowns, conjurors, Punch-and-Judy shows, bands, barrel-organs and girls in dirty white shoes and jaunty caps singing lustily to their accordions.

Consuelo's daughter Nell came out that year, 1897, and was the Season's most popular and beautiful debutante, "a glorious creature," who carried herself with "the poise that was the envy of many older women."

Consuelo's restless pursuit of frolic kept her constantly on the move: to Biarritz, to St. Moritz, to a rented house near Windsor for Ascot races week in 1899. Jennie came to stay, along with handsome, blond Guards officer George Cornwallis-West, Jennie's current beau, whom she would marry the following July, when he was twenty-five, her son Winston's age, and she was forty-six. "He has a future and I have a past," Jennie said with a laugh to Lady Adele Essex, "so we should be all right."

Consuelo was very worried about Nell's ill health. She'd gone to a ball some weeks before on a very hot night, rushed impulsively outside for a row on a nearby lake and caught a frightful cold that settled in her chest and wouldn't go away. Nell got very white and thin and began to spit blood. The doctors looked grave and packed her off to a Swiss sanatorium at Davos. On January 9, 1900, Lady Alice (Nell) Montagu, just turned twenty, died of tuberculosis. How could she bear it, thought Consuelo, as her second, beautiful, fun-loving daughter was laid to rest in the cold Kimbolton vault.

Consuelo took solace from her friends, particularly from Empress Eugénie, also widowed and alone, living modestly at Farnborough, Hampshire, where Consuelo often went to see her. The former Empress was seventy-four, superannuated from splendor, still beautiful, her face like old ivory. "You cannot unwrite history," she would tell Consuelo gently. Eugénie was still on stage; when she took leave of two or three guests who had come to tea, she swept them a low curtsy, graceful as a poem, before she sailed from the room.

At forty-two, Consuelo was growing stout and acerbic. She told Gladys de Grey that she had written several letters of introduction for a mutual friend visiting America, saying, "Please show some civility to the charming Countess of Shrewsbury, you will find her a valuable addition to any dinner party," and enclosed them with separate notes saying, "This old hag is no friend of mine!" Consuelo objected strenuously and publicly when on November 14, 1900, in Marylebone Parish Church, without her knowledge, her son, Kim, married a most unsuitable and vulgar American girl called Helena Zimmerman. Who had ever heard of the Zimmermans?

Queen Victoria breathed her last on January 22, 1901, at Osborne, Isle of Wight, where she and dear Albert had spent such happy holidays. A catafalque was erected in the dining room, and Victoria lay in state for eight days in her bridal gown. Then she was taken to Windsor for the funeral in St. George's Chapel, and thence to Frogmore for burial beside Albert in the mausoleum. A recumbent white marble Victoria, also in wedding garb, had been ready these thirty years to be placed above her coffin.

The Prince was crowned Edward VII in Westminster Abbey on August 9, 1902. Consuelo had to take a back seat, as mere Dowager Duchess, to the new Duchess of Manchester, the vulgar Helena, smug in coronet and ermine. In a special King's box, dubbed "the Loose Box," sat his dear friends who, as commoners, would not normally have been permitted to attend: Jennie Cornwallis-West, Minnie Paget and Sarah Bernhardt, the latter all in white.

King Edward was kept busy doing his kingly thing, ruling a global Empire of almost four hundred million souls, but he still had a great need of relaxation and amusement. Consuelo became totally absorbed in being hostess and houri to a King. She was caught in the Royal arms, somewhere between the lion and the unicorn, with no hope of release. Flocks of little white crowned notes landed on her desk at 45 Portman Square, her current London town house, all of them in Edward's loose scrawl.

> My dear Consuelo. The party you propose for Monday will do admirably. I shall bring Captain Fordham with me as you know he is a "Professor" at bridge... 12 I think the right number for a small party. I will bring S. Granville who can play bridge if we are three tables.... Many thanks for your kind invitation to dine with you. I hope it will be quite a small dinner and a little bridge afterwards.... Delighted to dine with you and Jennie on Tuesday instead of Thursday as you kindly granted choice of the two days.... Your suggestion of asking Lady Essex is a very good one. I suppose we shall be a party of 8 with two bridge tables? Believe me, yours very sincerely, Edward R.

Consuelo ordered the requisite lobsters and ptarmigan, truffles and foie gras, cigars and champagne. As well, a steady flow of presents made its way from Portman Square to the Royals: a cigarette case for the King's birthday; a "lovely little pencil" for his daughter; a pretty lampshade for Alexandra; and a ring for her birthday.

King Edward was costing Consuelo a great deal of money, but her brother, Fernando, fortunately had made her sole beneficiary when he died on March 6, 1901, so that her money worries were over. She had more than $2 million with another $2 million in American realty. She could laugh now, remembering the dinner she'd given for Prince Edward when she was so hard up that she'd asked each of her friends to provide a dish, and Edward had smiled gleefully at meal's end and expressed his delight: "I know exactly where all the dishes came from," he had said, "for each lady has sent the one I always like served when I dine at her house."

Consuelo moved into grander quarters at 5 Grosvenor Square, but she was often out of London, following like a faithful dog in the Royal footsteps, taking houses wherever the King was currently waiting to be amused: Monte Carlo, Biarritz, Ascot, Richmond, Cowes. It was no easy sinecure, playing favorite to a

King. Food and wines had to be exceptional at every meal. Guest lists had to be forwarded ahead for approval. Current mistresses had to be identified and included.

Consuelo would stand night after night in her drawing rooms, in pearls and spangles, talking and joking with her rotund, red-faced King, balancing, one more time, on that perilous tightrope stretched between spontaneous fun on one side and correct form on the other, with the dark chasm of His Majesty's boredom and displeasure just below. It took some doing, that balancing act. Once Consuelo had been banished from the Royal presence for a year because she'd circulated a hilarious verse called "Babbling Brook" satirizing the King's sometime lover Daisy Brooke, Countess of Warwick.

On every night when she wasn't giving little dinners for the King, Consuelo dined out, with the same faces, the same jewels. After dinner, everyone would "go on" to three or four evening receptions. Consuelo was extremely good at going on.

Minnie Paget returned home from her usual dinner and receptions on August 1, 1904, gorgeously gowned as Minnie always was, stepped into the ground-floor elevator of her Belgrave Square home and fell twenty feet into the shaft, the elevator being still at the top of the house. She sustained fractures of her kneecaps and femurs that, despite fifteen surgical operations, would refuse to heal. The King penned one of his little scrawls to husband Arthur: "Is there anything I can send her? Flowers or fruit or both?" By June of the following year, Minnie could still only walk with a cane on one side and a person on the other. She told Daisy, Princess of Pless, that "if she remained a cripple another year she would poison herself."

The round went on without her. For Christmas every year, Consuelo joined a party of fifty guests, tended by two hundred servants, who converged on Chatsworth, the splendid country seat of Harty-Tarty, Duke of Devonshire, and Double Duchess Lottie. The usual crowd, which included the King and Queen, gathered for Christmas 1904 for the usual theatricals and elaborate charades and the usual dancing after dinner to a Viennese orchestra.

"HRH very good-natured and jovial, nudging and patting his neighbours and putting his nose in their ears," one guest recorded rather acidly.

Consuelo took a break and breathing space from her Royal duties in the autumn of 1907 and sailed away to the United States aboard the *Lusitania* with her friend the novelist Elinor Glyn, whose racy novel *Three Weeks*, about a passionate Balkan love affair of that duration, had been extravagantly praised in England but banned in Boston. Elinor and Consuelo went to stay with Willie K.'s brother Frederick Vanderbilt and his wife, Louise (Lulu), at their Hudson River estate at Hyde Park.

Consuelo found herself in a strange milieu, a very Puritanical, provincial one. They arrived in time for tea, all very grand, with powdered footmen passing the cakes and Louise in long white gloves and $250,000 worth of pearls. The matrons sat on one side of the room all in a row, and their husbands sat opposite on straight gilt chairs, and the conversation had no double entendres, no risqué stories. Consuelo was used to the polish and gallantry of European men; she had forgotten that Yankee ones could only talk of stock markets and machinery patents.

When Consuelo and Elinor went up to bed, the latter remembers that the Duchess made her come to her room so that they could compare notes. "Everything seemed to her as amazing as it did to me, apparently, after her long absence," writes Elinor. "She said that she was sure that things had been quite different when she was a girl, and that it was not merely living in England which had made her see it all as quite incredible, especially the loud voices." Consuelo didn't realize how much she had changed, while American Society had stayed the same.

Back in England, Consuelo took a new lover, four years her junior. On June 1, 1905, Joe Chamberlain had suffered the first of a series of strokes, which affected his speech and confined him to a wheelchair. Consuelo's new beloved was the novelist Robert Hichens, son of a Kent clergyman, born November 4, 1862. Robert had begun his literary career as journalist, writing a weekly column on music called "Crotchets and Quavers" for *The Gentlewoman*. He went on to publish sixty popular novels, many of them made into plays with titles revealing their romantic bias: *New Love* (1895), *Flames* (1897), *Tongues of Conscience* (1900), *The Call of the Blood* (1906) and *Bella Donna* (1909). Robert was tall, well-built, with handsome face and wide, generous mouth. He first met Consuelo at a musical evening, which he describes in his autobiography *Yesterday* (1947): "I sat next to her, and was immediately attracted by her *bonhomie, savoir vivre*, and buoyant vivacity. She had a zest for life which was immediately apparent. She made one feel that with all its troubles and disappointments, of which I knew later she had certainly had her share, life was emphatically worth living."

Robert found her "a mine of information about the London Society of that time, for she knew everybody and had a very shrewd judgment of both women and men."

It was shortly after they met that Consuelo sent him a telegram from London — Robert was in Sicily — asking him to take a motor tour through Italy with her that spring, and to telegraph his reply. Neither was quite sure that traveling together was a good idea, but Consuelo loved to follow her whims, and take chances. Hichens writes: "I wasn't at all certain that the tour would be a success, and even, coward that I was, arranged to have a telegram sent to call me away if my fears proved well founded. Afterwards, she confessed that she had done the very same thing, in case she found out that she just couldn't stand me." They met in the lobby of a Genoa hotel. "She welcomed me cordially, but I had the feeling that she was looking me over rather as one looks at a horse one is thinking of perhaps buying. 'Now for our tour!' she said."

They started on a bright morning and found themselves mutually attracted. Consuelo had a big, powerful motor car and Italian chauffeur; her maid went ahead by train and met them at each hotel, where Consuelo engaged, in addition to quarters for the maid, a bedroom for Robert on one side of a shared sitting room, a bedroom for herself on the other side, and an extra bedroom beyond so that there would be no noise to disturb her nights, for, as she explained to Robert, she suffered badly from insomnia.

They went to Siena to hear the nightingales singing in the moonlight, to Ravenna, Bologna, Perugia, Florence. There, at the Grand Hotel, Robert was horrified to see on the board where names of guests and their room numbers appeared: "The Duchess of Manchester and Mr. Robert Hichens, Room 28." When he told Consuelo, she laughed and said, "I'm not very prudish, and I hope you aren't, but this must be changed at once or we shall be the scandal of Florence. Do go down to the bureau and tell them my name must be put under my numbers, and that yours must be put under your number." Their tour ended in Milan; they were both "very tired" but "had had a wonderful time."

After that Robert was often at Consuelo's big house in Grosvenor Square, where, as another guest reports, the Duchess knew how to stimulate Robert's amusing talk. "He was also no mean musician," and he and Consuelo "who herself played delightfully by ear, monopolized both conversation and piano." Consuelo's liaison with Robert would last until her death. She often visited him at his country house in Broadway, Worcestershire.

Consuelo, in spite of these "deevie" distractions, kept her preeminent place on the Court carousel. Harty-Tarty died on March 24, 1908, in a hotel room in Cannes, with Lottie beside him. Her face raddled and tearstained, she told Consuelo that at the very end he'd muttered, "Well, the game is over and I am not sorry." After that Lottie left her memories moldering in the corners of stately Chatsworth and repaired permanently to the Monte Carlo Casino, where a detective followed her from table to table, returning to their owners the chips she'd filched as she sailed by.

For Consuelo, too, the game was almost over, but she kept on stoically playing her last hand. The daily "Court Circular" for June 11, 1909, informs its readers that "the Queen honoured

Consuelo, Duchess of Manchester with her presence at dinner at her Grace's London residence and remained for a small dance held subsequently." On July 6, Consuelo attended the opening at London's Hick's Theatre of a play called *His Borrowed Plumes*, which clever Jennie had written. (Its heroine was played by Mrs. Patrick Campbell, whom George Cornwallis-West would marry after he divorced Jennie.) Jennie and George and her son Winston sat proudly in one box; Consuelo sat opposite, laughing in all the right places. There must have been moments when Consuelo felt depressed, given her disastrous marriage, the death of both daughters, the self-destructive path her son had already chosen, so like his father's. But she never let her sadness show; the gay clown's mask never slipped in public.

Edith Wharton was in London that July and attended several of Consuelo's lunch parties, but it would be another ten years before she began sketching Consuelo with great accuracy in *The Buccaneers*.

The first week of August, as always, Consuelo spent at Egypt House, Cowes, arranging little parties for the King. One afternoon she joined sister Emily, Daisy, Princess of Pless, the King and his last-but-not-least mistress, Alice Keppel, for a sail on the King's yacht *Britannia*, but "there was no wind so a cruiser towed us around the island." The King was perennially short of breath, with bloodshot eyes and a port-wine face, and every laugh ended in a terrible fit of coughing. Her duty done, Consuelo went to Paris on August 10 to rest and bathe her spirit in its amethyst light. She was feeling sick and tired.

Not until November 1909 did she stop going on. "Consuelo, Duchess of Manchester is indisposed. She was not quite as well last night," the *Times* "Court Circular" reported on November 14. In the predawn hours of Saturday, November 20, at her Grosvenor Square house, opposite the present-day American Embassy, Consuelo died of heart failure following neuritis, aged fifty-one.

The funeral took place on Wednesday, November 23, at 12:45 p.m. in the Lady Chapel of Kimbolton Church. Jennie journeyed from London to attend, along with Adele, Countess of Essex. The

*10   King Edward VII and Queen Alexandra
on the royal yacht at Cowes, 1909*

King and Queen sent a wreath that bore the message: "In sorrow-ful memory of our dearest Consuelo, sincere and thoughtful friend who after suffering much pain both mentally and physically was taken to her final rest and reunited with dear ones gone before." There were more than one hundred wreaths. At the same hour as the Kimbolton funeral, a memorial service was held in London's Chapel Royal at St. James's Palace.

Consuelo, Duchess of Manchester, left a United Kingdom estate worth £324,360 with a net personalty of £116,384 and an American estate in excess of £400,000 personalty, her legacy from brother Fernando. "I bequeath to her Majesty, Queen Alexandra," read Consuelo's will, "my ruby and diamond bracelet, which I would ask her to be graciously pleased to accept as a token of my respectful affection and regard for her Majesty." It was the splen-did bracelet that had sparked such dreams upon Consuelo's wedding, gift of the Luckmeyers. To her friend and mother-in-law, Double Duchess Lottie, she left "a ruby and diamond tassel." On November 22, the *Times* printed a letter from an anonymous correspondent concerning the Duchess, Consuelo:

> One of the first of the American ladies who married into great English families, and who brought into this country that rare combination of high intelligence, a sunny nature and uncommon personal charm, which has since made such a conquest of English society, and must as time passes have a profound physiological influence on a certain stratum of the upper classes, the deceased lady from the first took a position in England which she retained for over 30 years. Her path was strewn with many sorrows, the most poignant of which was the death of her lovely twin daughters.... But in proportion as she lost or suffered, so she braced herself to the day, even where it involved an effort of giving pleasure to others in the space that might be left to her. No hostess in London or in the country dispensed a more profuse or coveted, but at the same time, discriminating hospitality; and those who had the privilege of sitting at her table and hearing her witty and

sparkling talk, framed in an accent all her own, will possess a memory of rich and enduring value. She herself would have deplored a lingering illness as inconsistent with her eager and exuberant vitality. Clearly her image stands forth from the background of conventional types, alert and truly cosmopolitan in its sympathies, irresistible in its buoyant and sometimes dazzling humour, but profound in its womanly undertones and capacity for affection.

It is a fine and fitting tribute, and one wonders if Robert Hichens was its author; more than one Society member records how grief-stricken and bereft he was after Consuelo's death. King Edward would survive her by only five months, dying on the afternoon of May 6, 1910, in his Buckingham Palace bedroom, after taking a light luncheon and playing with two pet canaries in a cage by an open window.

Consuelo Yznaga had come a long way from her Louisiana home where the Mississippi pursued its own erratic course beside a topsy-turvy house painted the color of sunshine. She had married her Duke on a whim and a wish and lived to regret it. But Consuelo was never one to sit in a corner and moan. She made herself perfectly at home in English Society by changing and enlivening it to suit her own bright person; then, with a cheerful song, she placed her bits of shiny straw at the very core of the world's mightiest Empire: in the center of a grateful King's heart.

II

LILY HAMMERSLEY

She thought of the resultless life, the life of white idleness that
awaited nearly all of them. What were they but snowflakes born to
shine for a moment and then to fade, to die, to disappear, to become
part of the black, foul-smelling slough of mud below. And by what
delicate degrees is the soul befouled in the drama of muslin,
and how little is there left for any use of life.

—GEORGE MOORE,
A Drama in Muslin (1886)

LILY RAISED HER OPERA GLASSES and took a long, hard look at the gentleman seated beside Marietta Stevens in her box. He wasn't handsome or distinguished looking; his face was plain and pale, and his dark hair turning gray. Lily sighed, remembering her late husband Louis's small stature and very large head. The passionate crescendo of the "Liebestod" from Wagner's *Tristan and Isolde* crashed its climax into crystal chandeliers. Lily dropped her opera glasses into her lap. Why couldn't real life ever approximate romance? The less-than-perfect man there in Mrs. Paran Stevens's box in New York's Metropolitan Opera House, on an autumn evening in 1887, was George Spencer-Churchill, 8th Duke of Marlborough, divorced, disgraced in English Society, but still, indisputably, a Duke. Louis, for all his odd appearance and witless ways — for he had been both physically and mentally

73

abnormal — had given her what she wanted most: wealth. And the Duke of Marlborough could give her what she currently craved: social eminence and a fine role as moral reformer to an errant male. Thirty-three-year-old Lily raised her glasses again, and, in concert with other female necks stretching toward Marietta's box like hungry swans, Lily focused her full attention on the Duke.

Mrs. Stevens's box, like Lily's, was in the double tier of the Golden Horseshoe, in the wine-and-gold, gaslit interior of the new opera house that had opened four years before. Previously, Old Money Knickerbockers had attended opera at the Academy of Music in Irving Place, where they saw to it that New Rich couldn't get boxes. Willie K. Vanderbilt, at Alva's command, met with fifty-five other swells in 1880, each of whom contributed $10,000 to secure a box and to finance a new yellow brick Opera House on Broadway at Thirty-ninth Street. The Metropolitan opened on October 22, 1883, with Christine Nilsson as Marguerite in Gounod's *Faust* swooning over a casket full of jewels that certainly couldn't compare to those winking and flashing around the Golden Horseshoe. Pushed to it by their New Rich wives, the Met's Board of Directors asked the General Manager to keep all lights on during performances — usually German opera in those early days — so that the rival show taking place in the Golden Horseshoe could be seen. Naturally, the Manager refused. Three years after the Met's opening, the old Academy of Music, unable to compete, closed its doors and disgruntled Schermerhorns and Rhinelanders either had their old rose-cut diamonds reset and went to the Met or sulked at home in their modest, unturreted houses. (After a fire at the Met in 1892, the New Rich, by then riding high and feeling secure, reduced the double horseshoe to thirty-five luxurious parterre boxes selling for $60,000 each, and reporters soon named them, aptly, the Diamond Horseshoe.)

Lily Hammersley missed the Met's first exciting 1883–84 season because she was in mourning for her husband, but after that she was always present in her box. Born Lilian Warren Price, in Troy, New York, in 1854, daughter of Elizabeth Homer Paine and Comdr. Cicero Price of the United States Navy, Lilian grew into a tall, Junoesque young woman with a pretty, open face and honey-colored hair. The town of Troy, in upstate New York, where the Mohawk and Hudson rivers converge, had once been a thriving site of industry, with a large ironworks owned by the rich Burden family. But when trains replaced river barges for low-cost transport, Troy dwindled to a backwater where mongrels slept in the dusty streets and the fashionable world never came. Lilian was therefore pleased when the Price family moved to New York and she could set about achieving her goals.

Lilian Price was the one future peeress out of five who wasn't born into a rich family close to, or within, Society's circle. She was middle class and comparatively poor. She was also all-American, completely homegrown, not educated abroad, like the other four, to high cultural and multilingual standards. This lack of cosmo-politan sophistication would prove, later, a considerable handicap to Lilian. She did, however, have two great assets: her beauty and her goodness. The first would serve her well until she was in her thirties; when beauty vanished, benevolence would take over and see her through.

Whereas Consuelo Yznaga was a little wicked and wayward, Lilian was utterly virtuous and conforming to mid-Victorian norms. Raised to True Woman ideals of piety, passivity and purity, Lilian had no ambitions for an independent life of self-fulfillment. She saw herself as wife and mother, as helpmate and minion to a man, to a *husband*, united unto death by sacred, respected marriage vows.

Like Undine Spragg in Wharton's *Custom of the Country* and Lily Bart in Wharton's *House of Mirth*, Lilian Price, when she arrived in New York, knew that in her society's marriage mart, a young woman could, sometimes, with skill and luck, barter beauty for wealth. Lily Bart's mother, in Wharton's novel, when the Barts lose their money, assures her daughter with "fierce vindictiveness": "You'll get it all back, with your face." *The House of Mirth* is Edith

Wharton's most complete appraisal of Society's values. The heart of the fool, as the Bible tells us, is in the house of mirth, but what a sumptuous, seductive house it is! As the social historian Richmond Barrett notes, the novel "neither condones the intellectual poverty of the fashionable world nor attempts to rub off the rich material bloom." Being of no intellectual pretensions whatever, faithful to Victorian poet Charles Kingsley's dictum "Be good, sweet maid, and let who will be clever," Lilian Price didn't mind, or even notice, the intellectual poverty. She lusted after opulence and laid her plans to get it.

She was an old-fashioned American female to her core, but Miss Lilian Price had one thoroughly modern streak — so modern that it was positively twentieth century. She knew the importance of packaging, of promotion, of manufacturing an image. It was as if she'd communed with some Warner Brothers press agent in Hollywood's heyday, who had explained how an anonymous starlet, no prettier than a hundred others, could be turned into a star. Lilian seemed to know by instinct that *le style c'est la femme*, or, as Henry James put it, "it is by style we are saved."

As soon as Lilian arrived in New York, she changed her name to Lily — a most felicitous choice. Flower names for women — Violet, Rose, Daisy, Pansy — reinforced the era's image of women as decorative and delicate. The name Lily suggested purity as well, for white lilies, immaculate, unspotted, were the flowers most often associated with the Virgin Mary. The name Lily brought to mind the most famous Lily of the field: the Prince of Wales's beloved Lily Langtry, the Jersey Lily, so poor when she came to London that she had only one dress, but so beautiful that she captured a future King's heart.

Having rechristened herself, Miss Lily Price turned her attention to apparel. Being a conventional woman of her time, content to float downstream on its values and fashions, she knew, as the *New York Times* social reporter noted on June 28, 1875, that "a man is rated by his money, a woman by her dress." "If I were shabby, no one would have me," Lily Bart explains to a male friend in *The House of Mirth*. "A woman is asked out as much for her clothes as for herself.... Who wants a dingy woman? We are expected to be pretty and well-dressed till we drop." Lily Bart's creator, Edith Wharton, in her autobiography, *A Backward Glance* (1934), notes that she was only three years old, wearing a new winter bonnet, when she "woke to the importance of dress and of herself as a subject of adornment." When, a few years later, an aunt asked her, "What would you like to be when you grow up?" Edith promptly replied, "the best-dressed woman in New York."

Like Edith Wharton, Lily Price never underestimated the power of a wardrobe. She pondered; how could she best accentuate her pink-and-gold coloring? She decided always to wear white, to have the softest white muslins, the finest white laces, the deepest white ruffles. Again, it was a more felicitous choice than she realized. Her white costumes not only set off her youthful, unflawed porcelain skin, but also, like her name, proclaimed her very real purity and naivety, which would long outlast her youth, for Lily had the irreducible innocence of women who spin all of life's diverse strands into pure sentiment.

(Later, when wealth allowed, Lily further enhanced her image by feeding her spaniels on chicken fricassee, cream and macaroons and bedding them in silk sheets and satin covers. She also rejected the usual decorating scheme for the salon behind her opera box. While other ladies made do with draped brocade or modest silver baskets of carnations, Lily had her salon riotously festooned, positively pavé, with fresh orchids, so many orchids that walls and ceiling hardly showed.)

Soon after she arrived in New York, Lily's attention to image-making paid off. The New York socialite Elizabeth Drexel Lehr recalls that Lily was Marion Langdon's "only dangerous rival to the claim of being the loveliest woman" in New York. "She was Lily of Troy, with no money or social position, but a face as fair as the legendary Helen's." Lily was one of eight beauties entertained by the banker William Corcoran at his cottage at White Sulphur Springs. It was an innocent, well-chaperoned party, we must hasten to add, conducted with the Gilded Age's full propriety. Corcoran was Washington's most flamboyant figure, always with a big red rose in his buttonhole, collector of paintings which would find a permanent home in the Corcoran Gallery of Art, collector of pretty young girls like Lily.

The New York Lily, according to Elizabeth Drexel Lehr, "used to create a sensation when she appeared at the Coaching Parade," held in Central Park the first Saturday in May, "in white from the ostrich plumes trimming her big hat to the French shoes on her tiny feet." New York swells had imported coaching as a pastime from England, where the Prince of Wales and the 8th Duke of Marlborough were keen participants. The New York Coaching Club was founded by Col. William Jay, that good sport who had served Kim, Lord Mandeville, as best man when he'd married Consuelo Yznaga. All her life, Lily treasured the memory of those fresh May mornings when the long line of splendid coaches waited for Colonel Jay's starting signal, while grooms in smart livery held the heads of high-strung horses as they snorted and pawed the ground, impatient to be off. Lily and Alva Vanderbilt and the other ladies, with much merriment, would climb up, up to the high seats reserved for them, while beaux and husbands, in checked suits, tan aprons, buckskin gloves and red-and-white boutonnieres, stood gallantly below, arms outstretched, ready to catch them should they fall from the heights. But Lily never slipped or showed too much leg as she climbed to her seat. Then, with a tiny, satisfying click, she would open her white silk parasol, and the horns would sound their flourish and her white silk cape would float and fall around her like petals as the horses pounded ahead.

In 1877, when this American Beauty was twenty-three, she got herself invited to the Patriarchs' Balls, those thrice-yearly dances organized by Ward McAllister where Society's daughters angled for husbands. The *New York Times*, years later, would fully appreciate the odds against Lily as she began her remarkable rise, like Cinderella's, from rags to riches, on the strength of a beautiful face and small feet: "When Miss Lily Price, from Troy, appeared at the Patriarchs', none present thought what a personage she would become in London and New York Society. She was merely a tall, slight blonde lady, dressed in white. Her parents were in moderate circumstances, which fact always checks the belledom of any young girl, for, in a New York ballroom, a plain, rich girl, with bad manners and a sour disposition, is more likely to enjoy attention than a poor girl of rare beauty and charming manners and disposition."

Lily waltzed and fanned and flirted and waltzed again in all her white radiance, and two years later found her prince — still in his frog phase, awaiting the magic that would transform him. He was Louis Carré Hammersley, a bachelor conspicuous for his odd mannerisms, and the very first time he saw Miss Price, he made up his mind to marry her, heeding the Chinese proverb "If you have two pieces of silver, take one and buy a lily." Son of Andrew Gordon Hammersley, a New York merchant who had married a daughter of John Mason and invested wisely in bonds and real estate, thirty-nine-year-old Louis was fourteen years older than Lily, with frail physique, failing health, eccentric habits — and great wealth. When he stammered out a proposal, Lily said an enthusiastic yes! They were married in 1879 and moved into palatial quarters at 257 Fifth Avenue.

The real-life Lily, with her white packaging and soft sell, *had* found a rich husband, whereas Lily Bart in *The House of Mirth* failed in her quest, in spite of her beauty. Good fiction, of course, can never be as daring or exaggerated as real life, which proceeds, without fear of literary censure, to conduct itself with all kinds of astounding miracles and coincidences.

It was shortly after her marriage that Lily Hammersley discovered to her chagrin that she had to share her husband's love and attention. Not with another woman, but with a man. Louis and his father had a strange, symbiotic relationship. "Father and son," according to one newspaper, "were nearly inseparable. They hardly ever went upon the street, to the club, the opera, the theatre or church, except in each other's company. Their remarkable display of mutual affection was the wonder and remark of all who knew them and the cause of many sarcastic remarks."

Lily also realized all too soon that even though Louis's uncle, John W. Hammersley, was one of the twenty-five Patriarchs, Society considered Louis too "queer" and his wife too "common" to admit them to its innermost circle. In any case, Louis was increasingly unwell, and hated parties, the crush, the noise; he preferred a quiet game of cards with Father. For the next four years, even without much socializing, Lily was happy enough, just reveling in her remarkable new life.

In the summers, Lily and Louis and Father went, with the rest of New York Society, to Newport. In the seventeenth century, it had been a seaport whose distilled rum was exchanged for African slaves who were traded for Barbados sugar, which was shipped back to Newport to be made into more rum. By the beginning of the eighteenth century, Newport was already a fashionable resort as wealthy planters from the South and West Indies came in summer to savor its cooling breezes and take advantage of its twenty-two distilleries. Until the 1870s, it remained an unpretentious town of white clapboard houses and rambling, wild eglantine. Then Newport grew self-consciously showy and formal, marshaled into rigid order by Ward McAllister, who gave Cotillion Dinners at his Bayside Farm, and served his famous punch of local rum diluted with champagne and one small block of ice.

By the time Lily arrived in the early 1880s, Newport Society was quite as snobbish and select as New York's, and the Hammersleys were kept on the fringes. "When Mrs. Hammersley spent her summers here," a Newport journalist would later remember, "she did not mingle in the class known as Ward McAllister's 'Four Hundred.'" Each May when she arrived, Lily would don one of her spun-sugar white confections and appear hopefully on the Casino lawn on Bellevue Avenue where Mullaly's string orchestra played and the "rubber plants," as humble townsfolk were called, squinted through hedges at these exalted gentlemen and ladies. The latter always turned their pastel-colored backs on Lily, murmuring from under their parasols, "Such a silly affectation, Mrs. Hammersley's white gowns," not knowing that in another ten years they'd all be wearing white. Lily consoled herself with the knowledge that her gowns were beautiful. Still, she sometimes envied her friend, pretty young Mrs. Henry Clews, who most residents seemed to think was Newport's best-dressed lady, and who confided to Lily that each year she set aside $10,000 for mistakes in clothes.

When autumn came, the Hammersleys returned to New York. Every day Lily rushed in and out of her Fifth Avenue mansion, her costume different each time, to dressmaker's fittings and shopping sprees and five o'clock fireside teas where silver trays were piled with delicious little cakes, their icing thick and gleaming. When fresh snow fell, Louis's cousin, J. Hooker Hammersley, took Lily, muffled to her chin in furs, for a ride through Central Park's white fairyland in his troika, imported from Russia. Then in January 1883, Louis's father died, and four months later, on Thursday, May 3, in their Fifth Avenue house, Louis died of unknown causes, aged forty-three. The funeral took place at Grace Church, where Consuelo Yznaga had been married, on Monday morning, May 7, at ten o'clock, and Lily reluctantly laid aside her spotless raiment and donned black mourning clothes, with her crepe veil exactly the fashionable length. She wept heartfelt tears for Louis, for she was both emotional and softhearted, and looked forward to the day one year hence when plain crepe would give way to jet and passementerie, and to the day two years hence when black would yield to the palest shade of mauve.

Louis's will was presented for probate on May 18, and Lily found herself possessed of an estate of more than $4 million, for Louis had left everything to her, naming George C. Williams, President of New York's Chemical Bank, as executor and Lily as executrix. In the fall of that year, many distant Hammersley relatives, irate at being cut off without a penny, launched a bitter court battle, contesting the will, which dragged its acrimonious length through the next three years. The relatives tried to prove that Louis "had been under the influence of his wife and that the will embodied her wishes." There was much talk of his feeble brain and eccentricity, but Lily's spinster maid, Becky Jones, proved steadfast in her mistress's cause, refusing to divulge the truth about

Mr. Louis's addled wits. From May 20, 1884, to March 28, 1885, Becky served time for contumacy in Ludlow Street jail, and when at last she was released, she exclaimed, "Now say that a woman can't keep a secret, will ye!" Finally, on January 3, 1886, Surrogate Rollins ruled that Louis's money was all Lily's. By that time the estate's capital had grown to $6 million. She was rich, still young and full of bright dreams.

However, the publicity of the long court battle against the Hammersleys had pushed Lily even further to Society's periphery. As the *New York Times* observed: "While the widow Hammersley's comings and goings were noted, her carriage observed in the Park, and her presence scanned as she sat at the opera, the widow herself was not a popular personage."

But as she sat in her opera box, on that autumn evening in 1887, with one eye on the stage and one on the Duke of Marlborough, so close and yet so distant, Lily saw a way to augment her social status a thousandfold. Being a middle-class American, she believed in the American dream, namely that every member of her class could, with enough dollars and dedication, climb the status ladder to the very top rung. Boys could end up in the White House and girls in a golden palace.

Within her chosen, limited sphere, Lily was a female version of the Gilded Age's many self-made men, for she had the same drive and determination, if rather different goals. Lily set her sights on penetrating English Society, knowing it was the grandest, but unlike Consuelo Yznaga, she didn't want to lead it or change it or play a starring role. Lily's ambitions were far more modest: she merely wanted to get in, and she saw the Duke of Marlborough as a likely ticket. She was too much of an innocent to know how defaced and devalued that particular ticket was.

Lily had been tracking the Duke's movements in the daily press since August 28, the day he landed in New York aboard the *Umbria*. Since then, to Lily's frustration, he had been in Newport and Boston, and had only returned to New York in early October.

George Charles Spencer-Churchill, born May 13, 1844, was the son and heir of John Winston Spencer-Churchill, 7th Duke of Marlborough, the latter a pious, pompous gentleman against whose strict decorum and morality his eldest son would spend his life rebelling. George Charles, called Blandford all his life because his preducal title was Marquess of Blandford, was expelled from Eton for his extremely accurate work with a catapult. He served as an officer in the Blues and sowed so many wild oats that his chum, the Prince of Wales, no innocent himself, always referred to Blandford as "one of those wicked boys." On November 8, 1869, at the age of twenty-five, Blandford was married in Westminster Abbey to Lady Albertha Hamilton, daughter of the Duke of Abercorn. "Old Magnificent," as he was called, was related to half the noble houses in the United Kingdom, and was so proud that he insisted his housemaids wear white gloves when they made his bed to keep the ducal sheets from lower-class contamination. His daughter Albertha, nicknamed "Goosie," was pretty enough, with blue eyes, black hair arranged in tight curls and small feet and hands that she was very proud of, declaring that they had never needed a manicure. But Goosie was a woman of narrow horizons, as Blandford soon discovered, for, like most female English aristocrats, she had been given no proper education. Her husband, on the other hand, was extremely intelligent and well-read; he spoke many languages, including Urdu, was versed in higher mathematics, physics, chemistry and mechanics. His fox-hunting, shooting fellow peers viewed him with alarm; a future Duke who was a committed intellectual and who didn't seem to give a damn for the social conventions of his class was a chap to be shunned. Blandford, for his part, was bored with English Society's silly pomp and parade, finding there no outlet for his intellectual genius; he was also, almost immediately after marriage, bored with Goosie, and vented his frustrations by embarking on a series of widely publicized love affairs. Goosie then vented *her* spleen for her husband's blatant womanizing by resorting to such practical jokes as bits of soap placed among the cheeses at dinner to make guests ill, and an ink pot placed above a doorway to

12 *Blandford, the future 8th Duke of Marlborough,
looking young and wicked*

drop its contents on her scholar-husband's head. Yet Goosie bore Blandford four children, including the requisite heir, and presented a properly smiling countenance to the world, ignoring her husband's flagrant infidelities as a good wife should.

When, in 1874, Blandford's young brother Randolph impetuously became engaged to Jennie Jerome, Blandford's acerbic view of marriage surfaced in a poem he sent to Randolph which read in part:

Remorse shall seize upon thy stricken soul
When tinselled charms begin to pall.
Thy part is strife, a fractious grief thy whole
If thou doest thus in weakness fall.

And when thy better half shall whine or fret
Because thou dinest not at home,
Perchance the scene will turn into a pet,
Then wilt thou at thy fortunes moan!

Randolph, as we know, ignored Blandford's advice and married Jennie with no regrets, but rancor against his elder brother remained: "Really, the heartless, selfish way in which he talks is too much for me. He really is very bad," Randolph wrote to Jennie on April 20, 1875. Randolph's ire was fueled by the fact that Blandford had cast his appraising eye on Jennie's "tinselled charms" and found them sterling. He gave her a ring, which Jennie promptly showed to her mother-in-law, Duchess Fanny, rigidly corseted in righteousness, a proud grande dame if ever there was one. The horrified Duchess told Jennie that it was Goosie's ring, which Blandford had *no right* to give her. One of the many Marlborough family rows ensued, conducted, as they always were, on paper. Angry, name-calling letters darted about. Blandford's minor sin, however, was forgotten when, in 1876, a major scandal broke about his head, one that shook English Society to its core and made a deep crack in the virtuous mask it always wore in public, wanting to appear morally pure to the lower classes. Much worse than adultery was its advertisement, and when the so-called Aylesford Affair got into the papers, Blandford gave the public not just a peek but a panoramic view.

It all began with Blandford's admiring socialite Edith Aylesford's "pretty dresses" and Goosie's innocently having them copied for her own high-busted form. When Blandford took lodgings "for a winter's good hunting" in an inn adjacent to Edith's home, Packington Hall, near Coventry, Goosie didn't think it the least odd. Edith's husband, hard-drinking, fast-riding "Sporting Joe" had gone off to India with the Prince of Wales to stick pigs, shoot elephants and, on the borders of Nepal, kill six large tigers all in a day. Back in England, Blandford was making tracks through the snow, climbing through a conveniently opened window and finding his way, night after night, to Edith's bed. On February 20, while encamped on the Sardah River, Sporting Joe received a letter from Edith saying she was about to elope with Blandford and requesting a divorce. Prince Edward grew red-faced and, spluttering, called Blandford "the greatest blackguard alive" and dispatched his dear friend Joe, on a useful elephant saved from the slaughter, to the nearest railway station. When he landed in England, Sporting Joe swore he'd divorce Edith, naming Blandford as co-respondent, and fight the scoundrel in a duel for good measure.

Harty-Tarty, Lottie Manchester's longtime lover, ever cool and phlegmatic, managed to dissuade Joe from the duel but not the divorce. Divorce was to be avoided at all costs, for then everyone's dirty linen would be washed in public, so Blandford's brother Randolph asked the Prince to persuade Joe to stay married and to stop broadcasting his woes. The Prince flatly refused. Then Edith gave Randolph a packet of love letters written to her by Prince Edward when *he* had been her lover. Randolph rushed to Marlborough House and waved them in Princess Alexandra's face, telling her that unless her husband the Prince persuaded Joe not to divorce, he would make the letters public. "Public" was the word that made everyone blanch, including Alexandra, but when she contacted the Prince, he only got redder at the idea that Randolph was trying to blackmail him, and roared that he would challenge Lord Randolph to a duel, pistols at dawn, on a deserted beach in northern France; let him name his second. Lord Charles Beresford was dispatched from India with the Prince's challenge, but Randolph heeded Jennie's practical view that one simply didn't duel with one's future sovereign.

Meanwhile, still-innocent Goosie perpetrated an extremely pertinent practical joke. Edith had confided to Blandford that she feared she was pregnant with his child. When, sitting at breakfast one morning with Goosie, Blandford lifted his silver cover and saw beneath, not kidneys and bacon, but a pink celluloid baby doll, he choked and fled, and Goosie couldn't think why. Eventually, Sporting Joe lived up to his name and called off the divorce, and Prince Edward made it known that he would enter no house containing Lord Randolph or Blandford. Thanks to Jennie's charm and tact, she and Randolph were reinstated in the Prince's favor in 1884, but most of Society kept its doors firmly closed against Blandford.

He and Edith had to flee to France, where they set up housekeeping as Mr. and Mrs. Spencer, and in 1881 Edith brought forth a small pink baby, this one real enough. Sporting Joe got well away by going to live in America, where he ended his days in Texas as an alcoholic rancher, dying there in 1884, aged thirty-six. Edith stayed in France, and when passion cooled, Blandford returned to England. Goosie finally opened her blue eyes to life's hard realities and in 1882 launched her divorce suit. By that time, relations between naughty Blandford and his prudish, straitlaced father, the 7th Duke, were strained almost to breaking point.

(History obligingly repeats itself, for the relationship of the present Marquess of Blandford to his father, the 11th Duke of Marlborough, is also frosty, owing to the heir's wild ways. Thirty-six-year-old Jamie, Lord Blandford, has been far more strenuously dedicated to rebellion than his great-great-grandfather Blandford ever was. Since 1982, Jamie has been fined or jailed for multiple driving offenses, for assaulting a policeman, for breaking into a pharmacy to steal drugs and for possession of cocaine. He left his wife of two years, Becky, in January 1992, and in the following summer moved into a seedy apartment in London's Earl's Court district with girlfriend Arabella Tait. There are rumors that the 11th Duke may disinherit his wayward elder son in favor of his younger one, Edward.)

The 7th Duke of Marlborough, Blandford's distraught and disillusioned father, stopped short of disinheritance. He died in July 1883, of a heart attack, whereupon Blandford succeeded as 8th Duke of Marlborough, with only £7,000 left in the ducal purse. In November of that year his divorce became absolute, and the Duke invited Randolph and Jennie, who quite liked her reprobate brother-in-law, to spend the winter with him at Blenheim Palace, his huge country seat near Oxford, which had been given by Queen Anne to John Churchill, 1st Duke of Marlborough, the great military hero who had beaten the French at the Battle of Blenheim in 1704.

The brothers were soon at odds again, however, for Randolph disapproved of Blandford's selling 227 famous paintings that had always adorned Blenheim's stark walls, including Raphael's *Ansidei Madonna* and Van Dyck's *Time Clipping the Wings of Cupid*. Off they all went, most of them to Christie's auction rooms, and Blandford found himself richer by £350,000, which he spent on equipment for tenant farms and on splendid hothouses at Blenheim to be filled with extravagant orchids.

By summer 1887, the Marlborough coffers were empty again; the Duke's rent-roll income from his 23,511 acres was a mere £36,557, and what self-respecting Duke could live on that? Blandford went to Lavington Park, a large house that Clara and Moreton Frewen had rented that summer, to join a house party that included Minnie and Arthur Paget, Clara's sister Jennie, but not Randolph, and dashing Count Kinsky, Jennie's future lover. Moreton talked excitedly of finding gold in America. He had a harebrained scheme for extracting it from the refuse of mines with a machine he'd invented called "the gold-crusher." Blandford conceived a simpler, surer plan for acquiring gold and soon after sailed away on the *Umbria*.

The 8th Duke's arrival in New York on August 28 was greeted with loud hoots of derision by the American press, who weren't as innocent concerning ducal morals as they had been when Lord Mandeville secured Consuelo Yznaga eleven years before. One newspaper commented acidly, noting the Duke's thirty-five pieces of luggage: "Everything his Grace of Marlborough brought with him was clean, except his reputation." Another snapped: "Where the great Marlborough conquered campaigns, the little Marlborough conquers courtesans; the man of the past won battles, the man of the present wins bawds." When the Marquess of Stafford came wife-hunting, the *New York World* ran the headline: "Attention, American heiresses, what will you bid?" but the Duke of Marlborough, who was "badness personified," clearly wasn't worth a lead nickel. He had been severely censured in England for his sins, and in still-Puritan America moral standards were far more strict. When Thomas Hardy's novel *Jude the Obscure* appeared serially in a New York periodical in 1895, he had to turn the children born to Jude and Sue into adopted orphans; when a New York editor offered Edith Wharton a large sum for the serial rights to a proposed novel, he stipulated that no "unlawful attachment" should figure in it. That Lily Hammersley read of the Duke of Marlborough's licentious habits in the American papers and still wanted him as husband can be interpreted in several ways. She was desperate for a Duke; she had such a low self-image that she felt he was all she deserved; or, most probably, like so many True Women before her, she felt sure she could reform him; all he needed to keep him pure was the love of a good woman.

When the *New York Times* interviewed the Duke on the day of his arrival, he was deliberately vague about the purpose of his trip:

"I really don't know how long I shall remain in this country," he told reporters. "You see, I just came over for a pleasant trip. I am tired of the places in Europe that I have visited almost every year, so I thought I would come to America." To the Duke, everything in New York looked too shiny and everyone moved too fast and spoke too loud and the weather was far too hot. He went the very next day, Monday, to Newport to stay with Marietta Stevens, mother of his friend Minnie Paget, at her "cottage," Marietta Villa, on Bellevue Avenue.

Being a flower lover, the Duke admired the blue hydrangeas that bordered every lawn; their azure color was so intense that it looked like an expensive dye. The blue hydrangea was Newport's favorite flower, being, like Society itself, showy, puffed up, artificial and hard to ignore. When His Grace dropped into the blue hydrangeas, tomcat among the pouter-pigeons, Newport matrons were in a tizzy. Should they cultivate or cut him? They'd read all about his wicked ways, but a Duke was a Duke and this one was clearly in want of a wife. While the stuffier matrons shunned His Grace, those with marriageable daughters pushed them straight into his primrose path — which clearly indicates the frenzy to which peer-stalking had risen in America by the late 1880s.

On Monday evening, at the final Casino Dance, Edith Wharton, a bride of two years, observed the Duke closely — she was collecting material for future novels — while he danced with Adèle Grant, already peer-hunting, but with another six years to go before Consuelo Manchester would find her the Earl of Essex. On Wednesday, Marietta gave a dinner and dance at her villa for eighty people, including all the husband-hunting belles, which went on "until a late hour." Dinner parties were given on Friday at Ochre Court by the Ogden Goelets, parents of nine-year-old May, destined for a different Duke, and on Saturday by the Isaac Townsend Burdens, when Newport belle Eleanor Winslow was planted beside His Grace. On Sunday afternoon, Marietta paraded him up and down Bellevue Avenue in her carriage with Hélène Beckwith, daughter of Nelson Beckwith, beside him. Forty-year-old spinster Hélène was odds-on favorite for next

Duchess with half of Newport Society; the other half were betting on Cornelia Adair, John Adair's widow, who had consoled Consuelo Manchester at Tandragee in the first sad year of her marriage.

Newspapers across the country kept their female readers, including Lily, informed of the Duke's hot-and-cold reception at Newport, and on September 11, the *New York Times* pronounced the final word on His Dis-Grace, the 8th Duke of Marlborough:

> During the past week it [Newport] has had a fox terrier show, the Duke of Marlborough and little else. The esteemed visitor, it is said, visited the show and expressed his opinion of it in decidedly uncomplimentary terms. As he is thought in England to have gone, socially speaking, to the dogs, long ago, his opinion of terriers is probably a competent one... With the exception of 4 or 5 women, who are considered by their fellows and neighbours to be either extremely innocent or else very foolish, Marlborough has had the cold shoulder turned toward him more than ever in the past week, despite all reports to the contrary. There is a general and wholesome prejudice in this country against men, be they peers or peasants, Dukes or dirt heavers, who are lacking in chivalry or in that regard or respect for women and the sanctity of home which is a part of true manhood everywhere to maintain.

From Newport the Duke went to Boston, the very heart of Puritanism, where the prudish buzz and bluster reached its loudest pitch, and by early October he was back in New York, appearing in Marietta's opera box and Lily's dreams, and being shown about town by Leonard Jerome, father of adorable sister-in-law Jennie. The Duke also paid a visit to Menlo Park, New Jersey, where Thomas Edison still had his house and laboratory, the very first industrial research lab in the United States, soon to be moved to West Orange. There in the long room on the second floor, which ran the entire length of the building, with a pipe organ at one end for evening relaxation, a central table laden with instruments and wall shelves crowded with jars of chemicals, the forty-one-year-old Edison discussed the telephone with the Duke. Quite independently of Alexander Graham Bell's researches in the 1870s and Edison's refinements, the Duke had, at about the same time, invented a telephone system and installed it at Blenheim Palace with a large, delicate soundboard in the pantry and wires everywhere up and down the corridors. No one at Blenheim appreciated Blandford's invention; his autocratic father offered no praise, but then he never had; the housemaids complained about the wires everywhere, which tripped them. Now, at last, Blandford had found a kindred spirit who could appreciate his scientific prowess. Edison was extremely impressed with the Duke's knowledge, and wrote to their mutual friend Moreton Frewen: "I thought the English Duke was a fool with a crown on his head. But this one knows a great deal which I do not intend inventing until next fall."

In late autumn the Duke went west but, finding no gold there, was back in New York by early spring 1888, staying at the Albemarle Hotel. Lily Hammersley, meanwhile, had persuaded Leonard, her old friend from coaching days, to introduce her to Blandford. When the meeting duly took place, Lily was mesmerized by the forty-five-year-old peer's "diabolical charm" and the soft, mellifluous voice that more than one contemporary remembers. He was not at all like the blunt, big-fisted, seafaring men who had been her father's cronies, or like the loud, hustling business tycoons who had been Louis's acquaintances. His Grace the Duke was suave, sophisticated, never in a hurry, with hands as soft as a woman's, manners as gentle.

The Duke, for his part, saw a plump but still comely woman of no particular social distinction. He had, however, learned of Lily's $7 million from Leonard Jerome. Beyond that inducement, he liked the way Lily made him feel extremely clever and masculine and in control. As he held forth on a great variety of subjects, she gazed at him, rapt, adoring, as if she depended on him for the breath of life itself. Blandford had a complex personality, buried, private; his intellectual brilliance had scattered itself in too many directions; his passionate hedonism brought him no lasting satisfaction. He also had a dark, ineradicable melancholy common to the house of Marlborough. Lily made him feel almost cheerful and as if he really counted in the general scheme of things. She had endless patience and sympathy and kindness. Nothing seemed to rile her. Her charm and imperturbability and inexhaustible good nature soothed his inner restlessness and unfocused nervous energy.

In some ways it was a strange coming-together, but Lily and Blandford suited and complemented each other rather miraculously. Lily missed him, when in the middle of their "courtship," which is what she called it to herself as she primped before her cheval glass, Blandford went off to the Adirondacks with Leonard Jerome's brother Lawrence and some other men for a week's angling for trout. Leonard wrote to his wife, Clara: "I rather think he [the Duke] will marry the Hammersley. Don't you fear any responsibility on my part. Mrs. H. is quite capable of deciding for herself.... At the same time I hope the marriage will come off as there is no doubt that she has lots of tin."

Sometime later in that spring of 1888, Blandford did indeed propose to Lily and was quickly accepted. He gave her two most appropriate presents to mark their engagement: a handsomely inlaid table and box, both of which had growing orchids at their centers. One of his many hobbies, he told her, caressing the box's inlay with a well-manicured finger, was making such boxes from rare, exotic woods. Blandford had a love of beautiful things quite as keen as Lily's. They set the wedding date for Friday, June 29.

On the day before the wedding, a *New York Times* reporter tracked down a friend of Lily's who told him

that the Duke was a frequent visitor at Mrs. Hammersley's Fifth Avenue residence; that he has lately given Mrs. Hammersley a number of presents. "Just when the marriage will occur," said the lady, "I do not happen to know, but I am sure it will be within a very short time." Discussing the event further, the lady said: "The Duke is very fond of money, and

I know for some time that he was making inquiries as to Mrs. Hammersley's fortune. On the other hand, everyone knows that Mrs. Hammersley is not averse to marrying a title, and for that reason the engagement does not surprise me much. I am only sorry that Mrs. Hammersley is not better acquainted with the Duke's little affairs in England than she is."

Lily brushed the "little affairs" aside — they were all in the past, best forgotten — and looked forward eagerly to a brand-new chapter in her amazing storybook life.

At one o'clock on the wedding day, Lily's carriage, a coupé drawn by two dappled grays, drew up in front of the Chemical Bank at Broadway and Chambers Street, and Lily's "intimate friend," the widowed Mrs. John Cruger, an attractive woman with large blue eyes and smooth brown hair, wearing a corsage of pink roses on her black dress, was handed out by Lily's liveried footman, and entered the bank to return minutes later with its President, Lily's financial adviser, George C. Williams. He got into the carriage, which then made its way to the Chambers Street entrance to New York's Courthouse. There they were met by Leonard Jerome and by Creighton Webb, who was to serve as best man for the civil ceremony. Fortyish Creighton, whom one belle of the day called "fearfully dissipated," was the roué bachelor brother of Dr. Seward Webb, who had married Willie K. Vanderbilt's sister Eliza. Like Lord Mandeville before him, the Duke of Marlborough had managed to find New York's closest thing to a rake to befriend him. Tall, angular Leonard Jerome eagerly pumped Lily's gloved hand. His hair was iron gray now, his mustache drooping; Leonard was in his sixties and had retired from Wall Street to spend his afternoons in the Union Club shooting pool.

Everyone then hurried through the Courthouse, across the park, and into City Hall, going directly to the Mayor's office, where Blandford, having come down from the Albemarle Hotel in a hansom cab, awaited his bride. He was pacing impatiently about, according to one reporter, attired in a dark business suit; polka-dot four-in-hand; a white (rather than Newport blue) hydrangea in his buttonhole; and buttoned patent-leather gaiters. His hands darted nervously over his black silk top hat, lined in purple silk embroidered with his monogram. When Officer Gallagher could stand it no longer, he took the hat from the Duke's twitching fingers and placed it firmly on a nearby table. Mayor Abram S. Hewitt, who was to perform the ceremony, greeted Lily warmly, for he'd known her "since she was a little girl," as he told a reporter. Abram had graced Alva Vanderbilt's 1883 costume ball as "King Lear while yet in his right mind."

There were contract papers to sign before the ceremony, but for some reason there was a considerable wait, while Blandford stood stiffly guarding the table of documents, one hand on the back of a chair, and Lily moved aimlessly about, talking, sitting down, standing up again, gazing out the window, looking through the open door to the large room beyond where the ceremony would take place and where friends and reporters clustered eagerly. She was dressed completely in a creamy shade called écru — as close to white as an unvirginal widow could get for a marriage. She wore a cashmere dress with silk panels, trimmed in écru and gilt passementerie, with an écru straw bonnet. She carried — what else? — lilies-of-the-valley, held tightly in hands hidden by gauntlet gloves of écru undressed kid. "As she stood near the Duke, her stately imposing figure was in striking contrast with his rather small, spare build," one reporter noted. "Her heavy brown hair was brushed carefully off her forehead and arranged in a Greek coil, and she impressed the beholder simply as a magnificent woman."

Finally, the marriage contract having been signed, everyone moved into a large adjoining room for the ceremony, where about forty people waited, including Ward McAllister, smiling smugly because he took credit, publicly, for having engineered the match, and Mr. and Mrs. Nelson Beckwith, smiling gamely but grimly, because daughter Hélène had missed snaring the Duke at Newport. (In another two years, she would marry the Hon. Dudley Leigh, later 3rd Baron Leigh, eight years her junior.) Henry Clews was also there — he would host the wedding party —

husband of Newport's best-dressed lady. Henry had a sharp nose, muttonchop whiskers, the look of a wise ferret, and a bald pate which had once prompted a Society wit to stammer: "I s-s-say, Clews, since you are a self-made man, why the devil didn't you put more hair on your head?" Henry had come on vacation as a young man from England to America, liked its snap and bustle, decided to stay. Eventually, he founded his own brokerage firm on Wall Street, and in 1874 married Lucy Madison Worthington, grandniece of President Madison, who found herself married to a man whose views of women were extremely condescending. Henry declared in his autobiography that without a man, a woman is "like a ship at sea in a heavy gale without compass, anchor or rudder. They have no ballast apart from men, and are liable to perish when adversity arises." He also thought women hopeless about managing their money because "they do not seem to have the mental qualities required to take in the various points of the situation." Along with George Williams of the Chemical Bank, Henry Clews managed Lily's millions for her and she, quite as convinced as Henry of the limitations of her gender, was properly grateful.

The Mayor stood near his desk, and signaled to Creighton Webb that all was ready. Lily and Blandford stepped forward, and the Mayor began the short civil service. When he asked if either bride or groom "knew of any impediment why you may not be lawfully joined," Blandford bit his mustache nervously. When it came time for the ring, bride and groom faced each other, and the Duke pushed and shoved a small solitaire diamond onto Lily's fourth finger.

After declaring the couple married, the beaming Mayor turned at once to Lily: "Now, Your Grace, if you will permit me the only privilege I may enjoy as mayor, and perhaps the only opportunity of saluting a Duchess —" And then, according to the *New York Times*, "the Mayor's mouth was stopped by a kiss which he planted square upon the ripe lips of the Duchess, and everybody laughed heartily, including the bride who blushed just a little." Then everyone rushed up with congratulations, while "the Duke took the whole thing as a very matter-of-fact affair, but the Duchess seemed to be much affected. She threw her arms about the neck of one of her lady friends, and kissed her time and time again, and there was the faintest suggestion of tears in her eyes, and she tried to hide them by burying her face in her friend's bosom. Then she talked incoherently for a moment. She was happy." The company then repaired to the bride's Fifth Avenue mansion for a short respite.

At five o'clock, the Duke and Creighton Webb rolled up to the Lincoln National Bank — banks loomed large in these nuptials — picked up ex–Postmaster General Thomas L. James and proceeded on their way to the home of Daniel C. Potter, Pastor of Tabernacle Baptist Church on Second Avenue, where the Duke insisted that another ceremony, a proper religious one, should take place. He had wanted it to be in an Episcopalian Church, and Creighton had tried his best to find one, but the General Episcopalian Convention had passed a ruling that no divorced person could be married in its churches, so Creighton had persuaded Potter to conduct an Episcopalian service in his Baptist church. Pastor Potter, according to Society's wags, always retired to bed with a prayer on his lips: "Oh, Lord, Thou makest the clay, but we are the Potters."

Lily and Mrs. Cruger duly arrived, Lily now wearing a shot-silk street dress, "which perhaps reflected in a grosser way her agitated mind, in that in every light it bore a different shade," according to one of the more imaginative journalists present. She extended both gloved hands to Potter eagerly as Thomas James presented him. Then the party went into the church next door, arranged themselves around the chancel, and that old devil Creighton Webb, quick to transform himself, stopped playing best man and tried to look fatherly enough to give the bride away, while Mr. James took on the role of best man. This time, Blandford drew forth from a massive engraved case a heavy, wide gold band, which he placed on Lily's finger. He and Lily knelt for the final benediction, trooped into the vestry to sign the register and that was that. They were now civilly and religiously united.

Leonard had immediately dashed home after wedding number one to write a full account to Clara in England. "Well, Blandford is married! I went with him to the Mayor's office in the City Hall at one o'clock today and witnessed the ceremony. The bride was looking very well and all passed off quietly. I took charge of his cable to the Duchess [Blandford's mother, Dowager Duchess Fanny], also sent one of my own to Jennie. I dine with them at Delmonico's this evening."

The dinner at New York's favorite restaurant, given by Henry Clews for a dozen friends of the newlyweds, lasted from 6:30 to 9:00 p.m. After that, the Duke, oddly enough, went off by himself to the Albemarle Hotel, and Lily went back to her house, just as if two perfectly legal marriages had never taken place. Next morning, with Leonard Jerome, genial as ever, there to see them off, the Duke and Duchess sailed for England on the *Aurania*.

The *New York Times* ended its long and detailed account of the wedding, which had all the narrative thrust and sentimental touches of romantic fiction, with an optimistic note that probably coincided with Lily's own hopes for the future: the Duke "had conducted himself with the most exemplary propriety" during his American stay, the *Times* assured its readers. "Whatever he may have heretofore been, he is now a sober, serious and proper person of the house of Marlborough and will probably make his American Duchess a good husband."

As soon as Lily and Blandford arrived in London, he hurried her off to the Registry Office in London's Mount Street for yet another marriage ceremony. The Duke seemed obsessed with tying his nuptial knot so securely that Lily's millions could never slip free. His suspicion of the validity of marriage rites may have been fueled by the fact that his grandfather, the 6th Duke, had lured a Miss Susan Law — ironic name! — into a marriage ceremony with no hint of law about it, conducted as it was by a Guards officer friend of the Duke's dressed up as parson. Poor Susan bore several children before discovering that her "husband" was properly married to Jane, daughter of the Earl of Galloway, the first of his three legal wives.

Lily and Blandford stayed for two weeks with the Duke's mother, Duchess Fanny, an emotionally repressed woman who lived in Grosvenor Square amid plenty of tight-buttoned plush and heavy portieres, some of them hung in her mind to keep everything that wasn't perfectly proper and pleasant out of sight, including her eldest son's sexual escapades. Lily was scrutinized by the pop-eyed Duchess and her six daughters, all but one married to a title. They thought Lily's clothes, like Jennie's, far too showy, but could see that she was a sweet, old-fashioned female of their own persuasion, for they were solidly opposed to the shocking idea of female suffrage, and content to shine only on the domestic front.

That fortnight's close proximity to London Society in the middle of its Season was a terrible disappointment to Lily, for she realized all too soon that for as long as she was married to Blandford — and she trusted that would be forever — she would never be welcomed into Society's inner circle. Not only were most of its doors closed to him and consequently to his bride, but since Queen Victoria's very strict Court never countenanced divorced men, the Duke of Marlborough's wife couldn't be presented to the sovereign at one of the Court Drawing Rooms.

For the second time, as in her marriage to Louis Hammersley, Lily saw her hopes of social preeminence thwarted. Moreover, with the few titled families of the "fast set" who still recognized Blandford, Lily was not the scintillating success that the first wave of American girls had been, namely Consuelo, Jennie and Minnie, who'd arrived in the 1870s, for the simple reason that Lily didn't have their kind of vivacious, fun-loving, well-read, cosmopolitan personality. Lily was older, less animated, serious and literal minded, less accomplished, more provincial and bourgeois, and so self-effacing that in mixed company she left little impression at all.

In addition to her own personality, Lily had another disadvantage in England, for the British press was beginning to voice disapproval of Anglo-American matches. *Society* magazine deplored "the successful raids made by our American sisters-in-law on the English marriage market," and *Vanity Fair* in its July issue admitted that the new Duchess of Marlborough was "a very handsome woman" but denied that she had anything like £30,000 a year. "A recent marriage has all at once made her [the American girl] again a topic of discussion in England," wrote the *New York Tribune*'s London correspondent, George Smalley, on November 17, 1888, the "recent marriage" being Lily's. Smalley noted that "the English girl has always been dependent upon her mother to get her a husband," and those mothers interviewed by him were sounding rather hysterical, calling American girls in London "sad poachers," "the most formidable of competitors" and "forward hussies." One sniffed, "There are two things I wish the Americans would keep to themselves: their girls and their tinned lobster."

There was a double-edged anxiety underlying this British hostility. First of all, while a titled male could marry a British merchant's daughter to refill family coffers without loss of status, his sister couldn't marry a tradesman without losing hers, since her status was determined by her husband's; she had to find an aristocratic spouse, and once the Americans had picked the plums, there were jolly few left for her. Second, prestige and power in peers' families was constantly eroding, slipping down the social scale into the hands of immensely rich plutocrats — Jewish financiers such as the Rothschilds and Sassoons, colonial entrepreneurs such as Cecil Rhodes and Thomas Lipton — all most upsetting. New Rich American brides like Lily became the focus for Society's general antipathy to all upstart millionaires.

At the end of her two weeks in London, conscious of her social handicaps, Lily turned her back on Society, leaned more heavily on Blandford and went, feeling cheerful at the prospect, down to Blenheim Palace in Oxfordshire, her future home.

Blenheim was another severe shock and bitter disappointment. Home was the center of the True Woman's universe, hub and haven of her activity, responsibility and influence. "Our natural

*13 The magnificent Blenheim Palace,
the Marlboroughs' country house*

and happiest life," wrote Dinah Maria Mulock in *A Woman's Thoughts About Women* (1858), "is when we lose ourselves in the exquisite absorption of home, the delicious retirement of dependent love." "Woman's nature, physical, intellectual, moral and emotional, clearly points to home as her sphere," declared William Landels in *Woman: Her Position and Power* (1870), whereas man's sphere encompassed all the rest of the world. Ideally, the Womanly Woman needed four ingredients to be happy and fulfilled: a cosy, peaceful house; children; active domesticity; an attentive, sexually faithful spouse. At Blenheim Palace, to her intense chagrin, Lily discovered that she was to have none of these.

Take, to begin with, Lily's new domicile. Blenheim Palace was part tourist attraction, part historical museum, both showplace and monument, but it most certainly wasn't a home. Tourists trekked through it once a week, admiring its priceless tapestries of war, its stiff, high-backed two-hundred-year-old chairs. But tourists could then leave magnificence behind and return to their low-beamed cottages and snug hearths. Lily was stuck with Blenheim. Begun in 1705, and completed some forty years later, Blenheim Palace had been built by the famous general, the 1st Duke of Marlborough, to show off his wealth and power to the world; like Lily, he was ahead of his time in recognizing the need to advertise. The architect, Sir John Vanbrugh, on the Duke's instructions, had built a house with "State, Beauty and Convenience" in mind, but the latter was more or less an afterthought. Blenheim was a daunting, sprawling dinosaur of a house, made of immense blocks of ocher stone, with miles of cold corridors, just under two hundred gloomy, high-ceilinged rooms, an excess everywhere of gray interior stone and icy marble. How could one, poor Lily probably asked herself, as she pulled her wool shawls more closely about her with chilly fingers, make a real home of a house that covered three whole acres? The huge front Hall had a ceiling sixty-seven feet high and gigantic Corinthian columns. Walking through it, her heels echoing hollowly on the Portland stone floor, was like walking through some medieval cathedral that had never felt the sun. The Grand Saloon, behind the Hall, had immense white marble doorcases, a dado running round the room made of marble the color of dried blood and murals done by Louis Laguerre in 1719 full of painted columns ascending austerely to a forty-foot ceiling. With all those pillars everywhere, Lily felt as if she were living *outside* a house, under the White House's portico, say, rather than *inside*. The aptly named Long Library was 180 feet long; if Lily stood at one end of it, a person at the other could hardly be seen and certainly couldn't be heard.

When Lily gently expressed to Blandford her discomfort in Blenheim's overpowering, intimidating presence, he merely told her that the 1st Duke's wife, Duchess Sarah, had also disliked the "wild, unmerciful house" but found sanctuary in the Bow-Window Room, which was only forty-one feet long with columns of wood, rather than cold stone. As far as Lily was concerned, there was only one cozy room at Blenheim: the housekeeper's sitting room, and Lily found herself feigning excuses to go there. It was small, warm, homely, with a cat purring on the drugget carpet, souvenir china from Margate and Brighton on the mantel, one modern, comfy, overstuffed chair before the fire on which no sovereign or Prince had ever sat.

Lily used her money to do what she could. Central heating was installed throughout the house, but it made little impact on

Blenheim's almost two hundred years of chill. Electricity was installed everywhere, even in dairy and stables, and the leaking lead roof was repaired to the tune of £40,000 ($200,000).

Once she'd acquired the ideal home, a Womanly Woman was expected to fill it with children, but as in her marriage to Louis, Lily failed to conceive, to her great disappointment.

The third requisite for the happy middle-class homemaker was active domesticity. She might have several servants in her home, but there was still plenty for her to do in the way of baking, housecleaning, tidying, sewing, ironing, polishing, in addition to caring for her little ones. Blenheim had eighty-eight servants, and the whole household ran like a giant machine, and had been doing so, smoothly, efficiently, ever since bossy Duchess Fanny had started it up thirty-one years before when her husband succeeded to the dukedom. Lily merely had to consult each morning with housekeeper and cook, deciding on choice of flowers for the rooms, allocation of bedrooms for guests, daily menus and other such details. Blandford ignored servants in a room as if they were merely furniture, but Lily was always conscious of their presence, and felt sorry for them all, working long hours for little pay. The maids slept in tiny rooms, two to an iron cot, worked from 6:00 a.m. until late evening and got half a day off a month. The hands of the fifteen-year-old scullery maid were painfully red and raw, for she spent her days on hands and knees, for £8 a year ($40), scrubbing the floors of scullery, larder, kitchen and servants' hall. Lower housemaids, for £12 a year, removed ashes, cleaned hearths, laid new fires. Middle housemaids, for £15 a year, sprinkled damp sand on floors and carpets, swept them clean, carried cans of hot water up the back stairs to bedrooms, carried dirty bathwater from hip baths placed on the hearth back down. (Blenheim had only one bathroom.) Upper housemaids, for £18, dusted and tidied. The still-room maid got £20 annually for laying out early-morning and afternoon tea trays and cleaning the housekeeper's rooms. That lucky woman, snug in her parlor, received £50 a year, wore black silk instead of black cotton and dangled a large chatelaine of keys from her waist which unlocked all china and food cupboards so that she could dole out supplies. Then there were laundry maids, dairymaids, kitchen maids, Lily's own lady's maid and chief cook. Male staff included house steward (£100 a year), who controlled hirings and accounts; butler (£45), who controlled pantry, footmen, silver plate and wine cellar. He also ironed the *Times* each morning, to smooth away wrinkles and destroy lower-class germs. The dozen footmen, all six feet tall, looked impossibly splendid and regal in maroon livery with silver braid, maroon knee breeches, white stockings and white gloves. Each morning they dunked their heads at basins along one side of the powdering room, rubbed their hair with a stiff lather of soap and floured each other with huge puffs. The head footman, no matter what his Christian name, was always called James, which freed up Marlborough memories for more important matters. The groom of the chambers was so tall and stately that, like Blenheim's many columns, he intimidated Lily. For £70 a year he walked through the downstairs rooms three times a day, straightening cushions, drawing blinds and curtains, placing footstools strategically for outstretched ducal feet, stocking all letter racks with crested notepaper, opening doors for Lily to pass diffidently through. Then there was the outdoor staff: gate porter, grooms, coachmen, stable boys and gardeners. And the whole servant apparatus seemed to hum and turn with its own momentum, so that Lily felt quite superfluous. By nine o'clock in the morning every room had been cleaned, every leaf swept from the lawns and the Duchess's boiled egg had been placed by a large, white-gloved hand before her, with that day's date penciled on its top to assure Her Grace that, earlier that same morning, it had been snatched by a smaller, ungloved hand from beneath a Blenheim hen.

Worse than three acres of imposing house that lacked the patter of tiny feet but had plenty of stealthy servant ones, was clear evidence, on its walls and in its cupboards, of the Other Woman in Blandford's life, Lady Colin Campbell, his one true love and longtime mistress. Whistler's nude portrait of her hung, in plain view, permanently, above Blandford's bed. Lily's only rival for

Louis Hammersley's affection had been his father, but with Blandford, Lady Colin posed a far more serious threat.

Lily made discreet enquiries of Jennie and her sisters-in-law and learned that, like Blandford, Vera Campbell (née Blood) had, in Society's eyes, gone too far and been consequently cast out. When beautiful young Vera (christened Gertrude Elizabeth but called Vera) was old enough to marry, her mother took a house near the hunting lodge of Lord Colin Campbell, dissolute son of the 8th Duke of Argyll, and pushed Vera into Lord Colin's path. When he and Vera became engaged, his father, the Duke, candidly told Mrs. Blood, "My son is no man for a decent girl to marry. I spend my nights pulling him out of the maid-servants' beds, and he is steeped in vice of every kind." But Mrs. Eager-for-blue-Blood ignored the Duke, and Vera married Colin.

Like other Society wives, she took a string of lovers, rather too many, too soon, in husband Colin's view. He promptly sued Vera for divorce, naming four co-respondents: Blandford, Col. Sir William Butler, a Dr. Bird whom Vera called "my cockyolly Bird," and Captain Shaw, Chief of the Metropolitan Fire Brigade. The idea of a fireman aflame for a Lord's wife so delighted humorist W. S. Gilbert that he gave Captain Shaw a mention in *Iolanthe*, one of his comic operas written with Sir Arthur Sullivan. When called to testify in the divorce trial, all the men, including Blandford, lied like gentlemen, and the all-male jury, eyeing Lady Colin's svelte shape, dismissed the case. But from that time Lady Colin, who had transgressed Society's code by going public, became a social outcast. Vera Campbell was a strong, resourceful New Woman, however, who refused to follow the usual options of the time: either retreat to continental obscurity or continue a downward slide to prostitution. Instead she got herself hired by *The World* as art critic, and became a most proficient and esteemed journalist.

(A future Lady Colin Campbell, also a journalist, and divorced wife of a later Lord Colin, son of the 11th Duke of Argyll, would chronicle the life of Diana, Princess of Wales, in the 1992 best-seller, *Diana in Private*.)

To countenance the first Lady Colin Campbell's existence somewhere beyond her domestic sphere was bad enough for Lily, but in 1889, less than a year after she married, Blandford invited Vera Campbell down to Blenheim for a visit. We learn of it in a letter from Consuelo Manchester's friend Gladys de Grey to her sister-in-law. Gladys comments that Joe Chamberlain inviting Consuelo to his home Highbury just after he'd married Mary Endicott was exactly like "Lady Colin Campbell visiting the Duke and Duchess of Marlborough at Blenheim!... I did not think Blandford would be silly enough to get talked about again so soon, and I imagined he would try and electrify the world by his exemplary conduct, but not at all."

The whole incident was terribly upsetting for Lily, beginning with the moment when, as hostess, with blushing face and trembling lips and hands, she had to greet Lady Colin in the Great Hall. Moreover, Lady Colin in the flesh was stunning, incredibly beautiful, six feet tall, slim, elegantly boned, with ivory skin of a luminous pallor, smoldering dark eyes and raven's-wing hair. She dressed dramatically in sweeps of jewel-toned cut velvet and long, trailing scarves. She talked endlessly to Blandford of art and books and other intellectual subjects quite beyond Lily's ken. Lily suffered silently, but after Lady Colin had departed, the usually imperturbable Lily made such "an awful row," according to Gladys de Grey, that "Georgie Curzon [Blandford's sister] and the Duchess Dowager [his mother] had to go down and help patch it up."

Blandford's behavior went against all Lily's most sacred tenets. The majority of American husbands, she knew, stayed sexually faithful, and she had fully expected a European one to do the same, never having been exposed to European morality before she married Blandford. Then too, the Victorian middle-class home was supposed to be a sanctuary from evil, from everything unpleasant in the world beyond. As John Ruskin wrote in *Sesame and Lilies* (1865), home was "a sacred place, a vestal temple of the hearth" and so far as the "hostile society of the outer world is allowed by either husband or wife to cross the threshold it ceases to be home." To have all the six-foot swagger of the slinky, devious Lady Colin crossing her threshold and entering the vestal temple was too much for Lily. How could she play her Good Woman's role with a libertine spouse and his lover ensconced together on the hearth?

Lily may well have felt somehow responsible for Blandford's adultery, for, as William Landels notes in *Woman: Her Position and Power*, "a woman's character produces a wider and more powerful impression on man than man's character upon woman. The influence, whether for good or evil, is almost incalculable. She makes him better or worse, according as she is good or bad; for what she is, he more or less becomes." Why had she failed? Was it all her fault that Blandford strayed, Lily may have asked herself during long, wakeful nights.

She tried harder. She spent her money indulging her Duke; he had only to express a wish, and she set about making it come true. Remembering Thomas Edison's, Blandford asked for a pipe organ. Lily had a Grand Willis organ installed at the northern end of the Long Library and imported C. W. Perkins from Birmingham to play it after dinner. Blandford merely frowned and had inscribed on the organ's side: "C. W. Perkins. How often has thy genius beguiled my sad heart." Also recalling Thomas Edison's, Blandford wished for a laboratory. Lily had an elaborate one built on Blenheim's top floor, hoping to keep her husband close to home while he conducted his experiments in chemistry and metallurgy. Next, a proper telephone, made to his specifications, appeared in every room to replace the single, more primitive receiver he'd made.

Some of Lily's money — with or without her knowledge — was used by Blandford to set Lady Colin up for the summers in a palazzo in Venice where he sometimes visited her. When she was in London he went regularly, for the rest of his life, to her house off Victoria Street, where Vera awaited him, posed on a sofa, often dressed in yellow satin, and sometimes, in hot weather, with a snake draped around her long, white neck to keep her cool. Henry James was also a friend of Vera's, a strictly platonic one, who came often to chat about art.

After her initial shock and charged reaction, Lily did the only thing a good wife with a husband resisting reform could do: she tried her best to ignore Blandford's transgressions, to give him all her care and loving, to lay her gentle unction on his melancholy soul. "Dust. Ashes. Nothing." was the inscription on Blandford's bedroom mantelpiece. Lily was truly sympathetic of his periodic deep depressions, and did all she could to please.

14 *The Long Library at Blenheim Palace,*
with pipe organ at the north end

When Blandford's brother Randolph came to Blenheim for a visit, he wrote to his mother that "Duchess Lily talks about Blandford and to Blandford all day long, flatters him and exalts him to his heart's content. He believes himself to be a beneficent genius."

Lily was merely following to the letter those True Woman ideals that in the 1880s, under fire from radical notions of the New Woman, were being publicly reinforced. Leading the reactionary forces in England was Mrs. Lynn Linton, whose conduct-book essays appeared first in *The Saturday Review*, known for its antifeminist bias, then in *The Girl of the Period and Other Social Essays* (1883), dedicated "to All Good Girls and True Women." "Doves who are content with life as they have it in the dovecot" are "woman throughout without the faintest dash of the masculine," and every dove "loves her husband too well to desire an individualized existence outside his. She is his wife, she says, and that seems more satisfactory to her than to be herself a Somebody." Lily's strategy with Blandford was cleverer than she knew, for she had hit on the best way to keep an English husband happy, as the novelists Gertrude Atherton and Edith Wharton make clear. In *American Wives and English Husbands* (1901), a minor character declares that "no woman with individuality can get along with an Englishman." Atherton's heroine, Californian Lee Tarleton, has followed the advice of Lord Barnstaple: "It's a risky thing to say to a woman," he observes when she marries his son Cecil, Lord Maundrell, "but to live with an Englishman comfortably you've got to become his habit and to be happy with him you've got to become his second self." In Edith Wharton's *Buccaneers*, the American Duchess of Tintagel has done this so wholeheartedly that "there were moments when the vain hunt for her real self became so perplexing and disheartening that she was glad to escape from it into the mechanical duties of her new life. But in the intervals she continued to grope for herself, and to find no one."

Sometimes Lily would come across a photo of Lady Colin Campbell in one of Blenheim's many cupboards. She would stare, dismayed, at her slender rival, knowing that her own growing stoutness and facial hair, like her lack of wit and learning, were more of a handicap in England than in America. There it was the single beauties who were acclaimed — as she had once been — the "belles," while matrons stepped into the shadows, and stayed chaste. In English Society, it was just the opposite: single girls yielded pride of place to adulterous married ladies, the so-called Professional Beauties, women like Gladys de Grey, Consuelo Manchester, Jennie Churchill.

"Uncle George says every woman ought to have a profession," observes a young lady in a *Punch* cartoon, "and I mean to be a Professional Beauty." "Do come," London hostesses would urge their guests, "the P.B.'s will be there," for no party was complete without them. One could buy their photographs in shops, and many have survived. There they stand, these sepia, long-necked swans, fixed forever to gilt-scrolled cardboard, their shapely arms propped idly on velvet-draped tables. Far more than intellect or talent, female beauty in English Society counted. Blandford's nephew, young Winston Churchill, Jennie's brash son and Britain's future Prime Minister, liked to stand in a doorway, watching the ladies enter for a party, asking himself: "Is this the face that launched a thousand ships?" "Two hundred ships for that one," a male friend would remark. "By no means," Winston would reply, "a covered sampan, or a small gunboat at most."

If Lily knew she was down to a one-gunboat rating, she nevertheless had her defense. Dress, as in her American life, became her comfort and shield and compensation. Newland Archer in Wharton's *Age of Innocence* muses on "the religious reverence of even the most unworldly American woman for the social advantages of dress." "It's their armor," he thinks, "their defense against the unknown, and their defiance of it." So it was with Lily. Sometimes it troubled her that in her second marriage, unlike her first, she had taken on the male role of provider. Her clothes would counter, would proclaim her completely feminine. She put herself in the hands of Paris's reigning couturier, Charles Frederick Worth, born in England in 1826, who had gone to Paris at nineteen, opened his own house, obtained the custom of Second

Empire beauties and all the rich Americans in Paris and never looked back. Lily and Monsieur Worth understood each other, for he didn't just "dress" a woman; he created a complete image. The fashions of the 1880s and early 1890s played into Lily's hands, for the bustle wildly exaggerated a female's posterior curve, and padding under the arms accentuated the curve of the bust and made the waist appear smaller than it was.

It was Jennie Churchill who persuaded her sister-in-law to lose some weight, and to bleach the mustache. Jennie was even more passionately clothes-conscious than Lily and spent wildly beyond her more modest means. In Jennie's London drawing room stood a tall, glass-fronted case. Within it, for all to see, on shelves lined with silk, were displayed her brocade evening shoes, row upon row, their diamanté buckles glinting behind glass, like rare objects in a museum. Some of the shoes were twenty years old, for Jennie never threw a pair away and was inordinately vain about her small, pretty feet. In 1923, when sixty-seven-year-old Jennie was hurrying down the stairs at Mells Manor, an ancient country house, on her way to dinner, wearing a pair of very high-heeled, frivolous Italian shoes, she slipped on the highly polished surface and broke her ankle. Gangrene set in; the leg had to be amputated; an artery burst and Jennie Churchill died, victim of her vanity, victim of the fashions of her time.

When Consuelo Manchester's friend Minnie Stevens Paget died of a heart attack in bed at the Ritz Hotel on May 20, 1919, her huge wardrobe was put on the auction block in London. "Lady Paget had a more extensive wardrobe than any other woman in the London social scene," a newspaper records, "and her frocks and furs, her fans and ribbons, her parasols and her hats were displayed before the public today for discriminating eyes to behold." In addition to hundreds of gowns, there were yards of beautiful fabrics, brocades, ninons, velvets, Japanese silks with gauzes to match, even embroidered priests' vestments. And for the final fifteen years of Minnie's life, since she had fallen down the elevator shaft in her house, all this finery had adorned a bunched-up figure huddled in a chair.

Certainly these American women could pride themselves on teaching dowdy Englishwomen how to dress. "It was easy to pick out the American girls," a London gossip sheet gushed, describing a Marchioness's dinner party. "They dress so well and know exactly how to put on their clothes." There was need of improvement among all those ill-fitting, puce-colored, droopy English gowns. When Mrs. Westgate, a chic American in Henry James's story "An International Episode," surveys the getup of an English Duchess, she thinks to herself, "she won't know how well I am dressed." By 1891 George Smalley could write in *London Letters*: "The American has taught her English cousin how to dress, and her cousin has learnt the lesson and now dresses almost as well as her teacher.... The number of really well-dressed women in London is today ten or twenty times as great as it was before."

If clothes were the pride and preoccupation of the typical American and English Society woman, they were also her most immediate prison, into which, with the help of a maid, she voluntarily committed herself each morning. First she put on her "combinations," a one-piece garment of fine wool reaching to the knees; then her corset, steel boned and shaped and padded to produce the admired swanlike silhouette; lawn or silk camisole, short-sleeved and front buttoned; lawn knickers, lace trimmed at the knee; silk stockings fastened with garters to the corset; full-circle petticoat; dress or skirt and blouse; if she was going out, huge, flower- or feather-laden hat skewered to her hair with ten-inch steel pins; high buttoned boots for walking; buttoned gloves. Altogether she put on about fifteen pounds of clothing, and in so doing lost all touch with her body's physical and erotic sensations. The tightly laced corset, pulling her waist in to the requisite eighteen inches, pushed her ribs against her liver and often gave her chlorosis (a form of anemia), loss of appetite, headaches and fainting fits. Petticoat and long, full skirt slowed her walk; at least four changes of clothes a day took up much of her time. Clothes were part of the conspiracy of patriarchal society to reinforce the good old female stereotype by keeping women modest, physically delicate and inactive. If their clothes gave Lily, Jennie, Minnie and others confidence and some creative expression, one hopes it was compensation enough for all that tight confinement.

Lily needed the comforts of her closet when in 1891 Blandford's name was again mouthed above the tea tables, as one of the fourteen former lovers of Daisy, Lady Warwick. Her husband was threatening to name them in court if and when he sued for divorce. Among Daisy's other honeybees were the Prince of Wales,

*15 Blandford, 8th Duke of Marlborough,
looking old and jaded*

Lord Randolph Churchill and Lord Charles Beresford, whom Daisy had seduced on learning that he'd sworn he'd never fall in love with her. One of Daisy's love letters to Lord Charles fell into the hands of his wife, whose sister circulated a "defamatory pamphlet," naming Blandford and Daisy's other lovers, which flew around London drawing rooms and eventually crossed the ocean to America. Lily made a quick trip to Worth in Paris, and Blandford retreated to his study to fire off letters to the *Times* on his favorite subjects: bi-metallism and the telephone. "It will be only a very few years now before every householder in London may have the instrument," Blandford informed *Times* readers on September 5, 1891. Lily was turning, more and more, to Good Works as a way of purifying the Marlborough image. She made arrangements to transport three thousand children from London's most squalid areas down to Blenheim, on a specially hired railway train, so that they could enjoy fresh air and innocent game playing in beautiful Blenheim Park.

In the first week of November 1892, Lily and the Duke hosted an all-American house party at Blenheim, attended by Consuelo, Duchess of Manchester, recently, but not regretfully, widowed, and all three Jerome sisters: Jennie, Leonie and Clara, with their respective husbands, Lord Randolph Churchill, Sir John Leslie, a tall, landed Irishman, and Moreton Frewen, still waxing lyrical on his gold-crusher. With Lily's money and encouragement, Blandford had recently brought his scattered abilities to bear on Big Business, and he had never been happier. He had invested heavily in Tennessee land, and in steel and ironworks in the Tennessee mountains. In London, he was Chairman of the Coal and Light Electric Company and a most enterprising member of the Telephone Company. Lily smiled at him serenely from her end of the long oak dining table as Consuelo, in her soft Southern drawl, began another naughty story, while the Blenheim footmen carried in rich desserts smothered in cream and filled the wineglasses with a sweet sauterne.

Guests departed on Sunday evening; on Tuesday, Blandford toured the estate, rejoicing in the tangy air, the golden fields. He and Lily dined well, as always. After dinner he worked on an article entitled "Modern Railway Cars" and retired to bed at his usual hour, eleven-thirty.

At eight o'clock next morning, Wednesday, November 9, the Duke's valet, Mr. Camp, tiptoed into the ducal bedroom to arrange the ducal wardrobe for the day, carrying the ducal cocoa on a tray. "I did not dare to touch him in order to wake him," recalled Camp later, "for his orders were strict to the contrary." So Camp went in and out of the room, first quietly, then with more noise and finally with a loud bang of the door, but still the Duke didn't stir. Camp went to look. His Grace lay on his back "with a terrible expression on his face," his right hand clenched above his heart, obviously dead. Camp rushed to tell Lily's maid, who informed the Duchess, who rushed into the room, took one look at her husband, gripped Camp's arm hard and screamed. She sent Camp out of the room and looked down at the bed. Why couldn't she keep a husband? She loved them, cared for them. Blandford had been snatched from her after only four years; Louis, the same. But Louis had been sickly for years; Blandford was full of life and future plans.

Lily summoned Dr. Caudwell, who told her that the Duke had died from a heart attack, later confirmed by postmortem examination. Lily took to her bed, weak, sick, unable to do anything except weep piteously for her genuine loss. She had truly loved Blandford, and she knew that in his own strange way he had loved her. Blandford's brother Randolph arrived from London at tea time, and Blandford's only son, Sunny, from Cambridge. Sunny was very fond of Lily, who mothered him; Randolph had always been more distant and critical, but now both rallied round her and helped her, as only men could, to organize and authorize all the details attendant on a death.

Playing family rebel until the very end of his life, Blandford had left instructions that he was not to be buried where all former Dukes of Marlborough rested. "I dislike particularly the exclusiveness of family pride," the Duke had written, "and I wish not to be buried in the family vault in Blenheim Chapel, but in any suitable place that may be convenient in which others of my generation and surroundings are equally able with myself to find a resting place together." Randolph made arrangements for his brother to be buried just beyond Blenheim's gates in Bladon churchyard where, in another three years, dead from syphilis, Randolph himself would join him.

On Monday, November 14, at one-thirty in the afternoon, preceded by the local fire brigade, the coffin, covered with a purple pall and a large bunch of arum lilies from the bereaved Duchess of Marlborough, was borne from Blenheim's Grand Saloon to its Chapel, where one hundred people had gathered for the funeral service. Lily, in black widow's weeds for the second time, sat in the balcony while the choir of Exeter College, Oxford, sang two extremely apt hymns: "Just as I am, without one plea" and "My God, my Father, while I stray." The new Duke of Marlborough, the diminutive Sunny (so-called from his title of Earl of Sunderland), stood near the coffin, pale and nervous, with mixed feelings for the father who had always ignored him. Sunny was still an undergraduate at Trinity College, Cambridge, and had turned twenty-one the day before the funeral.

The *Times* obituary of the 8th Duke of Marlborough was all too candid: "The late Duke was his own worst enemy and by the scandals of his private life — which became public property through more than one divorce suit — he threw away the certainty of attaining to a position of great influence in the country." The *Illustrated London News* was more charitable, noting that he was "a man of remarkable intellectual endowments."

Blandford's will, with probate valuation of £350,000, equivalent to $1,750,000 at that time, most of it Lily's dowry money, showed his confidence in Lily by making her his executrix and leaving her all the residue of his real and personal estate — with one glaring, infuriating exception. "I bequeath to Lady Colin Campbell," Blandford had written in his will, "as a proof of my friendship and esteem the sum of £20,000 absolutely." The next day, all photographs of Lady Colin and Whistler's nude portrait of her above Blandford's bed disappeared from Blenheim, never to be seen again.

Shortly after Blandford's death, Lily wrote a desperate note to Randolph, explaining that her late husband had written a tell-all article on his womanizing called "The Art of Living," and had told Frank Harris, editor of the *Fortnightly Review* and himself a notorious womanizer, that he could publish the article if he would accept one of Vera Campbell's as well. "I am anxious to get it back," Lily told Randolph, referring to "The Art of Living." "I could not have it appear in print. See Mr. Frank Harris, and get this article from him at any price." Randolph succeeded in his mission, and it is worth noting that Lily instinctively got a man to act for her in this indelicate affair. She did, however, send Harris a note on November 21, written in her pretty, flowing hand, thanking him for graciously acceding to her request.

Lily packed up her many gowns, her sentimental hoard of mementoes, and said goodbye, not all that reluctantly, to cavernous, draughty Blenheim. She rented 27 Brunswick Terrace at Brighton, where she trailed her black skirts along the pebble-strewn beach, filled her lungs with fresh sea air and buried Blandford's faults once and for all in the sand.

The fact that Blandford's relatives still included Lily in the family circle for the rest of her life proves their regard for this kind, generous, sweet-natured woman. In early January 1893 she journeyed to the Melton home of Lady Sarah Wilson, Blandford's youngest sister, to be godmother to her child. In February, she gave Jennie's son, nineteen-year-old Winston, who was fond of Lily and often came to see her, a typewriter, a historic gift to the man who would inspire Britain to win World War II through the ringing rhetoric of his words. On February 20, Jennie's brother-in-law Moreton Frewen visited Lily in company with Harty-Tarty, Duke of Devonshire, and his bride of six months, Lottie, the Double Duchess. "Lily is a good creature," Moreton wrote to wife Clara, "and very kind to me and Winston too."

In June 1894, the third astonishing chapter of Lilian Price's true romance began. After many years' service in India, Lord William de la Poer Beresford, younger brother of the 5th Marquess of Waterford, arrived back in England, with all his horses. Lady Sarah Wilson suggested to Lily that he be included in the house party Lily was assembling at her Surrey house. Lily had taken a twenty-one-year lease on The Deepdene, a not-too-large, comfortable house near Dorking, once the property of the Hopes, one of whom, a rich banker called Henry, owned the blue "Hope diamond." Forty-six-year-old Beresford, "Lord Bill," as everyone called him, was a slight, gray-haired Irishman with large mustache, expressive blue eyes and dandified dress. When nineteen, he'd joined the 9th Lancers as a cornet, gone to India in 1875, as aide-de-camp to the Viceroy, Lord Northbrooke, stayed on as military secretary to three more Viceroys, Lords Lytton, Dufferin and Lansdowne, revelling in polo, pig sticking and horse racing. In 1879, fighting the Zulus in South Africa in command of the irregular volunteer cavalry, Lord Bill saved a trooper's life and was awarded the Victoria Cross, Britain's highest award for bravery. The "death-or-glory boys," Society called wild Bill and brothers Marcus and Charlie, the latter a naval officer who would rise to Admiral. Everyone in Society knew the story of how Charlie, Lady Warwick's sometime lover, had once, during a house party, made his way at night down dark corridors to the room where he thought his lady love lay in wait, got undressed, climbed into bed and found himself up against the Bishop of Oxford and his wife.

It was during her Deepdene house party for Lord Bill and others that forty-year-old Lily, for the first time in her life, felt herself suddenly, passionately, falling in love. Lord Bill, for his part, whose "particularly charming manner would woo the birds off the trees," as one friend put it, perhaps saw a way to keep himself in luxury and horses, or perhaps he perceived, and appreciated, Lily's sterling character.

To the great astonishment of all his friends, the confirmed bachelor and the double widow married on April 30, 1895, in

16   The Deepdene, Lily's country house near Dorking

17   The front hall at Deepdene

18   Lily's hero and true love, Lord William Beresford

London's fashionable St. George's, Hanover Square. Lord Bill chose the day because exactly twenty-one years before he'd won the Curraghmore Steeplechase. Finally, on her third try, Lily got her full Society church wedding, with festoons of white lilies everywhere, and the Duke of Cambridge, the Prince of Wales's cousin, large in the front pew, and the choir singing "Thine forever, God of love," as Lily, glowing, exultant, like a large goddess, processed grandly up the aisle on Sunny's slight arm. The 9th Duke of Marlborough would, in another seven months, himself wed his American heiress, Consuelo Vanderbilt. "No better evidence of the good sense, tact, generosity, and kindness of the bride can be offered than this testimony of regard" on the 9th Duke's part toward his stepmother, according to the *New York Times*. As the service ended, the choir sang "O perfect love," and then a distinguished company of lords and ladies enjoyed a sumptuous wedding feast at 3 Carlton House Terrace, the magnificent town house that Lily had recently leased.

In its account of the wedding, the *New York Times* waxed lyrical, in hearts-and-flowers prose, on the romantic, remarkable life of the American Lily:

> If Lily Beresford chances to be in a reminiscent frame of mind, the various phases of her career as they flash upon her, after the fashion of magic lantern shapes on a stretch of white canvas, must dwarf her appreciation of the imaginative powers of English and American novelists. Who has dared to picture as an American girl's career a life so replete with change and incident as that which has marked the fleeing years of Lily, our Maid of Troy? The career of Helen, with but one Paris, was tame in comparison.
>
> Republican kinsmen of high and low degree hastened to bend the knee which, oiled by the title of Duchess, allowed them to do what they could not do when they knew the widow Hammersley. And now...the relict of the republican Hammersley and the aristocratic Marlborough will begin a new life as my lady Beresford. Why not? She has never injured anyone, has been gracious, kind and gentle. Long life and prosperity to Lady Beresford.

By law Lily was only entitled to her current husband's title, not that of a former spouse. She had been first a mere Mrs., then a Duchess, and now was expected to downgrade herself to Lady. Lily refused; she had paid plenty, in dollars and disappointments, for the title of Duchess. She let it be known that Duchess of Marlborough, not Lady Beresford, she would, until her death, remain.

At long last, in her third and final marriage, all Lily's dreams came true. First, she was fully accepted into Society, where her new husband was extremely popular, and properly esteemed; second, she was able to make at Deepdene a real home in every sense of the word; third, to her great joy, a year after her marriage, Lily found herself pregnant.

On February 4, 1897, at the age of forty-three, Lily gave birth to a son, christened William Warren de la Poer, and as exemplary mother, reveled in woman's other lauded role, in addition to wife-hood.

The *New York Times* headlined the birth with the words "The Romantic Career of the Former Mrs. Hammersley" and went on to tell yet again Lily's miraculous tale that so closely paralleled a basic myth. Lily's story tapped into one of the essential symbols of womankind in American culture, one rooted in its collective unconscious from time immemorial, namely the Cinderella archetype. Lily was the first of the heiresses in this study to be turned by press and public in America into a cult figure, but not the last.

Lily adored her son, and pleasant Deepdene, but her third marriage, like her other two, was, in a sense, a ménage à trois, for she had to share her husband's love not with a father or mistress, but with a stableful of horses. Horses had always been Bill Beresford's primary passion, and he couldn't change at this late date. "Since his return to England," a newspaper noted, "he lived chiefly in the racing world." With Lily's money, Lord Bill bought a string of racehorses, mostly American, ridden by American jockeys. In 1898, his best year, his stable won 170 races. He also bought steeplechasers and hunters and a fine team, which he drove at Coaching Club meets. Lily generously, graciously, as always, put aside her own concerns and, according to Lord Bill's biographer, "was most interested in his horses and was as anxious as he was that he should own the best."

*19   Lord William Beresford with his
and Lily's only child, Billy*

When the smell of horses was too much for her, Lily went about her charitable works, scattering largesse to Dorking's poor and underprivileged. To celebrate Lord Bill's July birthday, the schoolchildren of Dorking, some eighteen hundred of them, were always given a party in the grounds of Deepdene Park, famous for its rhododendrons.

Then, suddenly, the Deepdene idyll ended. Ever since his Indian sojourn, Lord Bill had suffered from dysentery. During one such attack, he ate some game that had hung too long and become tainted; he developed peritonitis, and died on December 28, 1900, five years and eight months after his marriage. Dazed and numb, Lily climbed for the third time into widow's weeds and accompanied the corpse to Curraghmore, the Beresford family seat in county Waterford, Ireland, for burial in the vault of Clonegam Church. The funeral took place on Sunday, January 3, 1901, at twelve o'clock, after which Lily had to hurry back to Dorking, arriving at ten forty-five on Monday, just in time for a Memorial Service held at noon in St. Martin's Church, where more than four hundred people assembled, including Jennie, with Clara and Moreton Frewen beside her. The choir sang "Blessed are the pure in heart," and the lesson was read by Rev. Edgar Sheppard, who had married Lily to Lord Bill. Did she carry some invisible but potent curse, Lily perhaps asked herself, tearful in the front pew, that turned every husband to dust, ashes, nothing, after so few years of married bliss?

Lily sold off all her husband's horses, gave an endowment fund of £3,000 in his memory to the local cottage hospital and quietly carried on her good works. But she couldn't live happily without a man as sun to her moon, with herself circling round and round, reflecting his large, resplendent ego. Lily was increasingly unwell, and on Monday, January 11, 1909, aged fifty-five, she died at Deepdene of "an attack of heart trouble." Her last rites, like her life, had three stages. First, on January 14, her body was cremated at Golders Green in London. Second, at her request, her ashes were interred beside her husband Bill's at Clonegam Church in Ireland. Third, a memorial service was held at St. Martin's Church, Dorking, where, on Monday, January 18, a huge crowd of genuine mourners sang "Sleep on, beloved," while "the business of the town was entirely suspended" so that townspeople could grieve as well.

She had married three husbands, one for wealth, one for social status and one for love. She had also buried three husbands, after only four or five years of marriage. Lily Warren Price Hammersley Spencer-Churchill Beresford was a conventional woman of her time, acting out her particular "drama in muslin," her ongoing dress rehearsal, in the form of a romantic tragicomedy in three acts.

The first two heiresses we've focused on were as different as black from white. Consuelo Manchester had a devil-may-care, some-times bumpy, always hilarious, ride on the Court carousel; Lily's home-bound round was more sedate and ordinary, and much more conscience driven. Whereas Consuelo on her marriage to a Duke quickly shrugged off her American conditioning and took on English ways, Lily, in spite of two British husbands and twenty-one years in England, stayed essentially American, in her moral, material and feminine values. Dove in a dovecot, Lily kept her purity, unlike naughty Consuelo, but poor Lily never seemed to have much *fun*. She was part fool, part saint, guileless, trusting, humorless, eager to love, to give, to make allowances, to put another person's needs before her own. Once she'd got her man, this sentimental heroine was content to float through life in the wake of his wishes, buoyed up by impeccable apparel. If she felt frustrations and doubts and anger as she dressed and deferred and dressed again, they're hidden now, forever, in muslin's generous, clinging, insubstantial folds.

III

CONSUELO VANDERBILT

20   Consuelo Vanderbilt, 9th Duchess of Marlborough

I still remember that early morning gallop on the Indian plains with the sun rising in the distance. Above my head an unhooded falcon soared in circles waiting on her game. I watched as she climbed immense heights to get above the bird she wished to strike. It seemed remarkable that a falcon should have the power and speed to travel 150 miles an hour.

—CONSUELO VANDERBILT,
The Glitter and the Gold

IT WAS HER FIRST APPEARANCE in the bright world beyond the schoolroom, where she had been long and closely confined. Now she circled round and round the Duc de Gramont's Parisian ballroom but, at the end of every dance, flew straight back to her mama, seated on a gilt chair against one wall. It was as if a leather leash, thin but strong, stretched from mother to daughter; one sharp tug and the young falcon swooped back to the controlling hand.

Consuelo Vanderbilt had plenty of partners on that May evening in 1894, when the Duc de Gramont launched his daughter into French Society at a *bal blanc* (a white ball) and Mlle Vanderbilt stole the limelight. Consuelo accepted each partner in her usual timid, shrinking way, with childish artlessness. She was a very innocent seventeen, but she knew that a *bal blanc* was the hub of the French marriage market where Society bachelors came hunting for prize wives among the fledglings all in white. Consuelo also knew that all the young men wanted to dance with her not because they liked her but because she was a very rich American heiress. One partner seemed different, a handsome young Frenchman with a slow, easy smile and kindly eyes. (Next day he would tell his mother, "I met at the ball last night the girl I would like to marry," but it would be another twenty-seven years before his wish came true.) He kept holding Consuelo's gloved hand when the music stopped, but she disengaged it and hurried across the room, in her Worth white tulle gown, back to Mama. Alva Vanderbilt smiled, gloated, congratulated herself, fingering her diamond chain — seven and a half feet long, once Catherine the Great's — as if it were a rosary.

Alva was the daughter of Murray Forbes Smith, once a cotton planter and commission merchant in Mobile, Alabama. The Smiths had fallen on hard times after returning to New York from Paris following the Civil War, and Alva never forgot the social humiliation of her mother, Phoebe, having to turn their home into a boardinghouse to make ends meet. As with so many of America's self-made men, this early poverty and social obscurity gave Alva Vanderbilt a fierce, driving ambition to succeed. She was the female version of the Gilded Age's New Rich millionaires. Living at a time when a real career was closed to her, Alva made one out of Society storming. Had she lived now, no doubt she would be a hardworking corporate executive.

Thus far, forty-one-year-old Alva had concentrated her considerable energies on three creations: her Fifth Avenue mansion, herself as social leader, and her daughter as the perfect *jeune fille*, far more European than American, groomed for a glorious Old World future life. Consuelo, at five feet nine, was too tall, with too-large hands and a much-maligned tip-tilted nose, but Alva was a determined, designing woman. She had enlisted in her cause dancing and deportment masters, language tutors, European governesses, Monsieur Worth's genius. She regarded Consuelo as an object that, as the latter remarks in her memoirs, had to "stand out from others, hallmarked like precious silver." It was her mother's

21 Alva Smith Vanderbilt Belmont

wish "to produce me as a finished specimen framed in a perfect setting."

Yes, Alva had done her work well; her *jeune fille* had exemplary posture as she waltzed so expertly, gracefully, around the room. Consuelo wore no jewels on her long neck, only a narrow band of ribbon. The awkward hands were hidden inside long white kid gloves reaching almost to her shoulders. Below a dark cloud of curls, Consuelo's prim little ivory face, with retroussé brown eyes like a Japanese doll's, was "symmetrical as a primrose," as photographer Cecil Beaton later described it, a pale bud still closed to self-awareness.

Out of the corner of her eye as she swirled and dipped, Consuelo could see the hard glitter of her mother's diamond chain, could feel her mother's critical eye on her, assessing every move, vigilant for a moment's hand-holding or shoulder-slumping. Consuelo's posture was proof against the latter because she had always done her lessons with a steel rod going down her spine, strapped at waist and shoulders, strapped again so tightly around her forehead that she had to hold her books high for reading and could barely write. For all her growing years, that steel brace had imprinted her mother's inflexible will on her daughter's personality, the ever-present rigid armature molding the character.

Alva's sharp eyes appraised the young men present that night: good only for dancing, not for marrying. Promptly at midnight, Alva got up from her gilt chair. "I must take Baby home," she said loudly in the hearing of the Duc de Gramont's daughter, Lily, who would remember the remark, and record it years later. Never mind that "Baby" was seventeen, learned in languages and philosophy, taller than many of the men present. To her mother, she was Baby, and Baby she would remain.

Alva took leave of the *Duc*, the *Duchesse*, the threadbare *Comtes*, bundled Consuelo into her cloak and, without further ado, took Baby home.

"Home" for the months of May and June was Paris's Hôtel Bristol, on the Place Vendôme, where Alva and Consuelo habitually spent the spring buying new Worth wardrobes and absorbing French culture in a favorite city. Real home was the fantastic white stone copy of François I's Château de Blois, which Alva had brought into being at 660 Fifth Avenue, its steeply pitched roof crested in

22   *The Vanderbilt mansion at 660 Fifth Avenue*

copper, its buttresses flying flamboyantly, its towers bedecked with fleurs-de-lis. In one turret Consuelo had her bedroom, connected to her mother's room directly below by a spiral staircase, the invisible leash made stone. Although Consuelo was born, on March 2, 1877, in a small, unassuming New York brownstone, it was the storybook fake château, product of her mother's wild imagination, that in turn formed Consuelo's. If, in fairy-tale terms, Lily Hammersley was Cinderella, Consuelo saw herself as Rapunzel, the archetypal captive princess in the tower.

When Consuelo came to write *The Glitter and the Gold*, her autobiography, she made of it a sentimental tale with gothic over-tones in addition to mythic ones, with herself as suffering heroine. *The Glitter and the Gold*, in form and style, leans heavily on those gothic novels, full of melodrama and the macabre, creat-ed by Anne Radcliffe, Charles Brockden Brown, Charlotte and Emily Brontë. Consuelo's description of the Fifth Avenue château's great central stairway shows her in typical gothic form:

"I still remember how long and terrifying was that dark and endless upward sweep as, with acute sensations of fear I climbed to my room every night, leaving below the light and its comforting rays. For in that penumbra there were spirits lurking to destroy me, hands stretched out to touch me and sighs that breathed against my cheek. Sometimes I stumbled, and then all went black, and tensely kneeling on those steps, I prayed for courage to reach the safety of my room."

The château's enormous dining room had Renaissance stone mantelpieces and a huge stained-glass window "depicting the Field of the Cloth of Gold on which the Kings of England and France were surrounded with their knights." It was a strange setting for a young American girl living in a brash, up-to-the-minute, on-the-make city and country, and it would cast a very long shadow.

It seems significant, in light of her dominant role as marriage partner and parent, that Alva's bedroom in the château was more than twice the size of husband Willie K.'s. His was a dismal room only fifteen feet by fourteen; even Alva's dressing room was larger than that. Consuelo remembers that to her and her two younger brothers, Willie K., Jr., and Harold, her adored father was "invariably kind, so gentle and sweet," but "alas, he played only a small part in our lives; it seemed to us he was always shunted or side-tracked from our occupations. It was invariably our mother who dominated our upbringing, our education, our recreation and our thoughts." Very rarely, Willie K. had the temerity to oppose his wife; then Alva filled the high-vaulted baroque rooms with thunderous sound and fury while the bronze nymphs rattled on their marble stands and Willie K. capitulated almost at once, retreating to his own pursuits: yachting, horse racing and other women. If Consuelo stepped out of line, Alva lashed her bare legs with a riding whip. With the help of two governesses, Consuelo studied French, German and English. By the age of eight, she could read and write in all three languages. Later, she had two "finishing" governesses, one English, one French, who added the patina to this future aristocrat. The English one, Miss Harper,

23   Consuelo at age ten

who stayed with Consuelo until she married, encouraged her
secret ambition of going to Oxford to take the modern languages
Tripos, but a college education wasn't a viable option for New
Rich girls like Consuelo. Like houses and dress, a governess
proved one's wealth and status, so New Rich parents saw to it
that their daughters were educated at home, at a time when more

and more middle-class girls, particularly in the East, were trooping off to college. The first one to open for women's higher education was New York's Troy Female Seminary in 1821; Wellesley and Smith Colleges in Massachusetts opened in 1875, Radcliffe in 1879 and Bryn Mawr in Pennsylvania in 1885. But Consuelo, like other heiresses, isolated at home with only one or two teachers, missed out on the camaraderie, competition, sense of community and common goals, fine role models among instructors and superior education that a college in England or America would have given her.

Reading became Consuelo's focus and solace, her escape route from solitude, Alva's inflexible will and the hated back brace. Consuelo read fairy tales first, then poetry and sentimental fiction, feeding her romantic fancy, taking Goethe's epigram as her personal motto: *Himmel hoch jauchzend, zum Tode betrübt — glücklich allein ist die Seele die liebt.* (To high heaven joyous, saddened to death — happy alone is the soul who loves.) Consuelo's disciplined days stretched before her monotonously, predictably: winter in New York; spring in Paris; summer in Newport; autumn at Long Island.

In 1892, when Consuelo was fifteen, her mother dreamed up another appropriate setting for a ruling queen and her princess in a tower. This was Newport's Marble House, designed by Richard Morris Hunt, inspired by the Sun King's Grand Trianon at Versailles, built at a cost of $2 million, with another $9 million spent on furnishings and decoration. Alva even imported its construction workers from Europe. By 1892 Newport generally was putting on the Ritz, and beyond the blue hydrangeas on Bellevue Avenue, other pillared palaces were slowly raising their incredible bulk, causing any sane onlooker to blink and look again. Surely in that rustic setting of sand dune and sea spume, those monstrous, formal mansions couldn't be *real?* "What an idea, originally to have seen this spot of earth," wrote Henry James, "as a mere breeding ground for white elephants. They look queer and conscious and lumpish." But such dwellings as Marble House gave the members of Newport Society, those too-new, too-

24   Marble House, the Vanderbilt mansion at Newport

unheralded plutocrats, exactly what they needed: a secure sense of self-importance.

Among all those white elephants, Alva's creation rose first, and reigned supreme for sheer sweep and braggadocio. Alva Vanderbilt missed her calling; she would have made a great set designer in Hollywood's heyday. What could have been more fitting for an American Brünnhilde than Alva's bedroom? Over its doorway, cherubs clasped shields emblazoned with florid A's. More cherubs guarded the canopied bed, grouped above the windows, spread out round the ceiling, where a robed and helmeted Athena, goddess of war, flexed her powerful muscles, ready to take on all adversaries. Alva had chosen Marble House's High Gothic decor better than she knew, for it would soon serve as backdrop for events equally melodramatic.

At Marble House, in spite of its seaside-resort location, the rigid discipline of Consuelo's training never sagged into self-indulgent fun. "How full of tedious restraint was this artificial life!" she comments. Luncheon provided the only break in her studies, but it was formally served in the huge red marble dining room, copied from the Salon of Hercules at Versailles, and the high-backed bronze chairs were so heavy that footmen had to move them in to the table.

Consuelo saw little of other young people; Alva wouldn't allow her to go on picnics where boy-girl flirtations might erupt. Sometimes Consuelo went to Bailey's Beach with cousin Gertrude, daughter of Cornelius II, Willie K.'s elder brother, who in 1895 would move into his pretentious white elephant, called The Breakers. At Bailey's Beach, corseted, hatted in a huge, flower-laden confection held on with steel pins, veiled and gloved, wearing a muslin gown with high, tight whalebone collar even on the hottest days, Consuelo walked with Gertrude along the sands, or bobbed sedately in the shallow water — she was not taught to swim — wearing hat, dark alpaca dress and drawers and black silk stockings. She and Gertrude, two years her senior, who would later become a talented sculptor and found New York's Whitney Museum, formed a close bond, for, as Consuelo explained years later to Louis Auchincloss: "Gertrude and I were *heiresses*. There seemed never to have been a time when this was not made entirely clear," and as Auchincloss recalls, her tone made it obvious "that this was no easy thing to be."

Consuelo and Gertrude and other girls born and bound in cloth of gold served their fathers and their country as important success symbols, committed, as Thorstein Veblen points out in *The Theory of the Leisure Class* (1899), to "conspicuous leisure and consumption." In 1861, America had only three millionaires; in 1892, there were 4,047, and the splendidly caparisoned daughters of these New Rich, as Veblen points out, were akin to liveried servants since in both "there is a very elaborate show of unnecessary expensiveness" and a "notable disregard of the physical comfort of the wearer."

After three generations of capital accumulation in railroads, Vanderbilt wealth was considerable. The *New York World*, in 1889, estimated it at $274 million. Willie K.'s grandfather, Commodore Cornelius, born in 1794 to a Staten Island Dutch farmer and a New Jersey farmer's daughter, turned the $10 million he'd made in steamboating into $105 million within twelve years following the Civil War, by dint of speculating wildly, bribing whole legislatures and hiring tough gangs to fight his railroad wars. Cursing "Corneel" had a contempt for women as large as his fortune. When his wife, Sophia, after producing thirteen babies without a murmur, refused to live in the too-large, too-grand house Corneel had built in New York at 10 Washington Place, he pronounced her insane and clapped her into an asylum. There she cooled her heels for a year before moving, properly tearful and penitent, into the hated Greek Revival town house.

Meek Sophia died in 1868 and next year seventy-six-year-old Corneel married thirty-year-old Frank Crawford, feminine and pliant in all but name. When Corneel lay dying in 1877, just two months before great-granddaughter Consuelo was born, Frank was at his side, singing, at his request, "Come Ye Sinners, Poor and Needy." Poor and needy he wasn't, with $105 million in his coffers, $90 million of which he left to his eldest son, William Henry, even though he had annoyed his father by marrying the impecunious daughter of a Brooklyn clergyman, Maria Louisa Kissam. Again showing his contempt for females, Corneel left only $500,000 each to his wife and eight daughters. William Henry was less prejudiced; when he died in 1885, leaving an estate of $200 million, he bequeathed $10 million to each of his four daughters and two youngest sons, and $80 million each to his two eldest, Cornelius II, father of Gertrude, and William Kissam, father of Consuelo.

The two poor little rich girls, arm in arm, both prodigally dowered, would stroll along Bailey's Beach, agreeing on how really awful it was to be an heiress. Gertrude poured out a poignant lament on the subject in her diary:

You don't know what the position of an heiress is! You can't imagine. There is no one in all the world who loves her for herself. No one. She cannot do this, that, and the other simply because she is known by sight and will be talked about. Everything she does or says is discussed, everyone she speaks to she is suspected of going to marry, everyone she loves loves her for what she has got.... And so she sits on her throne, her money bags, and society bows to her because her pedestal is solid and firm and she doesn't seem perhaps quite human.

As they commiserated at Bailey's Beach, Consuelo and Gertrude would brace themselves against the sea winds, clutch their over-laden hats, summon their carriages and return to the cold torpor of their marble palaces.

Idlehour, at Oakdale, Long Island, the rambling frame house where Consuelo spent the autumn months, was less intimidating than Marble House. There she could fish in the river, ride her pony sidesaddle, plant a garden, help sail a boat. When leaves withered and fell, and grass blades stiffened with morning rime, she went back to New York for another close-bound winter, then Paris in the spring, Newport in the summer...always too much constraint, too much gold, always her mother's hectoring voice in her ear. In the summer of 1893, the Maharajah of Kapurthala came to visit Marble House, Newport's own Taj Mahal, and Consuelo's parents received the first of many proposals for Miss Vanderbilt's generously proportioned hand. The Indian Prince was a little *too* exotic, even for Alva's Arabian Nights fantasies; moreover, Baby was only sixteen. Alva said a decisive no!

Relations between Alva and Willie K. were going from bad to worse that summer, and their constant quarrels, according to Consuelo, "embittered the sensitive years of my girlhood and made of marriage a horrible mockery." In November of that year, the warring Vanderbilts with Consuelo and her two brothers steamed down the Hudson on their new yacht, the *Valiant*, bound for whatever diversions Gibraltar, India and Nice could offer. It seems significant, in light of future events, that Willie K.'s earlier yacht, the *Alva*, 285 feet of steel and hard mahogany, had gone to the bottom in 1892 after a collision in the fog off Martha's Vineyard. The 312-foot *Valiant* could cross the Atlantic in seven days, cost $500,000 to build and $10,000 a month to run. For the cruise to India, she had a crew of seventy-two, as well as a French chef, a doctor, a tutor for Consuelo's two brothers, a governess for Consuelo — and two gentlemen friends of Willie K.'s, who, as India's heat and color neared, revved up the yacht's onboard drama to highest pitch. Consuelo fell in love with one of them: tall, tanned, charming Winthrop Rutherfurd, sportsman and attorney, thirteen years her senior, "of really breathtaking good looks," from a rich old Knickerbocker family. Alva, for her part, cast an appraising eye on lively little Oliver Belmont, five years her junior, from a rich, not-so-old, partly Jewish family. Consuelo leaned on the starboard rail with Winty. Alva leaned on the port one with Oliver. Odd-man-out Willie K. paced the deck alone.

When the tense little group reached India, however, Alva refocused her energies on Consuelo. The Vanderbilts went to stately Government House, Calcutta, for a week's stay with India's Viceroy, Lord Lansdowne, and his wife, Lady Maud. There, Alva noted enviously that Lord and Lady Lansdowne lived with a pomp and privilege that no amount of money could buy. Alva had done what she could in New York's bourgeois milieu, putting the Vanderbilt footmen into silver-laced maroon livery, painting Vanderbilt carriages maroon, ordering a maroon carpet to be unfurled for Vanderbilt feet between the Fifth Avenue pavement and their mansion's wide steps. But in Calcutta, Alva saw all the deference and display, the custom and ceremony, that only true aristocracy and true Brits could muster. Alva then and there made up her mind. Consuelo must marry either Lord Lansdowne's son and heir, or Lady Lansdowne's nephew, Sunny, 9th Duke of Marlborough. Alva rejected the future Lord Lansdowne quickly enough; he had not yet inherited the title and would in any case be only a Marquess. But the young Duke.... Lady Lansdowne was daughter of "Old Magnificent," Duke of Abercorn, and sister to

Goosie, Lady Blandford, divorced wife of the notorious 8th Duke of Marlborough who had come wife-hunting to New York and carried Lily Hammersley off to what everyone presumed were ducal delights.

Alva made discreet enquiries about Sunny, who had succeeded to the title the previous year. His aunt Maud declared herself excessively fond of him, but Sunny was, like most Dukes, land rich and cash poor; he needed, before all else, a well-dowered wife. Lady Lansdowne fanned herself with fresh vigor, and Alva's eyes glittered.

Alva Vanderbilt already had all the status symbols money could buy — except one. Her social preeminence in America was based on the shifting sands of speculative finance, where getting to the top was a matter of push and shove, and a great deal of hard work. But the Lansdownes, the Marlboroughs — now there was real security, real class, based on the solid rock of heredity and primogeniture. Alva knew, as Henry James put it, that "Americans are greatly impressed by a coronet," and she had never forgotten that in her girlhood days in Mobile, her family had been beyond the social pale. If one's daughter wore a Duchess's crown, one's grandson would be a Duke. It was a delicious, dependable certainty. And Alva had seen enough of dear friend Consuelo, Baby's godmother, since she became Duchess of Manchester to note that Her Grace got top priority in the pecking order of British *and* American Society. Alva narrowed her eyes at the golden lions on the Viceroy's throne chair and stiffened her resolve. Consuelo had been groomed since birth for a spectacular marriage; she had to marry Sunny Spencer-Churchill, 9th Duke of Marlborough!

Alva and Willie K. had a final horrendous battle in Calcutta, and parted once and for all, with Alva determined to come out of the marriage with a good settlement. With Consuelo in hand, she headed for Paris, checked into the Hôtel Bristol, went straight to Carolus Duran and ordered him to paint a portrait of Consuelo, not with his usual red-curtain background, but with the classic English landscape that Gainsborough and Reynolds had always used for English peeresses. There was no doubt in Alva's mind that her daughter's portrait would join (as indeed, it did) earlier Duchesses hung on the silk-brocade walls of Blenheim Palace.

A few days later, in that spring of 1894, Consuelo made her European debut at the Duc de Gramont's *bal blanc*, fledgling on a string. Five proposals of marriage followed, all of which Alva rejected, including one from Paul Deschanel, a future President of France. She hesitated, just for an hour or two, over the one from Prince Francis Joseph of Battenberg. A real Prince...but he had no palaces, no retinue, and she was not to be deflected from her English Duke.

Willie K.'s brother Cornelius arrived in Paris from America to see if he could patch up his brother's marriage, but Alva was adamant. Willie K. was keeping mistresses in Paris, she told Cornelius, one of whom had committed the unforgivable sin of dressing her servants in maroon Vanderbilt livery. Willie "Kiss-em" Vanderbilt, raised to Continental standards of sexual morality during his growing-up years in Geneva, was committing adultery, and she would divorce him for it. Not even dreams of Winty Rutherfurd and the chestnut blossoms and lilacs of her favorite city could lift Consuelo's gloom that spring; her darling father had permanently departed the scene; now she was, more than ever, brailed and bound by her mother's iron will.

Alva and Consuelo left Paris at the end of June and moved closer to the quarry, putting up at Brown's Hotel in London. At once Alva commandeered a copy of *Burke's Peerage*, noted that Marlboroughs took up more than three pages, their lineage traced back to Edward IV on the Churchill side and Henry VIII on the Spencer. Alva's finger pounced on her prize, Charles Richard John Spencer-Churchill, and underlined his titles, resounding like clarions in her mind: 9th Duke of Marlborough; Marquess of Blandford; Earl of Sunderland; Baron Spencer of Wormleigh; Baron Churchill of Sandridge; Prince of the Holy Roman Empire; Prince of Mindelheim Suabia.

Next, Alva hustled Baby round to Minnie Paget's house at 35 Belgrave Square, for she and Consuelo, Duchess of Manchester, were to be enlisted as matchmakers. Young Consuelo adored her godmother, whom she calls "witty, gay and gifted" and who "delighted us with her charm," but Minnie she thought too worldly and brittle, "Becky Sharp incarnate." Over the teacups, Minnie assessed Consuelo with her "hard green eyes," and pronounced her too, too impossibly *jeune fille*. "Tulle must give way to satin, the baby décolletage to a more generous display of neck and arms, naïveté to sophistication." Consuelo was soon made seductive in new evening gowns from Monsieur Worth's London branch, then dined at Minnie's, placed at table — Minnie was never subtle — right beside the 9th Duke of Marlborough.

Consuelo's initial view of him was kindly enough. She thought him "good-looking and intelligent. He had a small aristocratic face with a large nose and rather prominent blue eyes. His hands, which he used in a fastidious manner, were well-shaped and he seemed inordinately proud of them." The American novelist Gertrude Atherton, when she first encountered Sunny, was more caustic: "I thought he would tear his hands out by the roots."

Charles Richard John, so inappropriately nicknamed Sunny, born November 13, 1871, was six years older than Consuelo and three inches shorter. He had inherited his father Blandford's sallow skin, unfocused nervous energy and melancholy, but not his father's propensity for pretty women, or his intellectual brilliance. Sunny's psyche had been permanently scarred at age ten when his parents had finally separated after years of coldness. "Up to ten years old," his aunt Maud, Marchioness of Lansdowne and Vicereine of India recalls, "Sunny was one of the most charming boys I ever met and most joyous; after that his spirits seemed to have vanished and he quite changed." When Blandford's divorce from Goosie was finalized two years later, Sunny was put in his father's care, and "entirely crushed," according to Sunny, who claimed that his father "never spoke a kind word to me." Sunny was then at boarding school, not Eton, where Marlboroughs had

25 Sunny, 9th Duke of Marlborough

always gone, but Winchester, his rebel father's choice. When home on holidays, Sunny retreated into his shell and crept through Blenheim's echoing rooms, lonely and neglected. His home atmosphere warmed after his father married Lily Hammersley when Sunny was sixteen, for she was loving and maternal and indulgent.

Blandford insisted that Sunny attend Trinity College, Cambridge, because Marlboroughs had always gone to nearby Oxford. At Trinity, according to Harold Frederic, a journalist, Sunny "behaved nicely and worked hard, but excited no personal enthusiasm. I should add that no one has any hints to drop of the sort which so customarily surround the wild-oats period of aristocratic youngsters." Sunny was still a student there when his father died and Lily departed his life and he found himself master of Blenheim at the age of twenty-one. Sunny had superrefined, formal manners, a dandified taste in dress and a finicky regard for neatness. He compensated for his small stature by a demeanor that was every inch a Duke's.

"I don't like tall women," Sunny once told a friend. To lanky Miss Vanderbilt that evening at Lady Paget's dinner, he was merely polite as they talked of art and literature and Alva watched them anxiously from her seat farther down the table's silver-laden length.

Now in full cry after the Duke, Alva took a house at Marlow on the Thames, midway between London and Blenheim, for the whole summer, but His Grace had, in ducal fox-hunting jargon, gone to earth — which only strengthened her resolve, for Alva dearly loved a challenge. Several undistinguished Englishmen asked for Consuelo's hand in marriage, but Alva brushed them aside, and Consuelo, for her part, realized ruefully that they were motivated only "by a desire for my dowry, a reflection that was inclined to dispel whatever thought of romance might come my way." In any case, she was still spinning airy dreams of what she calls her "Rosenkavalier," the attorney Winthrop Rutherfurd.

On September 28, Alva, aptly garbed in a dress with "epaulettes of green velvet," disembarked from the *Lucania* at New York, with Consuelo trailing behind in "dark dress and long cloth cloak." They drove directly to Grand Central Station, boarded a private Wagner palace car, dined therein and departed at 11:00 p.m. for Newport's Marble House. The Marlborough campaign was on hold for the moment; Alva had first to clear the decks legally of a superfluous husband. "Aunt Alva is getting a divorce from Uncle Willie," wrote Consuelo's cousin Adele Sloane in her diary on December 12, the day he landed in New York; "I am sure Consuelo must feel very badly about it."

On March 2, 1895, Consuelo celebrated her eighteenth birthday, and the Fifth Avenue house filled up with huge boxes of American Beauty roses. When she opened the smallest box and found "a perfect rose alone on its green foliage," she knew it was from Winty.

Later that day, she and Winty managed to outdistance Alva and the rest of the party while bicycling on Riverside Drive. Consuelo was not the only American girl to feel the liberating force of the country's latest craze: the bicycle, which brought not only new freedoms from chaperonage but an independent means of transport and the first chance since the collapse of Amelia Bloomer's crusade in the 1850s for girls more daring than Consuelo to wear trousers. During their ride, Winty asked Consuelo to marry him; she breathed a fervent yes; then, almost at once, Alva hove into sight, puffing and pedaling furiously to break up the twosome.

The very next day, Alva and Consuelo sailed for Europe. Two days later, with Alva safely out of range of press and gossiping Society, the Vanderbilts' divorce was announced, beginning a trend among Vanderbilts, who have been divorcing with great frequency ever since. Alva had done her work well; the case had been heard in camera and records sealed. Willie K. had obligingly provided evidence of adultery with Nellie Neustretter, a Parisian demi-mondaine originally from Eureka, Nevada. Alva got Marble House, custody of all three children, $100,000 annual income and a lump-sum settlement reputed to be $10 million. She was offered the Fifth Avenue château but declined as its upkeep was very expensive; then, too, she would soon have access to a setting far more impressive and authentic. And if, by her divorce, she had slipped back an inch or two on the social ladder, that also she would soon enough regain.

She and Consuelo stayed abroad for five months. Winty followed them to Paris, but Alva never allowed him to see Consuelo, and his frantic letters never reached her. Alva coolly went off to Worth and ordered a wedding gown befitting a future Duchess. In June, she and Consuelo arrived at Brown's Hotel in London, and went to the Duchess of Sunderland's ball at Stafford House, where Sunny, without much enthusiasm, danced several times with Consuelo. The 9th Duke of Marlborough already had a great love in his life: Blenheim Palace. His view of it was very different from stepmother Lily's, for Sunny thought Blenheim the grandest and most famous house in England, built as it was on a historic Oxfordshire site where Kings had paraded and dallied and hunted since Anglo-Saxon times.

Over the years, Britain's greatest craftsmen and artists had beautified Blenheim: Grinling Gibbons carved its interior columns; Nicholas Hawksmoor sculpted its ceilings; William Chambers swagged its mantels with neoclassical garlands; Capability Brown landscaped its grounds. For beautiful, beguiling Blenheim, Sunny reserved his highest veneration and his holiest vows, serving his palace with the zeal of a knight on a Crusade, wearing his house on his sleeve. As he held Consuelo in his arms, perhaps he pictured the veining cracks and threadbare brocades of his beloved; in any event, he invited Miss Vanderbilt and her formidable pug-nosed mama down to Blenheim for the weekend.

There Consuelo stayed noncommittal while her mother flushed with pleasure as she peered at everything: the lovely park with storied golden bridge spanning a big blue lake; the carved stone lions ferocious on Blenheim's roof; the famous battle tapestries made in seventeenth-century Brussels; the ancestral portraits by Kneller, Reynolds, Gainsborough; the marble doorways bearing the Marlborough coat of arms, with the double-headed eagle that only Princes of the Holy Roman Empire were entitled to. And nothing had been ripped from another building, to be reassembled halfway round the world, piece by painstaking piece. Everything at Blenheim had been right there in the same hallowed place for almost two hundred years.

After dinner, faithful Mr. Perkins from Birmingham played the organ in the Long Library, just as he had for Blandford and his American Lily. On Sunday, when the Duke took Consuelo for a drive around the estate where old women curtsied to his diminutive form and old men touched their caps, she got her first glimpse of Blenheim's age-old hierarchy. Alva had a private moment with His Grace, talked of old friend Lily Hammersley, and the wonders American dollars had already worked at Blenheim, invited him to Newport in August. She quitted the palace very pleased at how things had gone, while Consuelo "firmly decided that I would not marry Marlborough. I dreamed of life in my own country with my Rosenkavalier."

Once she was back at Marble House in August, Consuelo's life "became that of the prisoner with my mother and my governess as wardens." Alva had to keep Consuelo away from Winty until the Duke arrived. Friends who called were told Miss Consuelo was not at home; the porter had strict orders not to let her out unless accompanied. With high marble walls around it, and gates lined with sheet iron, Marble House was a model prison from which no princess could possibly escape. How could she get a message to Winty?

Consuelo was frantic. She prowled around the hall's tawny Siena marble, past the Gobelin tapestry where the Protestant Admiral, Gaspard de Coligny, was being massacred in 1572, on St. Bartholomew's Day. Past the tapestry where Etienne Marcel, Provost of Paris, was being murdered in 1558. She stared at the front doors: three tons of steel and bronze; Winty couldn't possibly slip in unobserved because the doors had no handles outside; they were opened always from within, always by a vigilant footman.

Alva relented enough to let Consuelo attend a ball; she managed one dance with Winty — he still loved, wanted her — then her mother dragged her back to Marble House, according to Consuelo's dramatic account in her autobiography, where the showdown took place that same night in Alva's bedroom. While Athena glowered from the ceiling, Consuelo stood mute as her mother ranted and raged. Alva screamed of Winty's multitudinous flirtations, of his love for a married woman, of his wanting to marry Consuelo only for her money, of insanity in the family, of — Alva was grasping at anything, never mind its truth — his sterility. She threatened to shoot him if he appeared on the scene. She strode back and forth, hair spiked, face wine red, arms flailing.

She would choose Consuelo's husband and Winty Rutherfurd was *not her choice and never would be.*

Consuelo's big hands clenched and unclenched. Her small head drooped on her long neck. Then, from somewhere, came a rush of courage. She stood tall before her mother and did something she'd never done before. She opposed her mother's wishes.

Consuelo told Alva that she had a "right to choose my own husband," words that were "the bravest I had ever uttered." Her opposition was like fat on a fire. Alva's will merely strengthened.

She would prevail, she screamed. Consuelo would marry the Duke of Marlborough, and no one else! Consuelo crept, sobbing, from the room.

Next morning, the house was ominously quiet. Consuelo stayed in her bedroom, which had none of the florid decorations of Alva's. It was a room austere as a nun's cell where, as in Rapunzel's tower, the windows were so high up, so narrow, that Consuelo could see only gray sky, but she could hear the surf pounding like a great breaking heart. Her mother had chosen and positioned the dark oak furniture, and every object in the room. On a table to the right of the canopied bed, copied from St. Ursula's in Carpaccio's painting, her mother had put a silver mirror, brushes, combs: tools for a well-groomed heiress who was herself a piece of hallmarked silver. There wasn't a single thing visible anywhere in her bedroom that expressed Consuelo's personality — but invisible, inside her, was a new, small grit of pride. She had stood up to her mother, and the sky had not fallen.

Alva kept to her baroque bed all that day, but sent her emissary, Col. William Jay's wife, who was staying in the house, to tell Consuelo that if she continued to cross her mother, poor Alva might well suffer a heart attack; the doctor had said so. "In utter misery," Consuelo asked Lucy Jay to let Winty know that she couldn't marry him. She would have to accept the Duke when he finally got around to making his formal proposal.

Once Consuelo was docile again, Alva bounced out of bed and went about her business, preparing for the Duke's stay, and Consuelo's "coming-out" ball, to be held on August 28. On August

10, the *New York Times'* Newport correspondent announced that "cards for Mrs. Alva Vanderbilt's ball," 350 of them, "will go out tomorrow," and in the same column, noted in feigned innocence that "Winthrop Rutherfurd today rented the Mason cottage, Francis Street, for the rest of the season."

In response to Alva's invitation, the Duke of Marlborough landed in New York aboard the *Campania* on August 23, accompanied by his first cousin, Ivor Guest. The Duke wore a blue serge suit, pot hat with orange band and russet shoes. He left almost at once for Marble House, where Alva proudly placed him in her best guest room and clanged shut the big front doors.

For the next three weeks, with Consuelo beside her, meek and mild in white organdy, Alva introduced the Duke to those of her deserving friends who had no marriageable daughters, and showed off her pint-sized prize on the Casino's emerald lawns. There, on the morning of August 26, Marlborough sported gray suit, tennis shoes, multicolored necktie and matching hatband. "In the great throng the little fellow could hardly be seen, and men, women and young girls tiptoed and craned their necks to an alarming degree," noted the *New York Times*. Consuelo's cousin Gertrude pronounced him "nothing on looks," and another Casino regular found him "a pale-faced, frail-looking lad with a voice as soft as a debutante's." That night, Richard T. Wilson, Jr., hosted a ball where Winty looked down angrily on the Duke as he danced and talked with Consuelo. Gossip about Winty's passionate suit for her hand and the Duke's pallid one buzzed about Newport, whose residents concluded that "a marble palace was the right place for Alva Vanderbilt's marble heart."

The marble heart was, in fact, missing a beat or two. Alva could easily dominate an ex-husband, a daughter, two sons, most of her friends and all of her servants, but she was finding it much more difficult to dictate to a Duke. Day after day passed. His Grace was polite, pleasant enough and intermittently attentive, but he did not propose to Consuelo. Alva glowered at her bedroom's cavorting cupids. People were beginning to titter behind her back, to suggest that it was Gertrude Vanderbilt, Consuelo's first cousin, whom the Duke was really after. More drives, more dinners, more dances. Alva had planned to announce the engagement at her coming-out party for Consuelo on August 28. But there was nothing, absolutely nothing, to announce.

On that morning, Sunny played lawn tennis at the Casino, carefully keeping grass stains from his immaculate white flannels, while talk around the club centered on "poor Oliver Belmont," who had been ordered by Alva to give a ball in honor of the Duke two nights hence at his mansion, Belcourt. Oliver had so exhausted himself in preparations fit for a Duke that his doctor had put him to bed with "nervous prostration" and a nurse in attendance.

On the evening of August 28, Alva showed Newport how to give a spectacular party, just as, in 1883, she had showed New York. In Marble House's yellow marble hall, a bronze drinking fountain overflowed with pink lotus plants, above which hovered

26 *The gilded ballroom at Marble House*

artificial butterflies and hummingbirds. Consuelo eyed the hummingbirds ruefully; they looked as jewel bright as real ones, but were condemned to hang forever in one spot, hooked to thin gold wires. Consuelo was bridelike in white satin and lace once worn by her Smith grandmother. Alva wore her famous Marie Antoinette pearls draped over one shoulder and under the opposite arm in the same way Queens wore a sovereign order. As the guests chatted with Alva and eyed Consuelo and the Duke, they asked the inevitable question. "Are they...?" Alva twitched her pearls and changed the subject.

Nine French chefs prepared the dinner and one course alone consisted of four hundred mixed birds. Dancing to two orchestras took place in the Gold Room, where everything — carved walls, ceiling, mirrors, candelabra — that could be gilded was. Ali Baba himself would have gasped in envy. Sunny danced languidly with Consuelo several times while golden cherubs on two massive chandeliers held their golden trumpets at the ready, and waited....

More days passed. Sunny announced, in his soft debutante's drawl, that he would be leaving Marble House, most regretfully, on September 18, because he wished to see Niagara Falls in company with a male friend. On the evening before his departure, by which time Alva had almost torn *her* hands out by the roots, Sunny took Consuelo into the Gothic Room and very formally, at long last, asked her to marry him. The setting was, according to our suffering heroine, most "propitious to sacrifice," for the Gothic Room had stained-glass windows that kept out the light and a collection of medieval crucifixes. Sunny made no avowals of love; he was thinking only of the piles of invoices on his Blenheim desk, of the £100,000 needed each year for upkeep, never mind improvements. The annual bill for coal alone to heat Blenheim's three acres of draughty rooms came to £2,500. His spendthrift father had squandered Lily Hammersley's millions on rare orchids and common women and his foul-smelling laboratory. Since Sunny had escorted Lily up the aisle the previous April to the eager grasp of Lord Bill Beresford, she was keeping her new husband in racehorses and never gave a thought to poor Blenheim, so worthy a recipient of largesse. Sunny was already married to his house, but he told Consuelo that he would try to make a good husband, while his words echoed hollowly in the Gothic Room's gray shadows. In a faint voice Consuelo said yes, she would marry him, burst into tears and ran to tell her mother.

Alva was in ecstasy as she and her future son-in-law fixed the wedding date for November 6. Sunny left Marble House next morning, Wednesday, and returned to New York accompanied by that debonair fellow who had acted as best man for his father's wedding, Creighton Webb, now older and leaner and more licentious. As soon as Sunny arrived at the Hotel Waldorf, he sent a telegram to his Blenheim estate agent, Mr. Angus: "HAVE THE LAKE DREDGED." It was a large lake and dredging up its nasty weeds and muck was a luxury that Sunny felt he could now afford. On Friday, Sunny announced his engagement to the reporters besieging him in the hotel lobby, in a way that clearly spelled out the less-than-romantic attitude typical of the British upper class. "A marriage has been arranged," he dictated to the poised pencils, "between the Duke of Marlborough and Miss Consuelo Vanderbilt. The engagement was arranged by Miss Vanderbilt's friends and those of the Duke of Marlborough." That done, Sunny went blithely off to view Niagara Falls, and to tour, on the Grand Trunk Railroad in company with its President, Sir Charles Rivers Wilson, the country that His Grace was forever maligning.

Almost every day through October the American press fed its eager readers tidbits about the approaching marriage of America's wealthiest heiress and Britain's neediest Duke. On October 20, the *New York Times* waxed lyrical on Consuelo's trousseau, every item of which Alva had chosen, giving orders to three Paris couture houses, one Irish one and various New York stores. Another article on the same day assured its readers that Miss Vanderbilt was an old-fashioned female. "There is nothing of the 'new' woman in her disposition and she detests knickerbockers and divided skirts," purred the reporter. "She has no opinion whatever as regards woman's suffrage, woman's rights. She is not quite sure that she will altogether like turning Englishwoman...she just loves America, and always shall."

At this point in her life, as the *New York Times* rightly noted, Consuelo was not at all committed to the cause of women's rights, which had been making progress in her homeland throughout the century, sparked initially by Englishwoman Mary Wollstonecraft's *Vindication of the Rights of Woman*, which appeared in two American editions, in Philadelphia and Boston, in 1792, and by American Margaret Fuller's *Woman in the Nineteenth Century* (1845). In 1848, Elizabeth Cady Stanton, who had insisted when she married Henry Stanton that the word "obey" be omitted from her marriage vows, organized the first Women's Rights Convention in Seneca Falls and read aloud the feminist version of the Declaration of Independence, which held "these truths to be self-evident: that all men *and women* are created equal." Between 1839 and 1850 most states passed legislation recognizing the right of married women to hold property. From 1850 to 1860, national women's rights conventions were held every year except 1857. The Civil War gave America's women, both North and South, the chance to prove their strengths in nursing stations and on a home front short of men. Since then feminists had been trying, without much success, to get nationwide female suffrage.

While Consuelo remained properly passive, as an old-fashioned female should, her menfolk were deciding her financial future. On October 26, Sunny, with Willie K. and their respective lawyers, decided on the delicious details of the marriage settlement, which all the papers immediately printed. The capital given by Willie K. was $2,500,000 in the form of fifty thousand shares of Beech Creek Railroad Company stock, and from this an annual dividend of $100,000 was payable to the Duke and Consuelo during their joint lives. Consuelo got another $100,000 annually, payable to her for her own use for life.

Next day, the Sunday supplement of the *New York Times* devoted a whole page to "The Famous House of Marlborough" and another to Consuelo's trousseau underwear, both copiously illustrated with line drawings. The lavish lingerie, hand stitched in France, imported by B. Altman and Company, was described in great detail, piece by piece, for by 1895 the American heiress, the republican version of a Princess, bore on her slender shoulders the burden of her nation's collective symbolism, projection and fantasy.

"Under her wedding dress," noted the *Times*, "Miss Vanderbilt will wear a Fasso corset. It is of white brocaded satin in a carnation pattern. The clasps are like the clasps of an ordinary corset, except that in this instance they are of solid gold. The top of the corset is finished with Valenciennes lace, arranged in points. At the lower edge is a lace beading, through which is run white baby ribbon, which comes out in tiny bows here and there. There is a line of white plush down the steel inside the corset." A Gilded Age heiress wasn't just given over to conspicuous show on the surface but right down to her skin.

(The hunger of the American people for every smallest detail of the 1895 wedding of Consuelo Vanderbilt preceded by eighty-six years their similar preoccupation with the wedding of another cult figure, media star and Princess-in-a-myth: Lady Diana Spencer, whose marriage to Charles, Prince of Wales, on July 29, 1981, kept newspaper readers enthralled for months.)

Sunny's preparations for his wedding to Consuelo were simple enough, apart from signing his name to all that money. He purchased sapphire pins surmounted with diamond coronets for the ushers — small pins, not at all showy or vulgar.

As for Alva, she had never been so busy. "It is no exaggeration to say that the preparations for this wedding," enthused the *New York Times* on Sunday, November 3, "are the most elaborate ever made in this country."

The wedding rehearsal took place at four o'clock on Monday, November 4, at St. Thomas's Episcopal Church, on the northwest corner of Fifth Avenue and Fifty-third Street, but the Duke didn't turn up. When a reporter asked him next day why he had missed the rehearsal for his own wedding, the Duke drawled, "That sort of thing is good enough for women." He had gone shopping instead; His Grace just loved shopping.

On Monday and Tuesday, the bridal gifts were displayed for friends, with donors' names in plain view and detectives on guard, at Alva's house on Seventy-second Street at Madison Avenue. Alva rewarded her obedient daughter with a yard-long string of pearls "the size of nuts," once owned, like Alva's diamond chain, by Catherine the Great. Romantic May Goelet, one of the brides-maids, gave Consuelo a pendant heart, encrusted with diamonds, and Winthrop Rutherfurd sent her a pair of antique silver candle-sticks, heavy enough, should the need arise, to deal a mortal blow. Godmother Consuelo Manchester, who had buried her unsatisfac-tory Duke three years before, contributed a set of rubies, including "a golden dagger with a jewelled hilt," and Ivor Guest, the best man, gave the bride a blue enamel watch "fastened with a true lover's knot to a golden chain."

Wednesday, November 6, the wedding day, dawned cold and gray; at noon the temperature would reach fifty-five degrees Fahrenheit. Consuelo spent the morning "in tears and alone" with a footman stationed outside her door as guard. Except for her maid, no one, not even her beloved governess, Miss Harper, was allowed in. "Like an automaton," feeling "cold and numb," she donned her corset, heard its gold clasps close with ominous little clicks, felt the heavy wedding dress with five-yard train settle on her thin young shoulders. Her bouquet of white orchids was to come from Blenheim, from the hothouses built there by Sunny's father, Blandford, but the orchids never arrived. Already Blenheim was starting up its long train of disappointments. A substitute American bouquet, three feet wide, was hastily put together.

Outside Alva's house, a crowd of two thousand overflowed the sidewalks, leaned from every window, waited patiently in the chill to see the lucky heiress emerge. They would have a long wait.

Meanwhile, guests were already arriving at St. Thomas's Church, in whose vestry no less than five clergy were donning their cassocks to conduct the service. St. Thomas's Church, one of architect Ralph Adams Cram's Gothic creations, was an apt setting for these particular nuptials, for some waggish young worker in

Mr. Cram's employ had carved a dollar sign into the tracery over the bride's door, and three moneybags above the choir stalls.

The ceremony would begin at twelve noon, but by ten-thirty, when Dr. George William Warren began playing music from Mozart's *Magic Flute* on the organ, most of the four thousand guests and spectators were already in their seats. The ushers had a hard time of it, for female guests absolutely refused to take their allotted seats in side aisles or in galleries, but insisted loudly on center-front placement. As some well-known woman such as Caroline Astor arrived, many women stood up on their seats to get a better view.

At eleven-fifteen, the organ music stopped and Walter Damrosch raised his baton to conduct a sixty-piece orchestra not too well hidden by palms in the north choir. They played Wagner's Grand March from *Tannhäuser* and Beethoven's Leonora overture, both being the kind of rousing, martial music that Alva preferred.

At eleven forty-five, Alva Vanderbilt made her entrance, while women guests noisily clambered onto their seats and craned their necks. Alva wore sky blue satin with borders of Russian sable, and a matching blue toque that bore a remarkable resemblance to Athena's helmet. One newspaper reporter thought "Mrs. Vanderbilt looked very bright and fresh and wore a decided expression of satisfaction on her face." She took her front-row seat with her two sons; no other Vanderbilts were present, for they had all stayed loyal to Willie K. in the matter of his divorce.

At eleven-fifty, the five ministers came out of the vestry, including the Bishops of New York and Long Island, and arranged their white-and-gold bulk importantly in the chancel. Sunny and his best man, Ivor Guest, whom Consuelo calls "the good-looking but supercilious cousin," took their appointed places to one side. Sunny's very smart suit of dark gray Scottish worsted with thinnest possible black thread had peg-topped trousers "cut very close" and coat "cut very small at the waist" with boutonnière of white orchids, not from Blenheim, in his narrow lapel. Sunny flicked microscopic specks of lint from his suit with his small, well-mani-cured hands and waited for his bride to appear.

At precisely twelve noon, there was a rustle of paper as sixty orchestra members put Wagner's Bridal Chorus from *Lohengrin* on their music stands and waited for Damrosch's signal to begin. All heads turned to watch for the bride's appearance in the doorway marked with the dollar sign. The bridesmaids were all there, whispering nervously, clutching their bouquets. Everyone waited in the sudden hush, hopeful, expectant. Waited and waited, but still no bride appeared.

By twelve-fifteen, Alva had "said" her diamonds over and over — was she at the last minute to be foiled somehow by Baby? — and Sunny's hands were running everywhere at once, like two little white mice, up and down the black threads of his worsted.

Back at Seventy-second Street, the weeping bride was still in her bedroom; her maid was still frantically sponging her red, swollen eyes with ice water in a vain effort to make her pre-sentable. At long last, while the crowds on Seventy-second Street cheered loudly, Consuelo emerged from the house, climbed slowly into the waiting maroon carriage and with her father beside her was driven quickly to the church. When Consuelo and Willie K., who had strict orders from Alva to give his daughter away and then disappear, arrived at St. Thomas's, thousands more spectators pushed and shoved, controlled by two hundred policemen. Willie K. helped the lovely white lace cloud that was Consuelo to step down from the carriage, while he held her bouquet. "It must have been a very cold-hearted cynic who was not affected by the scene at that moment," the *New York Times* reporter decided, seeing only the romance, not the grim reality.

Willie K., for all his fine-rigged person, jaunty top hat and smile, was no hero. He knew of his beloved daughter's love for his good friend Winty; he knew of her reluctance to marry Marlborough. He could so easily have prevented the match by merely closing his check-book and keeping it closed. One can only conclude that William Kissam Vanderbilt, grandson of the tough, go-get-'em Commodore, was, not to put too fine a point on it, a first-class wimp. Most likely, he too had caught the Anglomania of the times and wanted a ducal son-in-law as much as Alva did. In any case, he now took a firm grip on Consuelo's quivering arm, propelled her into the church and up the aisle to her unhappy future life.

Bride and father were preceded by eight bridesmaids chosen by Alva. In addition to seventeen-year-old May Goelet, who, in another eight years, would proceed up the same aisle to a taller, handsomer Duke, the bridesmaids included Edith Morton, daughter of Levi P. Morton, former Governor of New York and Vice President under Benjamin Harrison. Levi's daughter Alice, in another seven years, would marry Winty Rutherfurd.

On her father's arm, Consuelo went forward reluctantly to her groom, wearing cream satin with lace overlay and plenty of orange blossoms, dragging behind her a heavy train embroidered with true lovers' knots in seed pearls and silver, the expression on her pale young face mercifully hidden behind a Brussels lace veil.

As the bridal pair stood before the altar, a fifty-voice choir burst into "O Perfect Love," while Sunny's prominent blue eyes stared into space, carefully avoiding Consuelo's. "O perfect love...the love which knows no ending," warbled the choir while Alva beamed and female guests sniffled into lace handkerchiefs. Finally, the tall bride and the short groom rushed down the flowery aisle and out into the cold gray light of day and four thousand guests and onlookers reluctantly made their way home, while a select 115 raced to the Vanderbilt house for the wedding breakfast, after which bride and groom changed to street attire and went off to Idlehour for the first part of their honeymoon.

A boat took the newlyweds to Long Island City, where they boarded a palace car festooned with flowers for the journey to the Vanderbilt home at Oakdale. Consuelo sat tensely on the edge of a plush-covered swivel chair, getting a preview of the snobbish elitism that would mar her marriage, while Sunny read out to her all the congratulatory telegrams from England that, according to Consuelo, "expressed so much deference that they seemed to me ridiculous." Sunny's voice grew more syrupy as the sender's rank grew more exalted, culminating in a special sweetness for Queen

Victoria's message. He spent the rest of the time en route to Idlehour giving Consuelo a verbal rendition of *Burke's Peerage*, mentioning many of the two hundred families whose lineage and titles she must learn, and quickly. She had spent the first eighteen years of her life as the selfless "other," labeled daughter and heiress, her mother's pawn. Now she was a different "other" labeled wife and Duchess, her husband's pawn, "only a link in the chain," as Sunny put it, not a cherished, respected individual, but a mere source of revenue, and of sons.

They were both shy, nervous, as the carriage arrived at Idlehour (which four years later would burn to the ground). Alva's bedroom had been prepared for Consuelo and the room next door for Sunny. After an awkward dinner, they repaired to their rooms. "A sudden realization of my complete innocence assailed me," Consuelo remembers, "bringing with it fear." Alva imported her tapestries from Europe, but not her sexual code, which was Puritan homespun. Like most American mothers, she had given her daughter no sexual education at all. Consuelo undressed with shaking fingers, stepping into a new shroud of white lace. Sunny duly appeared — and the rest is silence. Consuelo's comment on the occasion in her memoir is cryptic: "In the hidden reaches where memory probes lie sorrows too deep to fathom."

Next day, the *New York Times* gave the wedding, "without exception, the most magnificent ever celebrated in this country," two columns on page one, all of page two and part of page three, with large drawings of bride and groom that didn't look at all like them. The *New York World* devoted seven columns on the front page to the wedding with the subhead "Now She's a Duchess." Eighteen ninety-five was the year when the fashion and furor for heiress-peer alliances peaked. In that year, nine American girls married British nobles, including the April nuptials of Maud Burke to Sir Bache Cunard, and of Chicago heiress Mary Leiter, whose father co-owned Marshall Fields department store, to the Honourable George Curzon, son of Lord Scarsdale.

But the press also aimed a few barbs, resenting the dollar drain. *Life* magazine drew the Duke as a ragged Columbus landing on American shores, confronting Vanderbilt Indians offering wampum and a daughter. The *New York Journal* complained that $161,653,000 had now followed American brides to Europe, and *Town Topics* suggested establishing a protective export duty on American heiresses.

In her novel *His Fortunate Grace*, published two years after Consuelo's wedding, Gertrude Atherton aimed the strongest criticism yet at heiress-peer matches, giving her story a feminist context. The listless little Duke of Bosworth, who bears a remarkable resemblance to Sunny, comes heiress-stalking to New York, proposes to Augusta Forbes, nicely dowered with $5 million. The ardent feminist Miss Maitland convenes a meeting of heiresses and argues against such betrothals. "We are so conspicuous," she cries, "that everything we do is tittle-tattled in the Press — we are such a god-send to them that it is a thousand pities we don't give them something worth writing about. Now my idea is this: that all we New York girls band together and vow not to marry any foreigner of title, English or otherwise, unless he can cap our prospective inheritance by twice the amount — which is equivalent to vowing that we will go untitled to our graves." Augusta ignores Miss Maitland, marries Bosworth and lives to regret it. Circa 1895, American criticism of transatlantic alliances was still in its second stage. The ingenuous enthusiasm for British peers that had prevailed when Consuelo Yznaga married in 1876 had been replaced by mild pique and disillusionment. Real vitriol was still some years away. If the rational side of Americans perceived heiress-peer unions as a bad thing for economic or moral reasons, their fanciful side was still reveling happily in every ermine-bordered detail.

As for the new Duke and Duchess of Marlborough, their Idlehour idyll was mercifully short. A week after the wedding, they were back in New York attending the horse show at Madison Square Garden along with Alva, Oliver Belmont and the William Jays. They sat in the front row, while hundreds of men and women "stood as if riveted to the promenade in front of the party," according to the *New York Times*, "and drank in every motion any one of them made," exclaiming to each other in carrying tones how incredibly small the Duke was. Policemen arrived to get the crowd moving, but they wouldn't budge. An heiress-Duchess, after all, was a cult figure twice over. "The Duke seemed very much annoyed, and the Duchess was evidently ill at ease in the face of that staring mob."

Three days later, Consuelo and Sunny began their honeymoon and sailed for Genoa, at eleven-ten in the morning on the North German Lloyd ship *Fulda*, a small cargo steamer where they, and maid and valet, were the only passengers. Consuelo had a brave little bunch of violets pinned to her blue dress, and Sunny sported pointed tan shoes and a white silk muffler. Both Vanderbilt parents came to see them off. "We will meet again in Paris," Willie K. told a tearful Consuelo, while Alva hugged and kissed her twice. Consuelo leaned sadly on the *Fulda*'s rail as her native land got mistier and dimmer, while Sunny took off his black derby and bowed again and again to the waving crowd on shore.

The Duke and Duchess had a storm-tossed crossing and Sunny, but not Consuelo, was seasick the whole way. "Seasickness breeds a horrible pessimism in which my husband fully indulged," writes Consuelo, "and it took all the optimism I possessed to overcome the depressing gloom of that voyage." They left the ship at Gibraltar and went on to Spain, Italy, Egypt and France, not reaching England until March 1896.

During the long, tedious honeymoon, Sunny focused voraciously on eating, addressing most of his dinner conversation to the maître d'hotel, and shopping. Just four weeks after their wedding, he told Consuelo that he had been in love with someone else (whose identity is not known). Consuelo spent a homesick Christmas in Rome, where she fell ill and kept to her bed. Back in America, on January 11, 1896, Alva married Oliver Belmont in a quiet ceremony at her New York house. She liked to boast that she had been the first American woman to emerge virtually unscathed socially from divorce; she had done this by marrying her daughter to a Duke and giving New York's best parties; now she was the first to shed one multimillionaire for another.

When Consuelo and Sunny reached Paris, he accelerated his shopping spree. Willie K. had told Consuelo — perhaps to appease a smarting conscience — to buy whatever she wanted as a gift from him. She was amazed to see Sunny spending her father's money on household linens, expensive antiques, clothes for himself, clothes for her, including furs and such jewels as a nineteen-row pearl dog dollar with a diamond clasp that chafed her neck and her psyche. Like Alva's, Sunny's taste in dressing Consuelo, as she observes, was dictated "by a desire for magnificence rather than by any wish to enhance my looks."

There was only one occasion on that protracted, painful trip when Sunny got really excited: the day they found a fine Boucher tapestry, which ever after hung in Consuelo's Blenheim bedroom to remind her of her inauspicious honeymoon.

When they arrived back in London in March, Sunny took Consuelo to Grosvenor Square to meet his formidable grandmother, Dowager Duchess Fanny, who kissed Consuelo, as she recalls, "in the manner of a deposed sovereign greeting her successor," hoped she would restore Blenheim "to its former glories," thundered that Consuelo's "first duty is to have a child and it must be a son, because it would be intolerable to have that little upstart Winston [Churchill] become Duke. Are you in the family way?"

A family dinner party followed, where Consuelo met her mother-in-law, Goosie, who in the course of the conversation revealed that she thought Americans "all lived on plantations with Negro slaves," with "red Indians ready to scalp" them "just around the corner." Goosie told Consuelo that she hadn't come to her wedding because Sunny wouldn't provide the fare. Sunny's aunt, Lady Sarah Wilson, with a malicious smile, remarked, "But the press did not spare us one detail." Consuelo shivered in the unaccustomed English chill, ate her tough beef and swallowed her pride.

There was also a visit to Sunny's uncle, the current Duke of Abercorn, Goosie's brother. Consuelo could see that Sunny had inherited his uncle's appearance, and his "restless and fussy" manners. The little Duke of Abercorn stroked Consuelo's green velvet coat, lined in Russian sables. "What a wonderful coat, what priceless furs!" he lisped. "I must send for my sables to compare them."

On the last cold and windy day of March, Sunny took his bride home to Blenheim, insisting that she wear her sable coat for all to see. They went by train to Woodstock, the nearest village, where the station was beflagged, the platform red carpeted, and the Mayor told her that "Woodstock had a Mayor and Corporation before America was discovered." Preceded by the local fire brigade, various societies and the Queen's Own Oxfordshire Hussars, of which Sunny was a resplendent officer, the Marlboroughs' carriage was pulled, not by horses, but by tenants and townspeople, at which Consuelo's "democratic principles rebelled," all the way from Woodstock to Blenheim Palace, that mighty dragon of a house, which crouched on its four-acre grassy forecourt, waiting to devour its new mistress's youth and energy and optimism. Forty indoor and forty outdoor servants, the footmen in maroon livery reminiscent of home, were lined up below the steps to meet her. "When the Duchess stepped down from the carriage," recalls one of the houseboys, "you might almost have heard us gasp at how young and how beautiful she was."

There were more speeches on the wide steps while Consuelo's arms sagged with their weight of bouquets, and her sable coat felt heavier and heavier, and wind buffeted her big hat and behind her loomed that scaly-pillared giant. "I suddenly felt distraught," she recalls, "with a wild desire to be alone," but instead she had to endure a long, formal luncheon for Blenheim's tenant farmers. Then, as the *Illustrated London News* ingenuously noted, "the day closed amidst brilliant illuminations and general rejoicings."

On the last day of May, Consuelo was presented to the Prince and Princess of Wales at an afternoon Drawing Room at Buckingham Palace, wearing her wedding dress and the white three-feather headdress requisite for married ladies. Goosie assured her daughter-in-law after the ceremony that her curtsies had been so graceful that "no one would take you for an American." Such recurring insults were goading Consuelo toward new feelings, small at first, of pride in herself as an American girl and in the country that had formed her. She replied to Goosie's barb, "I suppose you mean that as a compliment, Lady Blandford, but what would you think if I said you were not at all like an Englishwoman?"

When she came to write her autobiography, Consuelo headed the chapter detailing her marriage to Sunny "A Marriage of Convenience," but the convenience was all Sunny's, Alva's and Willie K.'s, not hers. The Duke had profited financially; Alva and Willie K. had profited socially; only Consuelo, inclined to intellectual rather than social ambitions, was the loser, locked into loneliness. Raised in formal splendor, Consuelo at Blenheim, unlike Lily Hammersley, could take the servant population in her stride, but, like Lily, she found Blenheim devoid of comforts, without a single "really liveable room...not designed as a home." Sunny, on the other hand, adored his mighty stone carapace, which compensated for his own physical and psychological inadequacies. "Blenheim is the most splendid relic of the age of Anne," Sunny would later write, "and there is no building in Europe except Versailles, which so perfectly preserves its original atmosphere." For Consuelo, as for Lily, that was exactly the problem; she was living in a musty museum where she was more custodian than mistress, where there was room only for the past and not for her own modern imprint.

She hated the fact that Blenheim had only one bathroom, but when she pleaded for more, Sunny told her that Vanderbilt money would be used not for innovations but for restoring Blenheim to former glory. He accordingly repaved the grassy four-acre forecourt with the hard stones that were there in the 1st Duke's day, and rebuilt, to the east of the house, the original formal garden where flowers were tightly confined in pots, and boxwood was tortured into unnatural shapes.

(Later Dukes of Marlborough, lacking the flow of dollars from rich American wives, had to be more inventive to maintain Blenheim's splendors. In 1990, the 11th Duke of Marlborough gave a sumptuous dinner at the Palace for seventy-five wealthy Americans, including Mrs. Henry Ford, Estée Lauder and John George Vanderbilt. Each guest contributed between £10,000 and £50,000 for dinner and overnight accommodation at Blenheim, but some complained of "bad value," disappointed that no British Royals were asked to join them.)

Consuelo awoke at Blenheim each damp, gray morning, to the mantelpiece motto opposite her bed, inscribed by Sunny's father: Dust. Ashes. Nothing. Then she raised her eyes sardonically to the deep frieze of gilded cupids holding gilded garlands, which ran round the ceiling. She squirmed inside the steel of ritual and tradition and rigid hierarchical order. Once she asked the butler to put a match to the fire; he told her that only a footman could do that; Consuelo replied tartly that she would light the fire herself.

To Consuelo, English upper-class conventions were "closer to the 18th than to the 20th century," with "a complete acceptance of aristocratic privilege." It irked her that every morning, in all weathers, a little girl walked two miles from an estate farm at Folly Bridge to bring Sunny two fresh brown eggs for his breakfast. And that Blenheim's six overworked housemaids lived in squalid, crowded conditions high in a tower called Housemaids Heights without running water, while Sunny's valet, higher up the finely graded servant scale, dined well in the steward's room in tails and striped trousers. The American Duchess of Marlborough dutifully, dully, went through her paces, but republican hackles were beginning to rise.

As always, Sunny took a house near Ascot in July for race week and paraded about in full ducal pomp. He had bought, with Vanderbilt money, a crimson state coach whose coachman wore a crimson coat, with double-headed eagles stamped on silver braid, and white plush breeches. On a platform at the back of the coach stood two powdered footmen. With a "blatant display" that angered Consuelo, Sunny insisted on driving from house to racecourse, fifty yards away, in his carriage. To get there, it had to make a sharp, dangerous turn out of a narrow gate onto a main thoroughfare, while a groom held up traffic. Sunny's bloated conceit, which another lady who knew him well would call "black, vicious, personal pride, like a disease which gets worse and worse," severely infected his marriage to Consuelo. "The accident of one's birth," she argues with feeling, "has always appeared to me no adequate reason for personal pride." Some years later, she would testify that the "arrogance" of Sunny's character "created in me a sentiment of hostility. He seemed to despise anything that was not British and my pride was hurt." Sunny Marlborough bore a remarkable resemblance to Gilbert Osmond, who marries the American heiress Isabel Archer in Henry James's *Portrait of a Lady*. The differences between Isabel and Gilbert are like those between Consuelo and Sunny. The introverted heiress wives live, unwillingly, with the world's eye on them; their very social, snobbish husbands live eagerly with their eye on the world so that everything they do is pose. Isabel, like Consuelo, felt "this rigid system close about her," felt "shut up with an odour of mould and decay" and "pleaded the cause of freedom, of doing as they chose." Isabel suffers and succumbs; Consuelo will eventually prove stronger, much more protagonist than passive victim.

Dowager Duchess Fanny came to Blenheim for Christmas 1896, trailing her satins and sables, complaining to Sunny's two unmarried sisters that Consuelo dressed far too casually: "Her Grace does not realize the importance of her position." Fortunately, Jennie Churchill came that Christmas too; she and Consuelo formed a firm pro-American, anti-British alliance. "Her constant friendship and loyalty were to be precious to me," writes Consuelo. Jennie's son, Winston, also became a close friend. "Whether it was his American blood or his boyish enthusiasm and spontaneity, qualities sadly lacking in my husband," Consuelo observes, "I delighted in his companionship." His views were "not drawn and quartered as were Marlborough's." Winston, whose political views were liberal and forward thinking, not Tory and reactionary like Sunny's, "represented the democratic spirit so foreign to my environment and which I deeply missed."

*27 Consuelo on the steps of Blenheim Palace, with
the young Winston Churchill about 1906*

When there were no houseguests at Blenheim, tensions between Sunny and Consuelo mounted. He invariably kept her
waiting at luncheon, because he'd been closeted with his estate
agent. At dinner, where the polished table stretched interminably
between them, he pushed the food about his plate, twirled a ring
on his little finger round and round and hardly ever spoke.

Whenever she could manage it, Consuelo escaped from her oppressive house and husband to Blenheim's grounds for long, fast-striding walks. Past the pewter waters of the lake, where coots paddled fussily about, going nowhere; past dark clumps of ancient cedars on the lawn, marshaled like great, ragged heraldic devices; past the aviary where jewel-bright songbirds pecked frantically at wire netting. Back inside the monstrous house, wherever Consuelo looked — above gray marble doorways, on threadbare needlepoint, on huge, useless silver-gilt ewers — double-headed eagles flaunted their self-satisfied stasis. She thought with a homesick pang of the real thing, America's bald eagles, drawing great lines across the sky — fierce, singular, purposeful.

Ongoing conflict with her mother before marriage was replaced now by conflict with her husband. In this transatlantic marriage, two very different temperaments rubbed each other raw, but it was their opposing ideologies that were driving Consuelo and Sunny ever further apart. It was the clash of American versus British ideals; of an egalitarian mix versus hierarchical order; of faith in the future versus preoccupation with the past; of change versus tradition; of liberal politics versus conservative ones. In a 1951 letter to her American publisher, Cass Canfield of Harper and Brothers, when Consuelo was writing *The Glitter and the Gold*, she speaks of "the drive to democracy which as far as I can remember always possessed me." It was this drive that would wreck her marriage and save her soul.

Tradition decreed that from January to March, the Duke and Duchess of Marlborough went to their lodge at Melton Mowbray, Leicestershire, for fox hunting. Consuelo was pregnant in the winter of 1897 and so couldn't join the hunt. Instead, she read German philosophy and looked out at a pond "in which a former butler had drowned himself. As one gloomy day succeeded another I began to feel a deep sympathy for him." When tales reached her of unemployment, hunger and misery in the villages near Blenheim, she sent off funds for relief work, without telling Sunny, who rebuked her roundly for doing so.

At the beginning of May 1897, Consuelo and Sunny received their invitations from Lottie, Duchess of Devonshire, for her costume ball to be held July 2, asking them to come in costumes "allegorical or historical before 1815." Consuelo would be seven months' pregnant and didn't relish being tightly laced into some period gown for another boring Society function. Sunny, however, was ecstatic and went straight to Worth in Paris — there wasn't a moment to lose — to order a spectacular costume. Monsieur Worth was nonplussed. The couture house had seen "a number of freak orders," as his son recalls, but had never made an outfit for a man. After a few "scandalized protestations," Monsieur Worth got to work, according to His Grace's most explicit directions, on a Louis XV costume of straw-colored velvet embroidered in pearls and diamonds, every one sewn on by hand. The waistcoat was particularly splendid, made of white-and-gold damask from an old, authentic pattern. The costume took a month to make and cost £300 (the equivalent then of $1,500) at a time when English laborers earned a pound a week. The other male guests, including Prince Edward and his brothers, the Dukes of Connaught and York, merely ordered costumes from the London theatrical suppliers, Messrs. Nathan of Coventry Street.

On the evening of the ball, Consuelo, in a Louis XV gown of palest green satin, and Sunny, so much more stunning, arrived at Devonshire House in Piccadilly, ascended the curving marble staircase with ironwork railing boasting a band of crystal, entered the ballroom and paraded self-consciously about with the other guests. Mrs. Alice Keppel advertised her new status as Prince Edward's chosen one with hooped petticoat embroidered in tinsel lovers' knots.

Consuelo, as the *New York World* reported, because of her pregnancy, "did not go into supper with the Royalties and played a comparatively unimportant part in the ball." She observed the splendid spectacle from very far away; the part she was expected to

28   *Consuelo, tightly laced, in her Louis XV gown*
at the 1897 Devonshire ball

play in Society's show was a burden, not a delight as it was for god-mother Consuelo Manchester. Pretend kings and queens…such silly strutting, pandering to history. Sunny's face, above his pearls and diamonds, had a supercilious smile permanently pasted on it. Consuelo was sick to death of leaning into the past. It might have cheered her that night had she known that World War I would sweep away Edwardian glitter forever, and that Devonshire House,

29 Sunny in all his splendor, at the Devonshire ball

with its crystal-banded staircase, would become an automobile showroom, given over to a different kind of conspicuous show.

"The ball lasted to the early hours of morning," writes Consuelo, "and the sun was rising as I walked through Green Park to Spencer House," which Sunny had rented for the Season. In her billowing silken skirt, Consuelo picked her way around "the human beings too dispirited or sunk to find work or favor" asleep in their dirty rags on the crushed grass. "The realities of life seemed far removed from the palatial splendor in which we moved," Consuelo noted, but never more so than in that clear dawn, after the stars had gone. "Much money, time and energy is spent in rounds of expensive and luxurious entertaining," she would later proclaim, "that leave her [the Society woman] empty and disheartened at the end."

On September 18, at Spencer House, at 3:00 a.m. after a long, hard labor, Consuelo gave birth to a son, christened John (after the 1st Duke) Albert Edward (after his godfather, the Prince of Wales) William (after Consuelo's father) and known as Bert. Alva quickly dispatched a grand, gilded antique Venetian cradle to hold the future Duke. It was while Consuelo was still confined to bed that Sunny met a young American named Gladys Deacon, who would figure prominently in the Marlborough story. Raised mainly in France, Gladys was the daughter of a wealthy Bostonian, Edward Deacon; he had gone to prison for fatally shooting his wife's lover when he found him crouched behind the sofa in her Cannes hotel room. Gladys was like "a lascivious young god," according to one friend, with gamine charm and eyes as blue as sapphires. Gladys had one dream only: to be mistress of Blenheim and wife to its Duke. When he'd become engaged to Consuelo, fourteen-year-old Gladys wrote: "Oh dear me, if I was only a little older I might catch him yet! But alas! I am too young, though mature in the arts of woman's witchcraft." Her charms, given time, would serve her well.

On the last day of that year, amateur theatricals were held at Blenheim Palace to raise money for a nearby church. Sunny got to wear his Worth-designed, pearl-covered, straw-colored velvet again for *tableaux vivants*, while Consuelo, taking part in a modern skit with Jennie Churchill, got to sing the following heartfelt lyric:

I am so tired,
Terribly, awfully tired.
I think I shall die
I don't know why
Except I'm tired.

The happiness her baby brought her, Consuelo writes, "lightened the gloom that overhung our palatial home," but she had to spend another bleak winter at Melton Mowbray while Sunny harassed little foxes and she awaited the birth of a second child. Another son — "you are a little brick!" noted a smiling Goosie — arrived on October 14, 1898, and was christened Ivor Charles, but usually called "Tigsy."

It was one year later when the free woman in Consuelo, her own woman, not her mother's or husband's accessory, began to emerge. The South African Boers, wanting their freedom from bully Britain, which was grabbing all their diamonds, went to war to get it (but ultimately failed). Sunny joined Lord Roberts's staff and went off, with a full complement of gorgeous uniforms, to bash the Boers into docility. Consuelo moved into London's Warwick House, near the Ritz Hotel, and joined the "American Amazons," led by Jennie Churchill, who were raising money for an American hospital ship sent to the aid of wounded British troops. The American women first met on October 25, including Lily, Duchess of Marlborough, wife of Lord Bill Beresford, Adele Essex, Minnie Paget and fourteen others. They met almost daily for the next two months, worked together with great zeal and initiative, staged various entertainments, and raised $200,000. On December 23 the *Maine* sailed for Cape Town with a triumphant Jennie on deck, going out to rendezvous with her fiancé, Lieut. George Cornwallis-West, serving with the Guards. Consuelo proved a most efficient organizer, and got a taste of what a strong-minded American woman could accomplish once she'd put her mind to it.

By now, Consuelo, like Nan, Duchess of Tintagel, her fictional counterpart in longtime friend Edith Wharton's *Buccaneers*, was "tired of trying to be English." She deplored the fact that in "the little circle I knew of American women married to Englishmen" there were "very few who remained definitely American." She was particularly contemptuous of Mary Leiter Curzon, who had married her adored George in the same year as Consuelo married Sunny. Mary had "shed her American characteristics more completely than I was to find myself able to do" and "had subordinated her personality to his to a degree I would have considered beyond an American woman's powers of self-abnegation."

Consuelo had been raised mainly in America, only intermittently in Europe, but her "finishing" under Alva's hand had made her more European than American. Paradoxically, it was living in England, married to an Englishman, that was slowly turning Consuelo into an American girl, committed to republican ideals, homesick for her native land. The Yankee rebel was surfacing regularly now in small ways. For a dinner in honor of the Prince and Princess of Wales, Consuelo left off the prescribed tiara and wore a diamond crescent in her hair instead. "The Princess has taken the trouble to wear a tiara. Why have you not done so?" snapped the Prince. Consuelo turned up in France at Longchamps races in the spring of 1901, wearing white, not black, gloves. The rest of Society was still in full mourning for Queen Victoria, who had died on January 22, no doubt from the shock of finding herself a live anachronism in the twentieth century. Double Duchess Lottie, whom Consuelo describes as a "raddled old woman, covering her wrinkles with paint and her pate with a brown wig," let out a stream of abuse at the sight of Consuelo's white gloves. "How could I, she complained," pointing to them, "show so little respect to the memory of a great Queen?"

Gladys Deacon came for the first of her annual autumnal visits to Blenheim in 1901, while Sunny laughed at her wit and admired her flat-chested, boyish figure. In the following winter, Consuelo and Sunny went to Russia so that the little Duke could indulge his "weakness for pageants" at the great court functions that ushered in the Orthodox New Year. Consuelo caught a severe cold that turned into an ear infection and left her permanently deaf. It was a hard sentence for a girl still in her twenties. With Queen Alexandra, similarly afflicted, she would later take lessons in lipreading, and later still acquire a hearing aid.

Back in England, Sunny hired the French architect Achille Duchêne and began spending Consuelo's Christmas check from her father by building the London town house the Duke had always wanted, to be called Sunderland House. At the corner of Curzon Street and Shepherd's Market, a chapel was demolished to make room, then the house slowly raised its impressive bulk, looking, Gertrude Atherton decided, "not unlike a mammoth packing box," and proving, eventually, fit quarters for a bank.

Sunny, with great enthusiasm, and Consuelo with less, joined the parade and pomp of King Edward's Coronation at Westminster Abbey on August 9, 1902. As one of England's tallest Duchesses, Consuelo was chosen to hold a corner of Queen Alexandra's canopy; Sunny carried the King's crown on a velvet cushion.

In the following November, Consuelo went off, with her two little boys, but not Sunny, to Vienna, for the first of many unsuccessful treatments for her deafness. In January 1903, she and Sunny and other English aristocrats sailed to India for the Great Durbar organized by its Viceroy, Lord Curzon, and graced by his beautiful, submissive American wife, Mary. There were two images of India that stayed with Consuelo and strengthened her emerging ego. When Mary Curzon took her female English guests to a purdah party to meet the wives of native Princes, Consuelo viewed the women as "a swarm of bright butterflies who were destined never to fly," cut off from the world completely, kept for their husband's exclusive use and pleasure. The second image imprinted itself on Consuelo's mind one glorious morning when a viceregal aide-de-camp invited her to watch a falcon hunt. She galloped on a "spirited horse" across the Indian plains "with the sun rising in the distance," to stand entranced while an unhooded falcon climbed to "immense heights" with incredible power and swiftness, silent and free and purposeful in its wide azure sphere.

Consuelo began making frequent pilgrimages alone to America to renew her spirits, and her resolve. She spent part of the summer of 1903 with Alva and Oliver Belmont at Newport's Belcourt. Like Lily Hammersley in her marriage to Lord Bill, Alva had settled for part of her husband's affection and attention, while his horses got the rest. Belcourt's ground floor was totally equine, with stalls for a dozen horses; in the salon above, two deceased favorites predominated, stuffed, at either end.

*30   Consuelo, Duchess of Marlborough, in her robes,
attendant to Queen Alexandra at the coronation
of King Edward VII, 1902*

At home in America, Consuelo, like Undine Spragg in Wharton's *Custom of the Country*, "among associations she shared and conventions she understood" felt "all her self-confidence return." When Consuelo came to the United States in September 1905, she was the first passenger to leave the *Campania* when it docked at New York, wearing a large hat with black feathers. She had grown into a beautiful woman: willowy, poised, distinctive, but "her greatest attraction," according to one male acquaintance, was "the pathos of her eyes." The playwright James M. Barrie, creator of Peter Pan, once observed: "I would stand all day in the street to see Consuelo Marlborough get into her carriage." She spent four days of that month-long visit in a private clinic on East Fifty-third Street undergoing an unsuccessful operation to cure her deafness, reflecting, in the silence, on the increasing tensions and conflicts of her marriage.

She finally broke free one year later, in October 1906. A dinner party was in progress at Blenheim, the table ponderous with Marlborough silver and poignant with Malmaison roses. Consuelo remarked that she was going to Paris to get her winter wardrobe. "Go and stay," hissed Sunny, in front of their guests. It was the last straw. Consuelo at once packed her things and left Blenheim forever. She went straight to Willie K. in Paris, now happily married to Anne Harriman Rutherfurd Sands, and told him everything. He came, reluctantly, back to London with her and got lawyers working on Consuelo's financial independence. Consuelo moved into Sunderland House with immense relief and began to think about divorce.

If godmother Consuelo Manchester's most daunting dragon in England was its rigid etiquette and Lily Marlborough's was its lax sexual code, Consuelo Marlborough's was the law. As a character in Burnett's *Shuttle* (1907) points out, "divorce courts in America are for women, but in England they are for men." According to the British Divorce Act of 1857, while a man had only to prove adultery, a wife had to provide undeniable proof of her husband's guilt in rape, sodomy or bestiality, or of adultery linked with incest, cruelty or desertion lasting at least two years. (Not until 1923 would the rules for men and women be equalized.) While as early as the 1860s, as Auguste Carlier reports in *Marriage in the United States* (1867), three thousand easy divorces were being declared in America every year, with a population of thirty million, as late as 1910 the yearly average in Britain was only 638, with a population of thirty-seven million. American divorce laws had been comparatively generous ever since most state legislatures had revised their statutes in the 1830s and 1840s.

Consuelo envied her mother her quick and painless divorce, and was persuaded, at this point, to opt for mere legal separation instead. As Alice Vanderbilt wrote to daughter Gertrude, now married to the boy next door, rich Harry Payne Whitney, "Willie K. will not listen to their [*sic*] being any divorce." Alice goes on to say that the "real reason" for the split between Consuelo and Sunny "seems to be that she is physically repulsive to him and that he cannot bear to be near her." A later letter to Gertrude reported that Anne, Willie K.'s wife, "made no charge against Marlborough in talking to me except to say he was impossible and that he had insulted Consuelo in every possible way and that for two years there had been trouble." Alice added that Sunny's family "certainly cannot put anything to Consuelo's charge." Years later, when Consuelo was discussing with Louis Auchincloss the writing of her autobiography, she told him, "Of course I can't put in a book what a beast Marlborough was."

At the prompting of Winston Churchill, who, in spite of being Sunny's cousin, sympathized wholeheartedly with Consuelo, his mother, Jennie, invited her to stay with her and husband George Cornwallis-West at their rented country house near St. Albans. "Poor little Consuelo," wrote George to Winston. "I do pity her with all my heart. What a tragedy.... Take my advice and if ever you do marry, do it from motives of affection, none other. No riches in the world can compensate for anything else."

Winston took this wisdom to heart, marrying penniless but beloved Clementine Hozier two years later.

The *New York Times*, on October 28, viewed the Marlborough split as a warning "against looking upon marriage as a business transaction" and reported that friction between the partners grew more acute "owing to the slighting, unsympathetic attitude of the Duke since the Duchess' deafness became more pronounced," and to the fact that "the Duke, in the opinion of the Duchess, paid greater attention than necessary to a girl friend of his wife" (the designing Gladys Deacon).

The breakup of Consuelo's marriage was the subject of many American and English newspaper editorials. One in the *New York Times* on October 30, 1906, reminded readers that in announcing his engagement to Consuelo the Duke of Marlborough had called it an "alliance," "arranged" by his friends: "There was no pretence that the loving and honoring and cherishing which he was presently to promise corresponded at all to his past or then present sentiments. This was strange language in American ears, especially in the ears of American girls. It was remarked at the time that if such an announcement as that of the ducal suitor in question had been made a generation earlier, by an affianced man about an American girl, it would have cost him his bride."

By 1906, hypocrisy in America was blatant, with a wide gap between professed sentiments and actual behavior. While the British, including Sunny, had always openly acknowledged their cold-blooded, practical view of upper-class marriage, where money was routinely exchanged for rank, the Americans wanted to eat their wedding cake and have it too. They used their money, in the Gilded Age, quite shamelessly to get them whatever they craved: political office or respectability or notoriety or European titles. In the latter case, however, they refused to relinquish one jot of their romantic yearnings for "true love" and "happily ever after."

Alva stormed into Sunderland House, come for an extended stay, in mid-December, and tried, in her usual steamroller way, to patch things up between Consuelo and the discarded Duke, but

Consuelo stood firm against her mother. Legal separation papers were signed in January 1907, eleven years and three months after the marriage, whereby the Duke retained the $100,000 a year from Willie K. settled on him at the time of the marriage, while the Duchess got Sunderland House and joint custody of their two sons, who were to spend half the year with each parent. The Duke was to control their education — they were then at Eton — and stipulated that they "shall not be taken to America for an extended period until they reach the age to choose a place of residence for themselves." Sunny was taking no chances on letting them turn into damn Yankees.

One feels sure that somewhere in the course of these financial negotiations, Willie K. must have pulled a pencil and scrap of paper from his pocket and soberly computed what he'd paid in total for the Marlborough dukedom. It worked out to just under $10 million, more than a tenth of his total fortune. Like most astute men of business, Willie K. liked to earn rich returns on his investments. But the 9th Duke of Marlborough had turned out to be, as grandfather Corneel might have put it, "one helluva stinking, rotten deal."

In the spring of 1907, as daffodil trumpets filled Hyde Park, Consuelo's true-gold life began to unfold. At long last, at the age of thirty, finally untethered from mother and husband, she could journey beyond stereotype and subordinate and find out who she was and where her interests lay.

Her timing was just right, for by 1907 the push for women's liberation in Britain was getting stronger every day. Enthusiastic articles entitled "The New Woman" had appeared in *Cornhill Magazine* (October 1894), *The Outlook* (October 1895) and *The Westminster Review* (March 1897), although, in general, with the exception of the vote, women's rights in Britain came later than in America. Queen's College and Bedford College were opened in 1848 and 1849 to give women higher education; Britain's first Married Woman's Property Act was passed in 1870; in both cases, these advances came more than twenty years later than America's. As for female suffrage, its advocates formed two groups, a moderate one, headed by Millicent Fawcett, called the National Union of Women's Suffrage Societies, and a militant one organized in 1903 by Emmeline Pankhurst and her law-graduate daughter, Christabel, called Women's Social and Political Union. Their full militancy would erupt, beginning in 1912, in a level of violence that American women rarely resorted to, including smashing shop windows, setting fire to buildings, jabbing ten-inch steel hatpins into police horses, and scratching policemen's faces with fingernails. That British suffragists employed such tactics shows the level of their frustrations within a society more patriarchal than America's. Not until 1918, two years before the Nineteenth Amendment to the Constitution gave American women nationwide suffrage, would British women be granted the right to vote.

Feeling all the excitement and agitation of "the woman question" brewing around her in England, Consuelo, in that spring of 1907, remembered that she was, before all else, an "American Girl," that free spirit known around the world for her strident individualism. In all his tales of transatlantic marriages, Henry James stressed the American Girl's independence. "I have never allowed a gentleman to dictate to me, or to interfere with anything I do," boasts the heroine of *Daisy Miller* (1879) and Isabel Archer declares in *The Portrait of a Lady*, "I can do what I choose — I belong quite to the independent class. I try to judge things for myself...I don't wish to be a mere sheep in the flock." James saw clearly, however — and therein lie the tensions for his heroines — that the American Girl's manifest destiny, for all her brave talk of liberty and the pursuit of happiness, was still marriage. It was no coincidence that Consuelo's emancipation began with her separation.

The majority of English Society women, lacking Consuelo's Yankee "drive to democracy," had little sympathy with women's rights. At one great London charity ball, when a suffragist in a tailored suit "with a wild, rather noble face" dashed amongst the glittering crowd, she was picked up shrieking in the arms of a policeman, while Society women in their silks and satins "closed in about her," as one horrified spectator records in her memoirs, "brutally beating the struggling figure with their fans." Consuelo was careful to find her freedom at the far edge of Society's norms, but not beyond.

She launched a committed career in social work and philanthropy. Since the 1870s, helping the poor and needy had been growing more fashionable among Society women, spurred on by the example of English heiress Baroness Burdett-Coutts, who had been created a peeress in her own right in 1871 in recognition of her organizing so many "good-works" societies. Consuelo realized that she could use her money and new freedom for similar philanthropic purposes, particularly for improving woman's lot. She leased premises where convicts' wives, who had no source of income while their husbands were imprisoned, could earn money sewing and doing laundry. She found and equipped and ran lodging houses for poor women and working girls, and set up an insurance society for female domestic servants. She began a school to teach mothercraft to working-class mothers, and became known — shades of her growing-up years — as the Baby Duchess.

Consuelo used her heiress's fortune and her superb London town house and her class privileges as Duchess, all of which had previously been only burdensome and inhibiting, as tools to further her own ends. Whereas Sunny had used Sunderland House to parade Marlborough pomp, Consuelo now used it as a kind of ingenious trap. She sent out invitations to large receptions, and everyone came, eager to hobnob with a Duchess, eager for caviar and champagne. On one such occasion, she lured churchmen, politicians, captains of industry and "butterflies of fashion" and made them listen, rather than mill about chatting idly, to twelve old women who had spent from twenty to fifty years working at humble jobs in industries under cruel conditions for very low pay. On another occasion, Consuelo's unsuspecting guests arrived at Sunderland House to find all the powdered, crimson-clad footmen holding out plates — not filled with strawberries or éclairs — but empty ones, ready for cash donations in aid of "Waifs and Strays," who themselves stood on every step of the marble staircase, like so many bronze statuettes, each with extended arm holding an empty plate.

As she organized her projects, chairing committees, making speeches, Consuelo's self-esteem grew by leaps and bounds, and British women looked in admiration and awe as Consuelo showed them what the formidable combination of American Girl and English Duchess could accomplish. She learned the art of speech-making from a master, friend Winston Churchill, and every well-received and wildly applauded speech gave her confidence to make a better one. She enjoyed the limelight now in a way she never had as Society Duchess when she opened bazaars and graced receptions, with the press commenting only on her clothes, never on her ideas, at a time when, as she puts it, "the film star had not yet eclipsed the Duchess."

Consuelo went often to the United States, whose freedoms drew her home. Landing at New York on October 24, 1907, from the *Kaiser Wilhelm II,* she "appeared as happy as a school girl and was extremely cordial to everyone and when the reporters approached her, she greeted them pleasantly," telling them "she was delighted to be back in her native country."

She made another trip home, arriving on the *Lucania* on March 7, 1908, and moved for an extended stay into a suite of ten rooms at the Martha Washington Hotel for Women on West Thirtieth Street, decorated to her taste with roses on the ceiling frieze and her own furniture and paintings.

Oliver Belmont died that year, and widow Alva, influenced by the suffrage leader Anna Howard Shaw, launched her last and most engrossing career: that of militant feminist, one that exactly suited her belligerence and fiery zeal, but that seems ironic in light of her earlier oppression of her own daughter's freedoms. Alva, like Anna, concentrated her energies on the ongoing battle for female suffrage. As in England, suffragists had formed themselves initially into a moderate and a radical group, based in

Boston and New York respectively. In 1890 these two groups had united into NAWSA: the National American Woman Suffrage Association. Alva opened wide the doors of Marble House in Newport for meetings; financed their national press bureau; leased a Fifth Avenue office as NAWSA's headquarters. In 1915, Alva would leave NAWSA, which was taking the state route to female suffrage, and, impatient with the fact that thus far only nine states had granted it, would join the more militant Woman's Party, which endorsed the federal route of changing the Constitution, and which in another five years would succeed. Alva got Christabel Pankhurst to come from England to fire up American women, and herself printed her feminist views in such magazines as *Hearst's* and *The Ladies' Home Journal.* Alva was convinced that the time had come "to take this world muddle that men have created and turn it into an ordered, peaceful, happy, abiding place for humanity." Consuelo got inspiration and approval from her

31 Alva Belmont speaking at a suffragist meeting held at Marble House, Newport, in 1914. Consuelo is on the far right.

mother, and a common cause brought mother and daughter closer together, equals and co-conspirators in the war against men's entrenched dominance. Later, Alva and Consuelo would go to Hungary for the 1913 Biennial Convention of the International Woman Suffrage Alliance.

"Baby" had come a long way since she'd danced on an invisible lead at the Duc de Gramont's *bal blanc* fourteen years before. Back in England, from her American visit, Consuelo stayed away from Society functions — Ascot, Greenwood, Cowes, the ritual round — which Sunny was now embracing more frenetically than ever. She was totally engrossed in her social work and philanthropy, which had become "my main way of life and gave it a meaning it had hitherto lacked." She did take time, however, to relax and enjoy herself over informal Friday-night dinner parties at Sunderland House, where she invited writers to spark the conversation, including Sir James Barrie, John Galsworthy, George Bernard Shaw and H. G. Wells, who in 1909 published his apparently feminist novel, *Anne Veronica*, advocating easy divorce and the end of legal financial contracts as a basis for marriage.

It was in 1909 that Consuelo published her own feminist manifesto, in the form of an article entitled "The Position of Women," which appeared in three installments in the *North American Review*. It was a lucid, well-researched article showing how the power and influence that women had enjoyed in some primitive societies, and in ancient Greece and Rome, had been taken from them with Christianity's advent. "It is in my opinion the necessity to adjust herself to man, to be judged by his individual standard and to conform her whole personality to his ways of thinking, that has robbed women of the power, strength and influence she could have exerted as a united and independent majority," announces Consuelo boldly. "Why should women have a standard of right and wrong," she asks indignantly, no doubt thinking of Sunny's suspect views, "adjustable to the moral sense of the men to whom they may happen to belong?" She does not wish to "decry marriage as a laudable and commendable goal" but to point out that "life does not end with its attainment as fairy-tales would make us believe. Woman's real life and purpose more often begin after marriage than before" — heartfelt words indeed. "Women who are not obliged to work for a living should work in one way or another, either politically, artistically or philanthropically, but always personally," she declares.

In the same year, Consuelo again stressed the Protestant work ethic, the ideology underpinning her nation, her family's fortune and her own life, for in a 1951 letter to her publisher, Cass Canfield, she admits to "a restless drive to work — so much more satisfying than the perpetual round of a mundane existence." In a speech that she made to open an East End London flower show, she told her audience that everyone, including the rich, needs the discipline of hard work on a daily basis, nurturing the flowers of "idealism, strength of purpose and good will." Not quite the speech one

32 Consuelo in 1919 touring the slums of Southwark, with the Prince of Wales, the future King Edward VIII

expected from an English Duchess at a flower show, but Ben Franklin would have approved.

During World War I, Consuelo became chairman of the American Women's War Relief fund, financed and ran a military hospital in Devon of four hundred beds, opened Sunderland House's basement as neighborhood shelter from Zeppelin raids and helped run the YMCA for American troops. When, in giving the 1916 Priestly Lecture on "Infant Mortality, Causes and Prevention," she openly referred to venereal disease, some of the ladies stalked out, blushing and furious, but the London *Times* next day applauded the Duchess of Marlborough's courage "in unveiling unpalatable truths." Consuelo turned politician in 1917 as elected Councillor to the London County Council for North Southwark, a poor, working-class district. She toured its slums, bettered its housing conditions, went about on public trams, not in a chauffeur-driven car. She launched the Children's Jewel Fund in 1918, appealing to Society women to give a jewel to save a child's life, and raised £50,000. When Willie K. gave her $15 million in 1919, she used it for her philanthropy.

Her happiness was crowned when she fell in love with the charming, rich Frenchman Jacques Balsan, who had first admired her at the Duc de Gramont's *bal blanc*. They had met sporadically over the years, sometimes in France, several times at Blenheim. He had sent her a postcard during the war, just before going on a dangerous flying mission from which he feared he might not return. Jacques was warm, caring, genial, good-natured, optimistic — all the things Sunny was not.

Before she could marry him, however, Consuelo had to endure the distasteful publicity of an English divorce, by proving desertion and adultery on Sunny's part. Sunny, too, wanted to be free so that he could marry Gladys Deacon, whom he visited often in London. (Cunning Gladys had taken a flat in the street that she knew Sunny was irresistibly drawn to: Savile Row.) Sunny visited

33 Col. Jacques Balsan during World War I

Consuelo one gray December day, then "deserted" her, sending a follow-up letter declaring that "it is impossible for us to live happily together." Then he registered with a hired co-respondent in a Paris hotel, as "Mr. and Mrs. Spencer" — shades of his father's caper with Edith Aylesford! — and was duly spied on by a private detective hired by Consuelo's lawyer.

On November 19, 1920, the English judge granted the Marlboroughs a decree nisi. Consuelo didn't appear, pleading an "indisposition," but Sunny turned up looking very smart in an astrakhan fur coat.

Willie K. Vanderbilt died on July 22, 1933, aged seventy-one, leaving, from an estate of more than $54 million, a $2.5 million trust fund to Consuelo and $1.6 million in cash.

The Marlborough divorce, to Consuelo's great joy, became absolute on May 13, 1921. She did not know then that there would be one more round in her fight to rid herself of her Marlborough chains. "Thank Heavens it is all over," wrote Sunny, drawing his cloak of self-pity about him. "The last blow that woman could strike over a period of some twenty years has now fallen." On June 24, Sunny married Gladys in friend Eugene Higgins's Paris drawing room, decorated with four huge paintings of female nudes, causing Gladys's mother to exclaim that they were "enough to put you off sex for life." Edith Wharton, one of the guests, watched the bridal pair united beneath a horseshoe of white gardenias.

Consuelo chose America's Independence Day, July 4, 1921, for marriage to Jacques. It took place in a London registry office in Covent Garden, with the bride in sea green satin with primroses pinned to her hat. It says much about the Vanderbilt-Marlborough union that whereas Consuelo's second marriage was a happy, lasting one, Sunny's was as disastrous as his first and his wife equally disenchanted. Friends noted, however, that Consuelo's marriage to Jacques worked because he was content to stay in the background, deferential and affable, leaving her the role of dominant partner.

When, sometime about 1950, Consuelo asked Louis

Auchincloss's advice as to the form her autobiography, *The Glitter and the Gold*, should take, he advised her to concentrate on the marriage "of the greatest heiress to the greatest duke," but Consuelo protested that "as her title would imply, Blenheim Palace was just the glitter and her real life, the one devoted to social work and to her second husband, Jacques Balsan, the gold." Certainly in the book she makes the contrast of her first and second marriages extreme; the gothic melodrama of exaggerated suffering gives way to a sentimental novel full of roses and sunshine. Consuelo's life recalls Anne Eliot's in Jane Austen's *Persuasion*: "She had been forced into prudence in her youth, she learned romance as she grew older — the natural sequence of an unnatural beginning."

The Balsans lived in style in France, with a Paris house at 2 Rue du Général-Lambert and a villa at Eze, near Monte Carlo, where yellow mimosa cascaded down terraces toward the jade Mediterranean. Later Consuelo found at St-Georges-Motel, near the forest of Dreux, the perfect setting for a shining knight and his lissome lady: a pink brick château with twin towers mirrored in a moat, and water gardens into which willows dipped their shimmering tresses.

Into this rosy idyll, in 1926, came one last thorn from marriage to Sunny, one that had its roots in the Roman Catholic Church's refusal to recognize divorce. Because of this, the Catholic Balsan family wouldn't receive Consuelo into the fold. Moreover, Anglican Sunny, drawn by its ritual and pageantry and hierarchical order, wanted to be received into the Catholic faith, but divorce from Consuelo barred his way. Consuelo and the Duke took steps to have the Catholic Church declare their marriage null on the ground technically known as "violence," which includes coercion. Alva appeared before the English Diocesan Court at Southwark and declared: "I forced my daughter to marry the Duke." Consuelo testified that her mother told her that she must marry him, that refusal to do so "was ruining her health and that I might be the cause of her death." Sunny declared that his bride "came late to the wedding and appeared much troubled." The Sacred

Rota Tribunal at Rome, composed of twelve members representing all the principal Catholic countries, returned a verdict of "nullity."

Newspapers in England and America splashed the affair across front pages, for this was the most discussed nullity case since Henry VIII had rid himself of wife Katherine of Aragon. The wrath of American clergy was mighty. How dared the Vatican pass judgment on a Protestant marriage? The Right Reverend William T. Manning, Episcopal Bishop of New York, called the Vatican's verdict "an unwarrantable intrusion and an impertinence, a discredit to the Christian church and an injury to religion." Monsignor Michael J. Lavelle of New York's St. Patrick's Cathedral, replying to charges that only the rich and titled could get a ruling erasing a twenty-five-year marriage that had produced two offspring, said severely that "the church makes no distinction between Dukes and tramps." *The Living Church*, the Episcopalian magazine, barked: "Let the Roman Catholic Church produce the tramp!" American press and public had found a new opportunity to vent their ever-growing disillusionment with heiress-peer alliances.

Finally, the tempest in a chalice subsided. Consuelo heaved a sigh of relief that her name was no longer headlined, and Jacques's family received her warmly. When, on February 1, 1927, Sunny's conversion to Roman Catholicism was announced to his mother, Goosie, a rabid Ulster Protestant, she telegraphed: "TO HELL WITH THE POPE!"

But a question remains to plague us. How much of Consuelo's point of view in *The Glitter and the Gold*, written more than twenty years later, was conditioned by the fact that, having testified for the Rota that her mother coerced her into marriage with Sunny, she had to be consistent? *Had* she been forced, or had her own romantic dreams also propelled her? There can be no definite answer, but one suspects that if Alva pushed her daughter toward a Duchess's coronet, Consuelo may have gone trippingly enough. When her friend Edith Wharton, who was a frequent visitor to Consuelo's French homes, characterized her in *The Buccaneers* as Nan St. George, she showed her marrying the Duke of Tintagel for the sake of her imagination. His Cornish castle, when Nan first sees it, "spoke with that rich low murmur of the past," and she pictures its walls "built on ancient foundations, and crowded with the treasures of the past." Like mother, like daughter; Consuelo, as well as Alva, may have felt the castle of Blenheim's siren call. She did, to be sure, tell a journalist at the time of the Rota rumpus that in marrying the Duke, "I may have been a little romantic and consequently over-enthusiastic." One wonders if only with the hindsight of its breakdown did Consuelo see, under the gossamer of her 1895 nuptials, the ugly bones of a money-for-rank exchange.

Alva had bought in 1926, near Consuelo's moated home, the Château d'Augerville-la-Rivière, the real thing, ancient and storied — not a Fifth Avenue fake — built by Jacques Coeur, who had financed Joan of Arc's holy wars. Alva erected a statue to that early feminist in a nearby church. Alva Belmont died at her Paris house at 9 Rue Monsieur — ironic name — at the age of eighty, on January 25, 1933, with Consuelo at her side. She and Jacques accompanied her mother's body home to New York for burial according to Alva's detailed orders. At the funeral service in St. Thomas's Church, the choir sang a hymn Alva had written for the occasion, which proclaimed:

> *No waiting at the gates of Paradise,*
> *No tribunal of men to judge.*
> *The watchers of the tower proclaim*
> *A daughter of the King.*

Alva had once told a feminist co-worker, "Pray to God. She will help you." An all-female escort accompanied the coffin to Woodlawn Cemetery, carrying a banner with the words Failure Is Impossible writ large. In Alva's final years, Consuelo had grown close to her, and genuinely mourned.

In June of that year, Gladys and Sunny had a most acrimonious final parting, during which he cut off electricity to their London home where she was living and tried to have her declared insane. Another Churchill wife wrote in sympathy to Gladys: "I know all the ungentleman-like tricks that the family we both had the misfortune to marry into can do — the lies and spite" and observed that "Churchills only fight women and children and persecute them — but never men in any position to retaliate."

Sunny's life was a sad one. He had been an unloved child; like his fellow aristocrats, he had been raised first by a nanny and then by boarding-school masters and spent little time with his parents. In their formative years, British peers didn't experience warm, embracing love within the family; perhaps that is why they made such unsatisfactory husbands. Nor did Sunny, the child of divorced parents, have a positive ideal of wedded bliss to inspire him in his own two marriages. His highly developed aesthetic sense, as well as an ego whose only real reinforcement came from his class status, compelled him to pledge his life to a cold, unresponsive love object, to Blenheim Palace, greedy, demanding Blenheim, which devoured time and money and energy and gave him nothing in return.

After he and Gladys parted, Sunny deserted his first love; he lived in his London house and stayed at a nearby hotel when estate duties called him down to Blenheim. He began negotiations with the Duke of Alba to retire permanently, as a layman, to a Benedictine monastery in Spain. But before he could do so, he developed cancer of the liver and died on June 30, 1934, at sixty-two. By 1934 English Dukes had lost most of their power and privilege, and one obituary called Sunny "a lonely peacock strug-gling through deserted gardens," who had "spent his life sowing seed after seed where none can ever grow."

Consuelo was more fortunate. After Sunny's death, she and Jacques enjoyed what she calls the "sweet careless gaiety" of the last summers before World War II. In early 1939, Consuelo gave her kind of costume ball at St-Georges-Motel and it was not at all like Alva's or the Duchess of Devonshire's, being a very small and informal party for her grandchildren. (Bert, 10th Duke of Marlborough, had married a Viscount's daughter in 1920 and had

34 *Consuelo, proud American citizen,*
photographed in 1942

four children.) "The best part of the fun," according to Consuelo, was that all the guests made their own costumes, and then danced to the music of a gramophone.

Consuelo still busied herself with good works and had built a sanatorium for sick children nearby. In 1940, when the Germans invaded France, she arranged for a fleet of vans to evacuate the patients; she and Jacques packed one small suitcase each and fled to Lisbon, where they boarded a plane for the United States. The last sentence of *The Glitter and the Gold* reveals how much of

Consuelo's heart had never left America: "As we moved through the waters and rose to our flight, I looked at the blue sky above and the slowly fading coast beneath and felt I had embarked on a celestial passage to a promised land." From then on, the Balsans divided their time between a house in Palm Beach, 2 Sutton Place South in New York and another house at Southampton, Long Island. Consuelo eagerly regained her American citizenship, lost at the time of her marriage to the Duke.

In 1951 she looked back on her eventful life and wrote *The Glitter and the Gold*. When her American publisher wanted to put Consuelo in her 1902 Coronation robes on the cover, she objected strenuously. "I really cannot overcome my dislike for the Coronation photograph," she told Cass Canfield on January 7, 1952. "It indicates to me a book entirely different from the one I have written. In these democratic days, I really do not think that a coronet, diamonds and pearls are going to have a specific attraction." She urged him instead to use a 1901 etching of her, wearing no jewels at all, by Paul Helleu. She also asked to have the words "Mistress of Blenheim Palace" removed from the cover, for that stage of her life was long over, and repudiated.

The book was published in New York on September 15, 1952, and in Britain on April 27, 1953. It was serialized in America in *The Ladies' Home Journal* and in England in *The Woman's Journal*. Consuelo was pleased when the book sold well and garnered enthusiastic reviews, but when both Sam Goldwyn and David Selznick wanted to make a movie of it, she said a firm no.

Nineteen fifty-six was a sad year for Consuelo; her son Ivor died of cancer of the brain, aged fifty-seven, on September 17 and her beloved Jacques died two months later, on November 6, at age eighty-eight.

We catch a final glimpse of Consuelo in 1958, when she was eighty-one, visiting a Fifty-seventh Street antique shop. The saleswoman didn't know who this "very tall, striking-looking woman" was, but felt her charm, her distinction, her sterling sense of self. "She was wonderful; you can't imagine. And she *apologized* for walking slowly upstairs."

On December 6, 1964, at her Southampton home, Consuelo died of a stroke, aged eighty-seven. The funeral took place on December 10 in St. Thomas's new Episcopalian Church, built on the site of the one where she had married the Duke sixty-nine years before, "at a time when rich Americans sought out impoverished but titled Europeans for their daughters," as the *New York Times* social reporter Charlotte Curtis put it, recalling that quaint phenomenon. Near the coffin of "one of the last survivors of America's Gilded Age," Charlotte tells us, stood a basket of pink and white carnations sent by a surviving bridesmaid, Mrs. Louis S. Brugière, the former Daisy Post. The large congregation assembled sang "Fight the Good Fight," the hymn Consuelo had considered appropriate.

Her son Bert, 10th Duke of Marlborough, and her grandson, the thirty-eight-year-old Marquess of Blandford, the future 11th Duke, accompanied the body to Kennedy International Airport for the flight to England, for Consuelo had asked to be buried beside son Ivor in Bladon churchyard, just beyond the gates of Blenheim Palace. Given the unhappy associations of her first marriage, it seems an odd, whimsical request, but perhaps the 9th Duchess felt she'd paid plenty for her right to lie there. Only a few people gathered in Bladon's fog and chill to walk behind the coffin, sprinkling white chrysanthemum petals, as Consuelo was laid to rest. One of the mourners was Tina, former wife of Aristotle Onassis, another rich girl whose money had enticed a British peer, for she'd married the Marquess of Blandford two years before, after he'd divorced his first wife for adultery. He would divorce Tina in 1972.

The London *Times* obituary of Consuelo was very short, part of one column, and merely emphasized her English connection, noting that she'd held one corner of Queen Alexandra's canopy for the Coronation of King Edward VII. The *New York Times* obituary and account of the last rites, on the other hand, ran to four columns, decked with large photos, and trotted out once again the twice-told mythic tale of the heiress and the Duke. Hardheaded Brits; starry-eyed Americans. Cynicism on one side of the Atlantic; sentimentality on the other. Perhaps it was that dichotomy before all others that underlay the friction in most transatlantic marriages.

Consuelo Vanderbilt was born to the insistent whiplash of her mother's will and to stultifying luxury, but she slowly learned to discriminate and discard amid so much swansdown, ending with everything she valued, and nothing she despised. Paradoxically, it was only when Consuelo found herself sealed in the cold marble of a loveless marriage and alien land that she put forth amazing new growth. While Lily Hammersley, after marriage to a Duke, stayed American, Consuelo Vanderbilt only then *became* American, in a decisive, demonstrated way, able at long last to take possession of her homeland and herself.

IV

HELENA ZIMMERMAN

35 *Helena Zimmerman, 9th Duchess of Manchester*

"We tried to rest ourselves," said the Duke this evening, "but there were a lot of people who called and then the newspaper men all wanted to know all we were doing and going to do."

—CINCINNATI ENQUIRER,
December 3, 1900, page 1

T HEIRS WAS A MARRIAGE made in headlines and consummated in the sheets of gossip columnists. The actual shared life of Kim and Helena, 9th Duke and Duchess of Manchester, pales, shrinks, retreats behind closed doors, unable to compete with that heightened life, vivid, visceral, bizarre, that splashed its way across the pages of British and American newspapers for almost half a century.

The Manchesters were born too soon. Their marriage should have been dished up in garish color in *People* magazine, or in *Life*, where a later British Duke and his brash American bride, the Duke and Duchess of Windsor, downgraded King and upstart commoner, regularly found themselves. The Manchesters had to settle for less hype and mere black on white, but at least they almost always made the front page.

Their story bears out the old adage that truth is stranger than fiction, for it is a soap opera full of astounding twists and turns and coincidences, played out against a very twentieth-century background: a greedy, me-first consumer society where everyone was obsessed with money and the media, frantically exploiting each in the service of the other. The Manchester marriage has moments of pathos but many more of hilarious farce. One can easily see why, when Charles Dana Gibson needed a really silly British peer for one of his cartoons, he always drew the unmistakable outline of Kim, 9th Duke of Manchester.

Kim and Helena's finest hour in print came early, just two weeks after their London wedding, when, on the afternoon of December 1, 1900, the honeymooners steamed into New York harbor, past the twelve-year-old Statue of Liberty's dignified welcome, straight into a crowd of newspaper reporters gratifyingly large, reverential and attentive.

And eager. Not wanting to wait until the American liner *St. Louis* tied up at its pier, the journalists had crossed the choppy bay by cutter to where the ship was temporarily anchored at the quarantine station. There they clambered aboard and quietly waited for the Duke and Duchess to appear. In 1900 reporters still had manners. They didn't just barge in unannounced to staterooms 3 and 5 where Their Graces were grooming themselves for their public with the help of valet and maid. The journalists waited respectfully in the corridor while the bride's father, Eugene Zimmerman, accompanied by two mystery men about whose identity the reporters speculated wildly, knocked on the door of Number 5, gained admittance for all three and closed the door firmly behind them.

Fifty-five-year-old Eugene Zimmerman, Cincinnati millionaire, tall, well-built, dark complexioned, had been in New York for a week, putting up as usual at the Lotus Club while he planned the route and stopovers for the newlyweds' trip to San Francisco and back in his private railroad car. Eugene was a typical self-made man of his day, totally absorbed in chasing his next dollar, with no time for social events or culture, no time even to spend the $2,000 a day that the *New York Herald* claimed he currently earned.

36 Eugene Zimmerman, Cincinnati millionaire

Born on December 17, 1845, in Vicksburg, Mississippi, to foundry-man Solomon Zimmerman, son of a Dutch immigrant, and Hannah (née Biggs), Eugene was raised in Ohio and orphaned at fifteen. When, one year later, Civil War sounded its thunder at Fort Sumter, Eugene at once left school and offered himself, with fifty cents in his pocket, in the service of the U.S. Navy. With a driving ambition to succeed, he rose through the ranks from lowly master's mate to Commander of the U.S.S. *Onachita* in only two years, so that at eighteen he was the youngest commander in the whole Union force. After the war, he went back to Ohio and turned his drive to getting rich. From lumber through petroleum — helping found Standard Oil — into coal and iron and railroads, Eugene advanced himself, ever onward and upward, getting richer and richer. He took a day off in 1876 to wed Marietta Evans, daughter of Abraham Evans, an Urbana, Ohio, horse dealer. Marietta had cultural pretensions, for her father's first cousin, Englishman Robert Evans, was the father of Mary Ann Evans, better known to posterity as the novelist George Eliot.

Marietta Zimmerman gave birth to a daughter, Helena, in 1879, and inconveniently died two years later. Eugene was about to become President of the Chesapeake and Nashville Railroad and was far too busy to raise a child. He dispatched baby Helena forthwith to her godmother and namesake, one of his wife's unmarried sisters, Miss Helena Evans, with strict instructions to make her a lady, no expense spared, and then return her about the age of eighteen. Accordingly, little Helena studied English literature at Miss Nourse's school in Cincinnati, learned riding and high-jumping from Professor de Gisbert, picked up assorted languages in France at a high-class school at Fontainebleau and was finally pronounced "finished" by the French nuns at Auteuil's fashionable Convent of the Assumption. Helena emerged a sturdy extrovert, physically and mentally fit, ready to dance, ride, golf, fence and express her wants in four languages, ready to take on all comers and to brook no opposition to her strong body and stronger will. When she returned to Cincinnati, Eugene regarded her with awe; he'd got rather more than he'd bargained for.

Denied a normal home with siblings and two nurturing parents, Helena had learned early to stand alone. The *Cincinnati Enquirer* called her "a self-willed, masterful, rebellious girl who accepted the world as made for her" with "the indomitable spirit of her father" and "an essentially independent temperament." Like most of her kind who tied their destiny to British lords, Helena would need all her strength of character on that painful road to experience that left even the most freewheeling American girls bruised and bowed.

Her father, meanwhile, had in 1888 hooked his wagon to that of the multimillionaire Collis P. Huntington, former Sacramento storekeeper, by persuading Collis to join him in building the Chesapeake and Ohio Bridge leading across the Ohio River into Cincinnati. Like Commodore Vanderbilt, Collis was one of that Gilded Age gang who proved themselves the boldest financial manipulators the world has ever seen, and he taught Eugene everything he knew. Eugene proved so apt a pupil that when, in 1892, the *New York Tribune* printed its official list of 4,047 "American Millionaires," there stood "Eugene Zimmerman" in bold face. It was his daughter's marriage, however, that was about to push Eugene into full notoriety. As the *New York World* noted the day after the wedding, an "obscure millionaire," owner of a "modest house in Cincinnati," who many people didn't even believe *was* a millionaire, had with "the somewhat spectacular marriage of his daughter" become overnight "a multimillionaire of handsome proportions."

The multimillionaire of handsome proportions had risen early, as usual, on that fateful December 1, 1900, as daughter and new husband headed toward him, about to crash into his closed, self-aggrandizing life. The clock had not yet struck seven when Eugene hailed the clerk behind the Lotus Club desk with the terse question, "Has the *St. Louis* been sighted?" Told that it hadn't, he ate a hasty breakfast and hurried to his office at 29 Broadway, for not even on an eventful Saturday could Eugene afford to neglect his business. By two-thirty, however, when a reporter from the *Cincinnati Enquirer* arrived with the news that the *St. Louis* had been sighted off Fire Island, Mr. Zimmerman was doing nothing more productive than pacing nervously up and down his private office.

At once he made his way to a neighboring barbershop for final grooming, wanting to hold his own with a dandified Duke. Then Eugene and the reporter went to the Battery's barge office, met up with Detectives Vallely and Stripp, boarded the revenue cutter, rode out to the *St. Louis* and all but the Cincinnati reporter gained entry to Stateroom number 5. He stayed in the corridor, explaining to his colleagues there, in answer to their queries, that Police Chief McClusky had dispatched the two detectives to guard the Duke. Some rabid patriot who objected strongly to Britain's impoverished peers stealing America's richest daughters had announced by letter to the Captain of the *St. Louis* his intention of pelting the Duke with rotten eggs when the ship docked.

After a few minutes' wait, Mr. Zimmerman reappeared in the ship's corridor, announcing that the Duke and Duchess would be most happy to hold a press conference. Then everyone pushed into a reception room, including an "interested crowd of fellow passengers," according to the *New York Times*, which, together with the *Cincinnati Enquirer*, would print the longest accounts of the event. Pencils were poised and all eyes swiveled to the chair where America's newest Duchess sat, with her Duke standing close beside her.

The Duchess from Cincinnati — "not known to New York Society" sniffed the *New York Times* — was pretty, not so much because of fine features, but because, at twenty-one, she glowed with youth, verve and health. In repose, her face looked stubborn, its broad mouth straight and unyielding, but when she smiled, dimples appeared at the corners, and her blue eyes caught the smile and sparked. She wore her springy, curly blond hair parted in the center, rolled back from her face in a pompadour, with a black velvet hat trimmed with ostrich feathers perched jauntily on top. Her fur-trimmed coat and dress were also black, and the latter had a fetching white lace collar. Black and white, the color of news: a fitting costume for Helena's first newspaper interview.

When it came to meeting, and manipulating, the press, the new Duchess was a novice, whereas her Duke was already a past master. In their concerted race for fame, Kim had an enviable head start. He'd been a Duke since he was fifteen, and Dukes, particularly naughty ones like Kim and his father, were always news, whereas daughters of obscure millionaires weren't.

Helena would prove herself a quick learner. That day, she let Kim take the lead, leaning slightly forward in her chair, watching him in action, her eyes darting back and forth from him to the journalists. "She seemed as much interested in the business of the reporters as they were themselves," commented the *New York Times*.

The twenty-three-year-old Duke, short, barrel-chested, muscled like a prize fighter, stood with feet apart, cool and confident.

37 Kim, 9th Duke of Manchester

He wore a gray pin-striped suit under a long black overcoat lined and trimmed with astrakhan fur and fastened with frogs. He looked more like a Spanish grandee than an English Duke, given his olive skin, small hands and feet inherited from mother Consuelo, his dapper, swaggering pose.

At the outset, he quickly and cleverly established both his genial cooperation and his rapport with the journalists. "Well, what do you want me to say? You know I'm a newspaperman myself, after a fashion." Having tossed them that bone, he didn't elaborate, but grinned boyishly, showing two front teeth broken off in the boxing ring. "It was a jolly good voyage, a bit rough," he continued, "but neither of us was ill" — he glanced proudly at Helena who "smiled and nodded emphatically." "We are both good sailors." It would prove the strongest bond in their marriage: that mutual physical fitness, coupled with a love of sports and, in the beginning, a strong sexual attraction.

"I am told that one of the New York papers said that right after the wedding ceremony we were in tears. It don't look much like it, does it?" Kim asked the reporters. "No, indeed," volunteered Helena, with an arch smile.

The Duke continued to interview himself. "I'll try to answer just the questions I'd ask a man myself if I were after an interview. What's next? Oh, how do I like America? That shows you." And he bowed in an exaggerated way toward Helena. "It looked as if almost all his pride was centered on his beautiful bride," decided the *Cincinnati Enquirer* man. "To her his eyes turn every minute or two."

Kim was giving a first-rate performance and enjoying himself immensely. In seeking and holding the limelight, he was truly his mother's son. "Shyness has never been a failing of mine," he admits in his autobiography, *My Candid Recollections*, "but then I have been accustomed from babyhood to living in a crowd" and "did my best to provide entertainment whenever possible." Kim's lifelong tendency to exhibitionism surfaced at age six, during that visit to New York when Consuelo helped Alva Vanderbilt plan her spectacular costume ball. One day the postman, holding a letter

38 Young Kim, aged six

addressed to Viscount Mandeville, remarked, "How I would like to see a real-life lord!" Little Kim drew himself up to his full forty-inch height. "Then look at *me!*" he squeaked.

Because of his American mother, Kim had been a frequent visitor to the United States since babyhood and had espoused its democratic ways. "Not a trace of snobbishness, there isn't an ounce of that in him," correctly decided the Cincinnati journalist about this Duke, who was the exact opposite of proud, pompous Sunny Marlborough. On previous trips to New York, Kim was often to be seen at Child's Eating House, chatting to the clerks and salesmen there, gobbling corned-beef hash and doughnuts.

The reporters wanted to confirm why the two detectives had been assigned to guard the Duke. "It was only a kindly and thoughtful consideration on the part of Chief McClusky," Kim replied. "My man isn't used to American ways, don't you know, and he couldn't manage all that luggage." There was no mention of a threatening letter or of rotten eggs. The Duke "looks you squarely in the eyes," scribbled the Cincinnati reporter, "and gives you an answer straight from the shoulder."

The interview continued while Helena "fairly beamed with gladness and when she watched her young husband manfully meet the attacks of the newspaper men, she laughed with glee and pride." When she gave her low-pitched, infectious laugh, the "vivacious, petite" Duchess closed her eyes; when she listened, she opened them very wide in intense concentration.

The journalists asked about the Fannie Ward affair, which had taken up much space in American papers. Just after their marriage, Kim and Helena had been visiting the London house of Mrs. James Brown Potter, who amused London Society at parties by letting her mane of red hair suddenly cascade around her while she recited "Lorraine, Lorraine, Loree" and who would eventually appear on the professional stage. At her house that day was the actress Fannie Ward, who, without realizing it, had dropped a diamond-studded purse full of jewels on the pavement outside. Helena's maid had picked it up and given it to her mistress. Helena had put it away and promptly forgotten about it. Fannie then told the newspapers that England's newest Duchess had stolen her jewels. The reporters in the ship's lounge waited, knowing Fannie's accusations, pencils raised. It was Eugene Zimmerman who replied. "The woman is an actress and is simply trying to advertise herself," he announced shrewdly, having unwittingly put his finger on the pulse of the new century, with its self-serving exploitation of the media. He refused to say more.

Eugene Zimmerman had always been as chary with words as with money, feeling that both should be doled out carefully. Speech meant commitment, showing one's cards. Silence was golden; piling up unspoken thoughts was emotional capitalism. He was the exact antithesis of his voluble, spendthrift new son-in-law. In the ongoing battle between them, one bent on hanging on and the other on letting go, it would be Helena who got caught in the cross fire and the Duke who gained ground, forcing his father-in-law into parting with both dollars and words in prodigal profusion.

Shortly thereafter the press interview ended because the *St. Louis* had reached its pier. Everyone disembarked: the interested passengers, the reporters and cameramen, the two Evans aunts, Miss Helena and Miss Martha, who had accompanied their niece on the voyage, two bull terriers called Prince and Dick, Kim's valet, Trowbridge, Helena's maid, Mary, Mr. Zimmerman, Detectives Vallely and Stripp and at the apex of the moving throng, a beaming Duke and Duchess. Their mode of departure was telling: Helena in one carriage with her father, the Duke in another with the detectives, and the Misses Evans with Trowbridge and Mary in a third. The Manchesters' twenty-eight pieces of luggage had to have a whole wagon to themselves.

The three carriages and wagon rattled uptown through a thoroughly modern New York hooting and clanging and hysterical, where horseless carriages and buses chugged up Fifth Avenue, their drivers, called "engineers," swearing at all the weaving bicycles, pedaled by young men in derbies and celluloid collars. A $35-million contract had been let for the city's first subway, and Broadway had no less than fifty theaters.

The Manchester party made its way to the Holland House hotel, where Kim and Helena installed themselves in the bridal suite, containing bedroom with bath, dining room, parlor and suitably modest quarters for maid and valet. The honeymooners remained behind closed doors for most of that Saturday evening, but round about midnight Kim deserted his bride, unable to resist coming down to the lobby, where reporters still lingered, to give one more public performance, leaving Helena alone with her private thoughts on her new husband, and on how far she had come.

She had first met Kim eighteen months before, in the spring of 1899, at the seaside resort of Dinard in Brittany where she was visiting yet a third spinster sister of her dead mother's, Miss Effie Mackenzie Evans. Perhaps inspired by her famous literary cousin, George Eliot, Effie had become a journalist, and was currently Paris correspondent for the *New York Herald*, owned by James Gordon Bennett, Jr., once polo-playing crony of Kim's father. Effie solicited advertising, wrote up "Society affairs," and was well-known among expatriate Americans in Paris as a "character." When, in August 1894, a young American girl had arrived there to try her hand at journalism, she sought an introduction to Effie. "Yes, I am Miss Evans," Effie acknowledged. "And I tell you one thing at the start. You can't get my place! Nobody can get my place. Look at me! I am the *New York Herald*! I am James Gordon Bennett! I have no thoughts, no wishes of my own. I submit myself entirely to the master mind!" Effie often borrowed money from her close friends, James Creelman, editor of the Paris and London editions of the *Herald*, and his wife, Alice. On June 2, 1894, Alice wrote to her mother indignantly on the subject of Effie: "I told her plainly she could go to the devil. She is as crazy as a loon but there is a very cruel method in her madness very often and she is quite sane enough to know it."

While Helena was staying in Dinard with this zany, bohemian aunt as chaperone, a visiting matron from Philadelphia gave a costume ball. Bent on making a spectacular entrance, Helena came floating down the broad staircase, dressed in white tulle with myriad rosebuds, as actress Edna May, star of the hit musical *The Belle of New York*, while an orchestra below played one of the show's tunes. Gazing up at Helena enraptured from the foot of the stairs was Kim, 9th Duke of Manchester. He was even more spectacularly costumed than Helena, as a bather, wearing a flapping dressing gown and nothing at all beneath except flesh-colored tights. The Philadelphia matron was so shocked at his daring costume, quite "beyond the bounds of propriety," that she asked him to leave, but the spark between Kim and Helena had already been struck, and would soon enough flame higher.

In the first of many coincidences in their story, Helena Zimmerman had hit on exactly the right costume to snare this particular peer. There had always been only two kinds of women in Kim's life: actresses, who gave him hopes of stardom, and heiresses, who gave him hopes of solvency. At age eight, by his own admission, he had fallen "desperately in love" with his mother's friend, the actress Lily Langtry, following her about, "with my childish eyes riveted on her countenance." After puberty, he gained closer proximity to such "footlight favourites," as he calls them in his autobiography, as Camille Clifford, Ethel Barrymore and French actress Cléo de Mérode.

Just before he met Helena, there were rumors of Kim's engagement to Cléo, who often danced at Paris parties on a silk-covered dais wearing a few wisps of orange gauze. Kim bought her a diamond bracelet with large Burmese ruby, purchased at Guy et Fils, Rue de la Paix, for $3,000, on credit, like all Kim's purchases. When rumors of the engagement reached his mother, Consuelo, she rushed across the Channel and scotched them at once, telling Guy et Fils that they'd never be paid, and most certainly never by *her*. If Kim's most incendiary passion for an actress was for Cléo, his longest lasting was for the friend whom he describes in his memoirs as "one of those lucky women who acquire more charm with each passing year," namely Edna May.

As for his propensity for heiresses, Kim let it be noised abroad while still in his teens that he was seriously on the hunt, and in 1897, in a bold attempt to stave off his creditors — like his father before him, he was always in debt — he told the press he was going to marry the American heiress May Goelet. (Her father promptly denied it.) At that point, Kim couldn't even pay his livery bill of £46, ten shillings, and his Irish housekeeper at

Tandragee Castle, to whom he owed weeks of back wages, was buying canned food and whiskey for His Grace's guests out of her own pocket.

Next year, Kim hopefully announced his engagement to an English heiress, Joan Wilson, daughter of rich shipowner Charles Henry Wilson of West Hull, but nothing came of that either. The *New York Times* noted that the Duke "has been reported to be engaged to almost every eligible heiress to whom he has shown any attention in society," and it was the needy Duke who always initiated the rumors.

No wonder, then, that when Helena Zimmerman, real heiress and romancing actress, wafted down the stairs toward him in her winking diamonds and white tulle cloud, Kim was well and truly hooked. He followed Helena to Paris when she returned there with Aunt Effie, who, thinking of all the good copy she could dispatch to New York concerning an American heiress and a designing Duke, welcomed Kim warmly and encouraged his suit. Helena laughed at His Grace's tall tales and funny antics, eyed his square shoulders and muscled arms and nicknamed him "Gracie."

In a matter of days, he made his first proposal as they sat, thighs touching, in a carriage. "What sort of ring shall I get you?" Kim asked. A dog seller offered his wares at the next corner. Helena stopped the carriage, jumped out, picked up a bull terrier pup. "Give me this," she said, showing her dimples. Rumors of their engagement surfaced in English papers, to be copied in America. However, their first quarrel soon followed, and Helena, needing time and distance to reflect on where she was heading, returned to the United States.

Through the summer, Aunt Effie, for her part, as the *New York Times* noted, kept her *Herald* readers "informed as to the personality and qualities of her niece and the movements of the Duke." She urged Kim to follow Helena across the Atlantic, and when he replied that he had no money to do so, she pinned a note to her next batch of copy suggesting to her boss that the *Herald* might do well to put a roving ducal reporter on its payroll. Aunt Effie and Aunt Helena both wanted a Duchess in the family, a handy thing to have. Where young Helena was concerned, they seem quite as self-serving as her father.

Kim arrived in New York on November 9, checked into the Waldorf Astoria and that very night granted an interview to a *Times* reporter from his box at the theater. He rattled on about his plans in his usual boastful vein, with no mention of heiresses or newspaper work. He claimed that Charles Frohman "in an indirect way" had offered him a role in the forthcoming Madison Square production of *Make Way for the Ladies*, in which Kim's friend the Earl of Yarmouth had the lead. "My friends have tried to convince me that I have great histrionic ability," Kim told the reporter, convinced that, like the Earl, he should turn professional. George Seymour, Earl of Yarmouth and later 7th Marquess of Hertford, had appeared in Newport theatricals that summer singing "When the Little Pigs Begin to Fly" in blond wig and flesh-colored tights. (In another four years, the Earl would marry Pittsburgh coal heiress Alice Thaw, who had led too sheltered and pious a life to know that the Earl was firmly, flamboyantly homosexual. Their marriage on April 27, 1903, was delayed for forty-five minutes because the groom had been arrested that very morning in Pittsburgh for outstanding debts and insisted then and there on renegotiating the marriage settlement. Five years later, Alice obtained an annulment on grounds of non-consummation and retrieved what she could of her $1 million dowry.)

Kim's role in *Make Way for the Ladies* never got further than his imagination, and he settled instead for one in the Strollers' amateur production of *The Lady from Chicago*, then rehearsing in the Waldorf Astoria. He was so keen that one day he fainted dead away at rehearsal, and another day gleefully kept the Earl of Yarmouth from looking on. "He's professional, don't you know. He mustn't be admitted. Keep him out," Kim told the Waldorf's doorman.

The *Herald*, it seems, declined Kim's services, so he went to the *Evening Journal*'s office in the Tribune building at 162 Nassau Street, in the heart of New York's newspaper world. The *Sun* and

Times were housed nearby, but the gilt-domed Pulitzer building took pride of place, where Joseph Pulitzer and his staff turned out half a million copies a day of the city's second-favorite newspaper, the *World*. Kim climbed the stairs to the Tribune building's second floor where, in the northwest corner, in an office full of antique furniture with windows overlaid with photographic transparencies, he found William Randolph Hearst, seated behind an elaborately inlaid ebony desk. Thirty-six-year-old Hearst had a large head, sloping shoulders, a white, flaccid face and pale blue eyes. He looked innocuous and inert but wasn't, being a man of tremendous voltage, always his own best news item. Everything about Hearst was as full-blown and extreme as the Gilded Age itself: his size, his breadth of vision, his business acumen, his collecting mania and his opinion of his own worth and importance.

He was a thoroughgoing modern in his ideas about newspapers, but there was also something medieval about Willie Hearst. One acquaintance called him "a walking anachronism in New York," a reincarnated feudal lord, lacking only a heavy sword to lay waste to his foes. When Orson Welles based his protagonist on Hearst in his 1941 film, *Citizen Kane*, he overemphasized the tyrant aspect at the expense of Hearst's deep complexity of character.

Hearst had begun his newspaper career as editor and proprietor of the *San Francisco Evening Examiner*, had come to New York in 1895, bought the *Morning Journal* (changing its name in 1902 to the *New York American*), established the *Evening Journal* in 1896, gleefully watched it outstrip the *World*'s half million circulation one year later. Hearst kept right on buying newspapers, spreading his new creed around the country. Circulation was his god, and the news that increased it best was sin, crime and corruption, reported with passionate engagement. "Important thing in making circulation," he once telegraphed his staff, "is to get excited when public excited. People will buy any paper which seems to express their feelings in addition to printing the facts."

When Kim appeared in his office, Hearst was busy laying out a front page, putting the *Journal* to bed, waking up America, yelling perpetually for more photos and bigger headlines. He looked across his desk at the Duke and recognized an original, a "character." He had hired Dorothy Dix to advise the lovelorn, Stephen Crane to expose the sex and sleaze of the Tenderloin district, Ella Wheeler Wilcox to rhapsodize in verse, Mark Twain to cover Queen Victoria's Diamond Jubilee. Why not a democratic Duke to chronicle Society and turn it inside out? Hearst hired Kim on the spot, tossing a $1,000 bill across the ebony desk when the Duke mumbled that he "hadn't a bean, don't you know."

Apart from hiring Dukes, Hearst was always an innovator, inventing the modern comic strip, elevating gossip to equal status with hard news, pioneering a new kind of journalism. In the late 1890s, the circulation war between Pulitzer's *World* and Hearst's *Evening Journal* raged around the colored Sunday supplements. Dick Outcault drew a popular yellow-shirted cartoon character called "The Yellow Kid" for the *World*. Hearst wooed Dick to the *Journal*; Pulitzer bought him back; Hearst raised the ante. Someone called the contest "yellow journalism," which soon came to mean any kind of sensational reporting. Clergymen preached against it; librarians refused to give it shelf room; but the populace bought it and loved it and yellow journalism came to stay. It was exactly the right medium to dominate the Gilded Age, whose mores and values embodied the same tendency to extravagance, hyperbole and puffery. And the 9th Duke of Manchester, bent on celebrity, soon to wed a like-minded heiress, was born at exactly the right moment to achieve his goal. He married himself to yellow journalism on that November day in 1899 when he pocketed his $1,000 bill and promised to provide Mr. Hearst with exactly the kind of copy he liked best. The Duke would keep his word till his dying day, but not quite in the way Hearst envisioned.

Next day, the *Evening Journal* proudly announced that "the Duke of Manchester — one of the most promising peers in England — joins the *Journal* staff," without specifying exactly where the Duke's promise lay. Kim began as he would continue: by offering himself, the newsiest peer on two continents, as the best possible copy. He granted an interview to another *Journal* reporter, on the subject of his "love affairs of the footlights." Like any well brought up English gentleman, he denied his involvement with Cléo de Mérode, Edna May, Ethel Barrymore and others, all of whom he carefully named, protesting that "lots of this talk about me is idle gossip." He was secretly pleased when his photo appeared on the front page with those of "twenty-two beautiful damsels," as he calls them, in close proximity around it. "The reputation given by the picture of being a terrible fellow," he writes smugly in his autobiography, "still clings to me!" Whether Helena Zimmerman, cooling her passion in Cincinnati, saw the spread is not known, but since it appeared as well in a Cincinnati paper, probably she did. No letters came from Gracie. He was much too busy cutting a swath in New York.

On the same day that he made the front page, Kim was invited by his godfather William K. Vanderbilt, Alva's cast-off husband, for a game of poker. Like his father, Kim was a compulsive gambler. He arrived to find a group of multimillionaires at the table, including the real-estate mogul John Jacob Astor III and the banking magnate Ogden Mills.

When Willie K. asked Kim, "Do you want some chips?" Kim offered his $1,000 bill. "Don't you have anything smaller?" Willie K. asked, looking stunned. Kim proffered a $10 bill and was told that would do nicely. "*The richest men in America were playing twenty-five cent ante!*" Kim recalls incredulously in his memoirs. The incident illustrates one important difference, which Kim never did grasp, between England's rich and America's. The English aristocracy threw their rent-roll money recklessly about, in gambling games, horse racing and other indulgences, because they hadn't earned it. It was easy come, easy go. The American plutocracy, on the other hand, labored long hours for theirs and watched every penny.

In the final week of November, Kim got his first *Journal* assignment. He was sent to cover the very Anglophile Horse Show, the social event that more than any other captured the vulgar, venal spirit of the times. It was not Kim, however, but Boni de

Castellane, a French Count who married an American heiress, Anna Gould, and who later became Paris correspondent for the *New York American*, who caught the Horse Show's essence. "Imagine an immense building packed with a crowd of 10,000 persons, a crowd in which every woman has tried to outdress and out-pearl some other friend or enemy, while the pitiless radiance of the electric light shines on faces," writes Boni, "and the hard American accent cuts the heavily perfumed air like the lashing of whips." As a new century dawned, New York Society had abandoned whatever pretensions to gentility and culture it had once had. As the novelist Gertrude Atherton recalls in her memoirs, on the streets and in restaurants she "never heard any word uttered but 'money,'" and people, as Edith Wharton notes in *The House of Mirth*, "were awed only by success, by the gross, tangible image of material achievement." If, in Philadelphia, Society still asked, "Who was his father?" and in Boston, "What does he know?" in New York it was always "What is he worth?"

Kim's career on the *Journal* lasted two months, and he never did get to Cincinnati to see Helena. His sister Nell died of tuberculosis in Switzerland in January 1900, and Kim took the next ship home to England to be with his mother. At about the same time, Kim's former boss, Willie Hearst, also sailed for Europe, taking with him his future bride, Millicent Willson, her mother and her father, George, a popular vaudeville performer known for his rendition of "I Met Her by the Fountain in the Park." Hearst returned to America in the spring of 1900, and so did the Duke, with the difference that Hearst brought half of Europe's goods back with him, and the Duke brought only his empty pockets and inflated dreams.

Willie Hearst was a collector in Alva Vanderbilt's style, a mere accumulator without specialization or taste, but Hearst's collecting, like so much else about him, was carried to extremes — the galloping consumerism of his time gone completely berserk. He stashed his plunder first in his bachelor quarters on the third floor of New York's Worth House on Twenty-fifth Street, and later in his California ranch, San Simeon, the world's most pretentious warehouse.

Gothic choir stalls, marble torsos, suits of armor, treasures still in packing cases lay all around Willie, higgledy-piggledy, without order or design. Like the New York Horse Show, Hearst's Worth House jumble was fit symbol for a country growing ever richer in material goods but ever hungrier for spiritual uplift from its European past, where America's collective unconscious still rummaged about. Americans began their indiscriminate collecting of Old World artifacts and titled gentlemen in the 1870s because they wanted the past's intangibles, its poetry and panache, the *soul* of class. They reached out — and grasped only price tags attached to old furniture and young peers, both coming apart at the seams. By 1900 it was clear, had anyone cared to notice, that the cash-for-class exchange whereby Americans like Alva Vanderbilt, William Randolph Hearst and innocent young Helena Zimmerman bought themselves a Duke simply wasn't going to achieve its ends, not then, not ever.

The current Duke for hire went off to Narragansett Pier in that early summer of 1900, in pursuit of his heiress. Along the coast from exclusive Newport, Narragansett was where the Zimmermans and other very New Rich, the also-rans who couldn't make it into Newport's select winners' circle, crowded onto the verandas of the big summer hotels to compare finery and parade self-consciously up and down the pier. It was there, in July, as the Duke later told London's *Daily Mail,* that he and Helena "discovered they had been in love with each other all the time." Kim's true sentiments concerning love appear in his autobiography, where he writes: "I have not made it a habit to fall in and out of love.... It's not much use to give a woman your heart and leave her with it, because ten chances to one she will start upbraiding you after a while and ask if you expect her to stand the fatigue of holding it for ever." For the second time, Kim and Helena announced their engagement to the press; Eugene Zimmerman promptly denied it, and tried, with far more words than he'd ever before expended, to change his daughter's mind.

Helena had never been close to her father and paid no heed to him now. She was used to making her own choices, and she wanted Kim. In addition to celebrity status, she craved love and the chance to make a real home and family, which she'd never had. In August Helena left America and her protesting parent and followed Kim, who had returned to Britain.

On September 10, newspapers in London and New York announced the Duke of Manchester's bankruptcy, with liabilities totaling $135,500, and Eugene Zimmerman, dining with a friend at New York's Waldorf Astoria, protested that "the daughters of American business men should always marry bright young American business men for their own good. I want my daughter to marry some thoroughbred American. I want no Duke" — Eugene thumped the table hard — "for a son-in-law."

On Tuesday, November 13, in London, Kim's friend Lord Lambart, a tall, fair-haired reprobate of a Baron, owner of Bletchley, a vast estate in Buckinghamshire, strolled to Marylebone Parish Church and told its rector, Canon Barker, to prepare himself to conduct a wedding next day, between the Duke of Manchester and "an American heiress with £10,000 a year now and unlimited prospects, as her father is one of the richest men in America." When questioned by the Canon, Lambart admitted that her father hadn't given his consent, then waved under the Canon's nose a special license obtained by the Duke from the Archbishop of Canterbury, so that he felt he had no choice but to comply.

Next day, Helena, in plain blouse and skirt, with approving Aunt Helena beside her, married her Duke, who was supported by Lord Lambart. No one else was present. According to Canon Barker, while the groom looked "nonchalant," the bride "looked greatly depressed, worried and anxious" with "no pretense of cheerfulness. In all my experience I never saw a more melancholy wedding."

On the following Monday, a reporter from London's *Daily Mail* got wind of the marriage and rushed to Consuelo Manchester's house at 45 Portman Square to question her. She told him there had been no wedding and evinced extreme displeasure at the idea of her son's marrying Miss Zimmerman. Subsequently the Dowager Duchess went to the church, inspected the records and found, to her great surprise, that the marriage had taken place. Quite apart from Helena's vulgar lineage, Consuelo was no doubt chagrined to find herself demoted to a walk-on part as mere Dowager Duchess while the pretty young reigning Duchess moved into the center spotlight.

So it was that on a gray November day the unknown heiress from Cincinnati tied herself to a notorious Duke. Consuelo Yznaga had married to wear Society's crown, with all eyes upon her. Lily Hammersley wanted status and a reforming angel's role. Consuelo Vanderbilt was pushed into Sunny's stiff arms by her domineering mother. Two Consuelos and one Lily were all true daughters, and victims, of their time, and so was Helena. She married at a moment when newspapers and magazines dominated popular culture and had great influence in swaying public taste. She was one of the first in that long line of twentieth-century women that leads to Ivana Trump and Elizabeth Taylor, for Helena Zimmerman, like them, was seduced into marriage, at least in part, by the lure of a front-page spread and her place in the *Sun*. As for Kim, 9th Duke of Manchester, his marriage to an heiress was the only one of his many get-rich-quick schemes that more or less succeeded.

Not until the following Tuesday, November 20, did news of the wedding hit the headlines. The *New York Times* gave it a column and a half headed "Duke of Manchester Weds Miss Zimmerman" (very large) and "Relatives Not Notified" (smaller). The *Times* included a brief biography of "The New Duchess" gleaned from acquaintances and a longer one of the Duke, selected from back files. The *Cincinnati Enquirer* spread the news over three columns headed "Duchess" in towering black letters.

The New York *World*'s headline read "Married For Love Not Title" and London's *Daily Mail* saw the marriage as "the outcome of a long and romantic attachment." The *Daily Mail* was England's version of yellow journalism, preceded in the 1880s by Stead's *Pall Mall Gazette*, T. P. O'Connor's *Star* and Alfred Harmsworth's *Answers*. Harmsworth had turned the London *Evening News* yellow in 1894, then launched the *Daily Mail* in 1896; Arthur Pearson

Not All in the Market

FOREIGN PURCHASER: "I think I will take one of those gals in the gallery, ye know"
PROPRIETOR: "No; they are not for sale. You must take your choice from these four hundred"

*39 and 40   Cartoons by Charles Dana Gibson, about 1902,
satirizing Anglo-American alliances*

added the *Daily Express* in 1900. All were halfpenny tabloids with plenty of racy Society gossip and accompanying photos. The yellow journals on both sides of the Atlantic kept one eye on women readers and, as a sop to their romantic sensibilities, still talked of "love" in connection with transatlantic marriages.

By 1900 the American press in general, however, was beginning to vent its bitter disillusionment with the cash-for-class marriage, which had been going from bad to worse for twenty years. It would take another decade before complaints reached full volume.

In that money-mad era, as one might expect, what made America hopping mad was all those hard-won dollars leaving the country, flooding into the empty pockets of European nobles who'd never worked a day in their lives and who owned nothing but disintegrating castles and morals to match. "Millionaire Zimmerman says there is no trouble about the debts of his son-in-law," observed the *Denver Republican.* "A statement of the Duke's liabilities, however, would indicate that trouble is the one thing he never borrowed." "Mr. Zimmerman is said to be quite easy-going," continued the *Republican* slyly, "and it will soon be demonstrated whether his money has the same characteristic." "The thrifty Mr. Zimmerman," according to the *Richmond News,* "acts as if he might have an idea of exhibiting the Duke of Manchester at popular prices." In Maine, the *Lewiston Journal* commented: "Of course the Duke of Manchester married for love, and being a sensible man he found it just as easy and twice as convenient to fall in love with a millionaire's daughter."

The millionaire who found himself suddenly exposed in the eye of the storm decided to put a good face on his offspring's marriage, unlike Consuelo Manchester, and to be gracious about it. Having received a cablegram from Aunt Helena Evans ecstatically announcing the wedding, a newly loquacious Eugene told a *Cincinnati Enquirer* reporter on November 19, "I have never disapproved of the match — all stories to the contrary notwithstanding. I believe it is a love affair, pure and simple. I do not know how to account for the fact of my daughter having failed to inform me in advance, unless it was that she wanted to surprise me. The story that I would disinherit her and all that stuff is rubbish." One account claims he gave Helena a dowry of $2 million; another more credible one reports that Helena received approximately $90,000 yearly from her father, to be shared with Kim as she saw fit.

Meanwhile, in London, the newlyweds put off facing Consuelo until the very day before they were to sail for America. Then they tiptoed sheepishly in and out of her darkened bedroom in Portman Square where the Dowager Duchess was claiming to be very, very ill. Later that evening, Kim told reporters, "I must now pattern after the Americans, and a very good pattern I have always found it. I sever myself from the past without regret and start for the United States full of hope for the future."

On the morning of November 24, he and Helena set sail on the *St. Louis*, with their entourage of aunts and dogs and servants, to be met in New York on December 1, as we have already seen, by one parent, two detectives and a fine gaggle of reporters.

Next day, Sunday, there was no rest for the Manchesters. They gave their first interview in the hotel lobby at 9:00 a.m., posed for snapshots on the street beyond and were still going strong at 8:00 p.m. when a *New York Times* reporter in their suite asked, "How did you spend the morning?" "Being interviewed," responded the Duke. "And the afternoon?" "Being interviewed." "Have you anything special on hand this evening?" "Well, if I can get off being interviewed long enough I expect to have dinner." The Duke said all this "in the best of humors."

When reporters asked His Grace if he would take part in the Strollers' production of *The Cruise of the Summer Girl*, whose rehearsal he had looked in on briefly that afternoon, the Duke replied, "I am through with that sort of thing now," and at the time, he really meant it.

Helena's hour to shine came on Wednesday afternoon, December 6, their final day in New York before they went west by train to the coast, when she was both photographed and interviewed at length. (Only New Rich ladies in America granted interviews; the consensus among Old Money was that a lady should see her name in the papers on three occasions only: when she was betrothed, when she was married and when she was buried.) Lively, extroverted Helena was thoroughly enjoying the fun of her new celebrity: flowers and phone calls, constant comings and goings in the suite, cameras clicking and necks craning when she passed through the lobby. She'd lived twenty-one uneventful years, much of the time abroad, isolated, outside the mainstream. At this early point in her marriage, Helena was looking into the mirror of her public self, face glowing, dimples showing, and she liked what she saw.

But suddenly, on that afternoon of December 6, she felt a moment of insecurity, and she did what most New Rich women do when insecurity strikes. She became a consumer. Not wanting to disappoint her public, or her husband who seemed so proud of her, Helena telephoned a "fashionable modiste" to send "twenty of her swellest gowns" at once to Holland House, from which the Duchess eventually chose four. She needed pearls for her photograph, knowing full well that the social importance of every woman in America was exactly correlated to the size of her pearls. Helena sent Kim off to the Frederic Diamond Company at 905 Broadway. He hurried back with three strings of "the best imitation fishskin pearls." In pearls, it seems, as in husbands, Helena didn't think herself worthy of the very finest. She ordered the jewelers to string the bogus pearls all together in one long rope; they did so in an hour, returning them to Holland House with a bill for $695, expecting to be paid cash, but Frederic's didn't know their Duke. Invoice after invoice would be ignored; one sent to Mr. Zimmerman got the same response; but Frederic's would have the last word.

When the photographer arrived, "more than 100 poses were taken" while Mary helped her mistress in and out of various

41 Helena posed in her pearls

gowns. When Emma Kaufman, a reporter from the New York
Evening Journal, arrived in the bridal suite at four o'clock, she
found Helena "cheeks very pink, eyes dancing," in black bolero
dress and high-heeled patent-leather boots, happily pouring tea

while a musician, Melville Ellis, played the piano, singing, "I don't want to be res-pect-able / I want to be as bad as bad can be," and Kim kept time with hands and feet. Kim had met Melville at the Strollers' Club rehearsal; he was orchestra conductor for a traveling theater company and had written the music for the Strollers' forthcoming farce.

In her article, Kaufman describes Helena's charm, and her "very natural, easy manner." The Duke boasted affectionately of his bride. "Let me tell you what she can do," he said, beaming at the reporter. "She can ride horseback superbly. Now I know what Englishwomen can do in that line and I tell you she can beat them. She plays golf splendidly and she knows a heap of other things. People think I control her. If ever a woman had a mind of her own it is Her Grace. She rules the house, let me tell you, and I follow in line as meek as a lamb." "I follow in line..." Kaufman scribbled furiously.

Like most female journalists in America, Kaufman always aimed her copy at female readers, who liked a bit of romantic embroidery here and there, so when she composed her article back at the *Journal* office, she gave the Duchess such unlikely dialogue as "My America is a garden of roses, a glorious tropical climate!"

Until the 1880s, most women reporters were required to write their articles at home, for newspaper offices were strictly male preserves. One of the first women to invade an office, where its male staff swore and smoked, played poker and shared a bottle, was Annie Howells, hired by the Chicago *Inter-Ocean* in 1872, and sent a disapproving letter by her shocked novelist brother, William Dean Howells. By the 1890s, most of the big-city dailies had a dozen women on their staffs, who sat at their desks in the city room in shirtwaists and gored skirts while editors shouted at them to "rush it lively!" Yellow journals not only paid them equal wages with men, but sent the more daring ones on moral crusades to sweatshops and slums to expose their grim realities.

A more forward-thinking reporter than Emma Kaufman, sensing the twentieth-century swing toward voyeurism and away from romance, paid Helena's maid $2,000 to hand over the Duke's underclothes. Photos of them duly appeared in the press captioned "Wedding Trousseau of a Duke." Being a thoroughly modern miss, Helena wasn't at all put out; she supposed she should fire Mary, but didn't. It was only five years since Consuelo Vanderbilt's lacy underclothes had been threaded through with sentiment in the popular press, but tastes were changing fast. What the public wanted now was not lace, but dirty linen, and the Duke of Manchester had plenty of that.

It was Kim's idea to invite the musician Melville Ellis to come along on the honeymoon trip to the West Coast as his "private secretary." What Helena thought about this is not recorded. The three young people and Eugene Zimmerman, who was only going as far as his home in Cincinnati, left New York on the evening of December 6, traveling in Eugene's private railway car, a plush affair with tufted armchairs and ball-fringed curtains. Kim's new auto, a Surrey steam contraption bought in New York, no doubt on credit, worth $4,400, followed in a freight car. "The Duchess and I will astonish the natives in Ohio when we ride in this," Kim said with a chuckle. This very modern Duke was all for whizzing fearlessly into the twentieth century; he'd been driving a car for four years, and taken a six-month mechanic's course as well.

Cincinnati had been preparing for its Duke and Duchess ever since their wedding announcement. Aunts Helena and Martha had gone straight there after arriving in New York to supervise the finishing touches. On December 2, the *Cincinnati Enquirer* headline proclaimed, "All is Bustle," reporting that workmen were re-graveling the driveway at the Zimmerman residence, 2438 Auburn Avenue, and "removing every stray vestige of fallen branch and twig" from its extensive lawns. The house, at the corner of Auburn and Macmillan streets, was set well back, a two-story cream-colored brick building with a two-story portico about the same size as that of the White House. Eugene had bought the house from one Elmer Cunningham in the late 1870s, and had just redecorated the interior. Local reporters were allowed to inspect it, notebooks in hand.

On Monday, December 3, four days before Duke and Duchess actually arrived, the *Enquirer* reported that outside the Zimmerman house a "small group" stood vigilant, expected to "grow into a good-sized mob" on the big day. By that time Police Chief Deutsch would have dispatched a special detail of police to keep intruders and "camera fiends" off the premises. Founded in the final years of the eighteenth century, mainly by emigrants from New Jersey and Kentucky, Cincinnati had been declared a village in 1802, a city in 1819, and prided itself on its urban sophistication. But Cincinnati had never before had its very own Duchess, and it was too much to expect its citizens to appear blasé.

On Tuesday, December 4, Abraham Evans, Helena's maternal grandfather, whose claim to fame as George Eliot's cousin America had never recognized, finally got his fifteen minutes of celebrity. When Abe came into Urbana from his farm, he was mobbed by reporters, as was James Lurigan in Cincinnati, who'd once lived near Tandragee Castle. "It's no castle," he told a journalist, "only a run-down house of rusty-colored brick" — one can almost see James spit — "an' you git there on a rutted road across a bog."

On December 5, two circus men wintering in Cincinnati, wearing "checked suits, plug hats, black mustaches and large diamond studs," rang doorbells up and down Auburn Avenue, wanting to rent lawns "on which to erect seats which they proposed to sell for $1 each" to anyone curious to see a performing native Duchess.

By early morning on December 7, people with cameras in hand dotted the street, yelling "Here she comes!" every time a carriage appeared on the crest of Auburn Avenue's hill. The actual arrival was an anticlimax — at eleven o'clock that night, in an "atmosphere of fog and sooty grime." Eugene's black horses, Theodore and Nix, sent with the carriage to meet the train, lightened the gloom "decked out in such a set of harness as the eyes of Cincinnati liverymen never snapped at before." Eugene had wired from New York to Tom Shea, his stable groom, to say he was sending a new $3,000 French-imported harness with metal pieces all of solid gold, to be used "by the ducal pair whenever they drive out."

In the end, the Duke upstaged Eugene; speeding about in a horn-honking auto was far more spectacular than sitting sedately behind a horse dripping gold.

Was the gold harness real, or just a gleam in a reporter's fancy? From a perspective nearly a hundred years down the road, it's impossible to separate the threads of rumor, fact and fantasy in this tightly woven tale of a high-profile Duke and Duchess as reported by the American press. What does stand forth from all the reams of copy is that the story's three protagonists — bride, groom and bride's father — not to mention Aunt Effie and Fannie Ward and dozens of others — not only saw the need for public relations but also divined the twentieth-century truth that the medium is the message.

Installed at Auburn Avenue, Helena gave a long interview on Tuesday, December 11, to Lavinia Hart of the *Cincinnati Enquirer*, who asked, "Are you happy?" The new Duchess "sank into a chair beside a bright log fire, pulled the silken folds of a blue-gray morning gown around her, blushed, sighed and said 'Yes.'" What else could a new bride say? Then Lavinia asked her if it was "wise for a girl who is so thoroughly American to choose a future husband and home that will keep her in a foreign country?" Helena pointed out that she had lived abroad so much that "I regard no one as a foreigner." When she thought Lavinia had probed enough, Helena signaled that the interview was over by rising from her chair, with the comment, "If you ask anything more you'll know me better than I know myself." Helena was learning quickly how to work the media.

Her friend Nick Longworth hosted a luncheon next day at the St. Nicholas Hotel. The Republican politician who would later become Speaker of the House was still a bachelor, living with his mother at Rookwood, the house his grandfather had built on Cincinnati's eastern hills above the river. Exactly five years later, Nick would become engaged to President Theodore Roosevelt's daughter Alice, always the pet of American newspapers, much to her vexation. When Alice went shopping in New York for her trousseau, as she tells us in her autobiography, she was "dogged by reporters, the sort of thing a royalty or a movie star endures." She and thirty-six-year-old Nick were married at the White House on February 17, 1906, and thereafter Alice used her rapier-sharp wit to protect her privacy and foil the press. Its favorite story of Nicholas comes from a later period in his life. The Senator was sitting, eyes closed, in a chair in his club when a friend passed behind him, touched Nick's bald head and remarked, "That feels just like my wife's behind." Nick opened his eyes, stroked his head reflectively, murmured, "So it does, so it does," and went back to sleep.

Nick's party for the Manchesters was followed by others, all described in detail in print, right down to the flowers. On December 18, Melville Ellis departed the scene, finding it hard going to keep a Duke amused, and Lord Lambart arrived from England to take his place. He would accompany Kim and Helena west and return with them to England. Helena was learning the bitter lesson that all American brides of European nobles had to learn: there would be no cozy, just-the-two-of-us intimacy. Helena countered by inviting Aunt Helena to make her home with them, which she did for many years.

Christmas at Auburn Avenue was subdued; Kim caught a cold and felt poorly. He'd recovered sufficiently by December 28 to apply at City Hall for a driving license, but when it came time to pay for it, the Duke hadn't a dollar anywhere on his natty, well-dressed person. The Mayor's clerk, quite unaware that he was being used, willingly paid the "two bones" for His Grace, and considered it a rare honor to be allowed to do so.

As 1901 dawned, Kim and Helena and Lord Lambart headed south in the Zimmerman private railroad car, bound for Natchez, where Kim's maternal grandmother, Ellen Yznaga, now spent the winters rather than at her plantation home, Ravenswood. But first the honeymooners had to stop at Talledaga, Alabama, where, as Eugene told the press, "I have my iron interests. The people are anxious for a visit from the Duke and his bride. They want to give them a rousing reception, and I did my best to plan the journey so that a stop could be made at this point." Eugene was not above doing a little ducal exploiting of his own. To be sure, he'd paid plenty for the right to do so.

At Natchez, Kim introduced his New Rich Yankee bride to his genteel Southern grandmother, Ellen Yznaga, who promptly took to her bed "with a severe attack of grip." The plush railroad car pushed on to New Orleans, where the *Times-Democrat* reported on January 15 that the Duchess was "pretty, winsome, unaffected...well versed in classical and contemporary literature and an accomplished linguist" and that the Manchesters, "the chief subject of table talk during the past month or so," were "interviewed time and again," including one interview given by Kim in the Turkish bath of the St. Charles Hotel, where he and Helena were staying.

The trio rattled west to San Francisco by easy stages, and on the way back made stopovers at Salt Lake City, Denver and Chicago so that Helena could show off her prize to friends.

On the day the Manchesters left New York for Britain, February 27, Helena suffered an embarrassment which, in different forms, would be repeated again and again. It seems Kim had purchased from a Mr. Kelly, of Boston, two more bull terriers, for $1,500, but had never paid. When Mr. Kelly approached the Manchesters' suite at Holland House, he was told that the Duke was "not at home." Kelly summoned his lawyer, lay in wait in the lobby, pounced on the Duke, listened stony-faced to his talk of being flat broke. Then the Duke appealed to Mr. Zimmerman, who happened to be with him, to pay the damn fellow $1,500, and be done with it. Eugene flatly refused. Kelly repossessed the dogs and stomped off, triumphant.

There was worse trouble waiting at Liverpool when the Manchesters' ship docked on March 6. Kim was served with a breach-of-promise suit on behalf of Portia Knight, an American actress who had played in a Lowell, Massachusetts, stock company before moving to London, to an apartment house called Stirmin's

Mansions, where the Duke had visited, courted and promised marriage — until Helena had arrived from America in August 1900. Portia, a sultry, olive-skinned brunette, no doubt hungry for celebrity, protested that she didn't bring suit for the publicity but "because I felt duty bound to all my friends here in England." The breach-of-promise suit dragged its sordid length through the newspapers — Portia threatened to produce love letters from Kim — until January 1902, when Kim settled out of court, paying Portia $5,000 and costs. Helena had dreamed of seeing her dignified, posed, coroneted likeness in the glossy pages of *Tatler* and *Queen*, London's Society journals. Instead her startled, candid-camera face leered at her from yesterday's tabloid lying in the gutter, or wrapped around somebody's garbage.

42   Helena (right) with four other ladies at
a Tandragee Castle shooting party

43 Kylemore Castle

Kim was leading her, in his bumbling, self-parodying down-hill slide, away from fame and into infamy. Helena did her best, as the years passed, to live a sensible, rooted family life at Ireland's Tandragee Castle. A daughter, Mary Alice, was born on October 27, 1901, and a son and heir, Alexander George Francis, Viscount Mandeville, always called Mandy, on October 2, 1902. (Another son, Edward Eugene Fernando, would arrive in 1906 and a fourth and final child, Ellen Millicent Louise, in 1908.)

In September 1903, the Manchesters left dilapidated Tandragee and moved into Kylemore Castle, fifty miles from Galway, a pretentious Victorian monstrosity that could be seen twice over: once where it stood, and again in the still waters of a lake. Kylemore had been built by a New Money Englishman, Mitchell Henry, the richest man in the Manchester cotton trade, at a cost of $2,500,000. Sometime later it was offered as a gift to Queen Victoria, but fortunately someone in the Queen's household went to look at it, and the mansion was ever so tactfully declined. Eugene

Zimmerman bought the castle for Helena for $350,000, a great bargain. Its wild remote setting was a long way from inquisitive reporters, being twelve miles over narrow, rutted roads from the nearest railroad station — but not far enough. Papa Zimmerman paid for new decor and improvements, so that American dollars left at Kylemore the shining, white memorials to American standards of comfort that Lily Hammersley and Consuelo Vanderbilt had been denied at Blenheim Palace: plenty of modern bathrooms.

Helena busied herself with her growing family and drove her own auto through twisting lanes of wild fuchsias, or over windswept hills where anonymous red-petticoated women tramped and innocuous blue peat smoke curled up from tiny white cottages. She tried to forget that other life in print that kept on relentlessly recording the adventures of a disaster-prone Duke, forever heading for a new pratfall. We can laugh at this Charlie Chaplin version of a Duke — but we can also sense his wife's very real pain, as she found herself caught fast in that crazy scenario.

Kim was restless, always wanting to be on the move, unstable, erratic. His enthusiasms came and went as fast as rain squalls on Doughraugh Mountain, which rose precipitously to 1,700 feet behind the castle, a wall of obdurate rock. Helena felt duty bound to travel with her husband — and that little black cloud that stayed above his head. When they arrived in New York on January 20, 1903, and booked into Holland House before going on to Cincinnati, their 125 pieces of luggage were seized by the Sheriff, on behalf of the Frederic Diamond Company, who'd been trying for three years to collect their $695 for Helena's fake pearl necklace. "It was a shock to the Duchess," noted the *New York Times*, always sympathetic to its American heiress, "when the Sheriff served the attachment on her baggage" and she found herself without clothes or toothbrush until the debt was paid.

The same fiasco recurred when Kim and Helena returned to New York from Palm Beach, Florida, on March 27. That time the Sheriff seized forty pieces of luggage because the Duke had paid Duveen Brothers, Fifth Avenue dealers in antiques and fine art, for an ornamental brass shield with a check for $225 — which bounced. "It was sad to behold His Grace," observed the *New York Times*, not really sad at all to be reporting yet another ducal misdemeanor, "begging the Deputy Sheriff for privilege to extract a suit of pink pajamas." Helena quietly paid the bill while the Duke pronounced the whole affair "a beastly bore." Kim was having the lesson forced on him that whereas class-conscious British merchants would wait patiently for years for their social superiors to pay them, democratic American ones wouldn't. A Duke who owed them money was no better than a clerk, and got the same treatment if he didn't pay promptly.

Kim soon found a new way to prostitute his dukedom for commercial gain. With Helena reluctantly in tow, and their children left behind, His Grace pimped his way around the world at the expense of New Rich Americans who wanted entrée to aristocratic circles. In 1905 the Manchesters went to Mexico with the George Goulds. Railroad king George, son of famous robber baron Jay, had married pretty actress Edith Kingdon, let her load up on fabulous jewels, including the Emperor of China's Peacock Feather brooch, then taught Edith's parrot to say, "Oh, what an extravagant girl you are!"

The Goulds with their Duke and Duchess traveled in five private cars on George's own railroad as far as El Paso, then hitched on to the Mexican Central Line, rolling through stony wastes and past clusters of tin huts where people lived in terrible poverty, with Edith resplendent at dinner in her wonderful pearls. When the travelers reached Detroit on the return trip, the Duke announced to the press that he and the Duchess would live there for a year while he helped run the Pere Marquette Railroad, bought the year before by Eugene Zimmerman — who announced acidly to the *New York Times* the next day, "the Duke's interests in American railroads will be confined to traveling over them."

From autumn 1906 to spring 1907 the Manchesters got a free trip to the East with New Yorker James Henry Smith, always known as "Silent" because, like Eugene Zimmerman, he never wasted words. Silent and his new wife, Annie (née Armstrong), just divorced from Rhinelander Stewart, invited the Manchesters to share their honeymoon voyage on the yacht *Margarita*, which Smith had leased from Annie's brother-in-law, Anthony Drexel. Silent knew that a yacht, like a Duke and Duchess, was a status symbol well worth its costly hire.

Fifty-two-year-old Silent Smith was a perfect example of a person seduced by the values of his age. A plain little man with drooping shoulders and balding pate, he'd been a recluse and bookworm in a dusty West Thirtieth Street apartment overflowing with books and papers until a cousin died and left him $52 million. Silent abandoned his scholar's life, bought the late William C. Whitney's Fifth Avenue mansion for $1 million, spent another million on decor, acquired an estate at Tuxedo Park as well and launched himself into Society with a splashy ball at the Waldorf whose gold cotillion favors Edith Gould helped him choose. Minnie Paget was trying her best to get Smith into London Society; he'd already bought the requisite country seat, Dunachton, in Scotland, but thought that investing in a friendly Duke and Duchess would do no harm.

The Smiths and Manchesters sailed in the *Margarita* first to India. Kim enjoyed the pig sticking at Jodhpur; Helena fell ill with fever at Delhi, and grew pensive at Agra when she saw that white marble elegy to lost love, the Taj Mahal. The party moved on to China, where Silent grew even more so, suffering severely from Bright's disease. They got the invalid as far as Kyoto, Japan, where he developed pneumonia and died on March 27, 1907.

Wherever the Duke traveled, disaster seemed to follow in his wake. "I was at his bedside constantly," Kim informed the *New York Times* concerning Silent's demise. "I was with him at the end." While the sad party steamed homeward to America with the body, newspapers there speculated wildly on who would inherit Smith's $52 million, the main contenders being his wife, his sister and various relatives from Illinois and points west who almost daily were announcing their candidacy to the press. Helena's aunt, the journalist Effie Mackenzie Evans, also got in on the act, telling a *New York Times* reporter that "the Duchess of Manchester will inherit a substantial sum by the will of Mr. Smith, but I cannot say how much."

When the Manchesters with Mrs. Smith and her deceased husband reached San Francisco on April 28 on the steamer *Siberia*, Eugene Zimmerman, called once more to the rescue, met them with his private railway car for the trip back to New York. The coffin followed in its own black-draped car, topped with a cross of calla lilies renewed at Chicago.

Silent's will, read on May 8, was full of surprises: he'd squandered all but $25 million of his $52 million; two nephews called Mason got the bulk of the estate; the Manchesters got nothing at all.

Rumors that Helena and the Duke were separating began in the press in the following year, but "the Duchess herself," as the *New York Times* reported on July 26, "has given indignant denial in a telegram." The Duke and his father-in-law, continued the *Times*, "have had some little difference of opinion on financial questions. The Duke of Manchester's anxieties were said so to have preyed upon his nervous system that his doctors were afraid the refusal by his father-in-law to meet his wishes with regard to a certain settlement would precipitate collapse." The Duke, deeply in debt and threatened with bankruptcy, played his invalid's role so well that Eugene agreed to pay off mortgages on the estates of Tandragee and Kimbolton whose interest payments were taking all the ducal rent roll, but canny Eugene saw to it that the estates were put in his eldest grandson's name, so that when Mandy became Duke there would be something left to inherit. The Sunday supplement of the *New York Times* on July 26 devoted a whole page to "The Castles Grandfather Zimmerman is Keeping in the Family," with large photos of them beneath, and "The Family He is Keeping in the Castles," with photos of Helena (oval), Kim (square) and fat-faced little Mandy (round).

The will left by Kim's mother, Consuelo, who died on November 20, 1909, showed what she thought of her feckless son. It was an "almost perfect example of the spendthrift's trust," according to Thomas B. Gilchrist of the United States Trust Company, which handled her estate. The will authorized the trust company to pay the Duke $350 a month or not, as they saw fit, contingent on his behavior. Thereafter the trust company's decision was to pay the money to the Duke's wife and eldest son but not a penny directly to him.

Kim, however, was quite incorrigible, "as bad as bad can be." In the next three years, he piled up $360,000 in fresh debts, including $55,000 spent on finding "a cure for consumption," which, using that word in a different sense, seems particularly apt.

Rumors of the Manchesters' marital difficulties persisted. Eugene retired from active business in 1910, aged sixty-five, keeping his company directorships, and thereafter was often at Kylemore Castle. A 1912 article by Walden Fawcett in the February issue of *Harper's Bazaar*, "Beautiful Kylemore Castle," makes no mention of its Duke, and it is Eugene Zimmerman who poses for his photo beside the massive front door. The article describes Helena's special hobby: "a model poultry farm which now has between five and six thousand feathered inhabitants. Her latest idea is the introduction of American turkeys."

Another 1912 article, by William Armstrong in the September issue of *Woman's Home Companion,* entitled "Three American Duchesses," sees Consuelo, Duchess of Marlborough, as "preeminent for her charities"; May, Duchess of Roxburghe as "a great figure in society" and Helena, Duchess of Manchester as "simple, lovable," her life "fully absorbed in her children and her home. She has clearly shown how little the outside world means in comparison. The Duchess likes Ireland much better than England; London and its gaieties she rarely visits; the smart set there sees little of her." The Duchess, "a thoughtful, clever woman of culture and character...takes life with a gentle seriousness," as well she might, for the independent American girl who had once thought the world made for her had long ago discovered that it wasn't. Family snapshots of Helena taken at this time show a stout figure and worried, unsmiling face. An Englishman who knew her calls

44 *Helena and Kim, in a country setting*

her "an exceedingly nice woman" in his memoirs; she deserved better than a down-and-out Duke.

Leaving the children at Kylemore, Helena accompanied Kim to New York to spend Christmas 1913 with the Frederick Vanderbilts at their Hyde Park estate. Fred was a surprisingly frugal Vanderbilt who built his house there for only $600,000. Louise (Lulu), his wife, outclassed other Society matrons when it came to pearls. She'd heard that Renaissance Venetian beauties had toyed with a single jewel on a chain. Lulu appeared at Society's parties kicking a great uncut ruby hanging near her feet, attached to her waist by a rope of pearls.

In January 1914, the Vanderbilts took the Manchesters for a Caribbean cruise on their yacht *Warrior*. There was one other passenger: Lord Arthur George Keith-Falconer, the Earl of Kintore's son. Arthur George was a distant relative of Kim's, his mother, Charlotte, being sister to Kim's grandfather, the 7th Duke. Kim's little black cloud sailed with them, for off the coast of Colombia the *Warrior* ran aground on a huge submerged ledge of rock, then a fierce storm arose. A United Fruit Company ship, the *Frutera*, answered the *Warrior*'s frantic SOS but the seas were too high to effect a rescue. Winds grew to gale force and waves became gigantic; all eight *Frutera* lifeboats were smashed or overturned as the *Warrior*'s shivering passengers watched in terror, lashed to its rail. Helena was "inclined to hysteria," but Lord Arthur George proved a rock: manly, calm and caring. The *Frutera* wired the *Almirante*, a sister ship forty miles away. By the time the *Almirante* arrived, the wind had died and rescue was easy.

The ill-fated cruise was Helena's last trip with Kim. She weighed sensible Lord Arthur George against her dizzy Duke, and decided that she'd had more than enough. She separated from Kim sometime that year and settled quietly at Kylemore with the children; Kim kept on the hop, and his pratfalls gained momentum.

On August 7, three days after Britain declared war on Germany, the *New York Times* shouted, "Duke Enters the Movies!" Kim had formed the International Educational League, with himself as President, and Charles Hite, an experienced moviemaker who owned the Thanhowser Film Company, as Vice President. Kim gave an interview from his suite in New York's Ritz-Carlton Hotel. He had $10 million capital, he explained in a manic rush, and the League would supply theaters, homes, churches, universities, missionary societies, hospitals and legions of other institutions with educational motion picture films "designed to facilitate the carrying out of social uplift." (At this point, reporters may well have sniggered; the Duke of Manchester's name did not immediately spring to mind in connection with "social uplift.") When, fourteen years before, on the eve of departing for America with his new bride, Kim had told English reporters, "I must now pattern after the Americans," he was, for once, telling the truth, for in his own foolhardy, madcap way, Kim had always done exactly that. He was in love with American drive and American technology, and may at this point have been patterning himself specifically after Willie Hearst, who'd founded the Hearst-Selig News Pictorial one year before, the pioneer newsreel for movie theaters, which would grow into the international Hearst-Metrotone News.

On August 13, Kim announced that he would live permanently in New York and had leased an apartment at 4 West Fifty-seventh Street, to be filled with heirloom treasures from Britain, where he expected "to entertain largely this coming season."

On Friday, August 21, Charles Hite, the Educational League's Vice President and only practical executive, was driving from the League's New York office home to New Rochelle when his auto skidded, tore through a viaduct's iron railing, dropped fifty feet, crashed through a high wooden fence and landed upside down beside the Central Casino, where a dance was in progress. Mr. Hite died the next day, and the League shortly thereafter. "The Duke expected to sell his stock with ease," noted the *New York Times* on September 24, "and through his own acquaintances to obtain valuable film rights in Eastern countries," but in actual fact "not a single share of the stock was sold." Kim himself was "suffering from a nervous breakdown said to have been caused by overwork and worry," and the furniture from the League's office at

18 East Forty-first Street, including paintings, etchings, bronze and marble statues, was sold at auction in a hopeless attempt to cover League debts. The ducal President's impressive mahogany-and-leather desk chair fetched the highest price: $55.

One can understand why Helena, after fourteen years of heartrending proximity to a man who was inveterate gambler, womanizer, liar, compulsive spender, rash schemer and all-round

45 Helena, 9th Duchess of Manchester,
who paid a high price for the Manchester tiara
and her Coronation robes

fool, wanted to get as far away as possible. But Kim, 9th Duke of
Manchester, for all that, was a pathetic figure who was, as much
as Helena, a victim of his time. His long exposure to his mother's
native land infected Kim with the American Dream as he
perceived it: one went to bed poor and woke up rich. He was a
Duke born too late in history to profit in his own country from
the power and privilege peers had once had. His aristocratic
upbringing gave him no profession, nothing but a gentleman's
manners and a gentleman's charm — useless in the cut and thrust
of American business. If, like the other heiresses who became
Duchesses, Helena was partly motivated by romantic daydreams,
it was Kim who was the ultimate dreamer, forever flying in his
hot-air balloon far above earth's hard realities. Kim looked in envy
and tried to emulate America's millionaires: Eugene Zimmerman,
George Gould, Willie Hearst. But he saw only their Midas-piles
of gold, and totally missed seeing the discipline, effort and genius
that lay beneath.

Even though his crazy business schemes for getting rich
overnight never paid off, Kim had one entrepreneurial skill: he
knew how to market and promote his dukedom. Over the years, it
netted him a job on the New York *Evening Journal,* a wealthy wife,
endless credit with class-conscious merchants and various trips
around the world. He may not have been the usual American
capitalist, but he was a capitalist nonetheless in his own hilarious
style. A later Duke, the Duke of Windsor, who, among other
ploys, never, ever picked up the bill in a restaurant even when he'd
initiated the party, was also adept at turning a dukedom into hard
cash.

"Harassed by many creditors," including a New York florist
claiming $482 and the New York Central Railroad claiming
$1,341.40, Kim boarded the *Adriatic,* bound for Britain, on
October 28, successfully evading two subpoena servers who stalked
the decks for him in vain, and telling the sole reporter who showed
up that he was going home to enlist. Childhood friend Winston
Churchill, then First Lord of the Admiralty, got Kim into the
Royal Naval Volunteer Reserve, while back in America, Eugene

Zimmerman told reporters, "As a former United States Navy man, I advised him to join the army. And I told him to go not only to the front, but to get out in front...and that if he got shot, not to get shot in the back."

Kim's naval career was as short-lived as all his others; two bouts of pneumonia and a damaged heart caused the medical board to reject him in September 1915.

On December 20 that year, sixty-eight-year-old Eugene Zimmerman went to New York on business, against his physician's orders, and joked at the Queen City Club with friends about the suit filed against him by one Ivy Wareham, a dog fancier from Elmhurst, Long Island, for breach of promise — a common Gilded Age trick used by women seeking instant fame and fortune. "I intend to fix her," said Eugene, chortling. He rose from his chair, coughed once deeply and fell into the arms of a friend, quite dead.

Helena left Ireland at once, reaching New York on the American liner *St. Paul* on January 4. It is significant that she avoided the press by traveling as plain "Mrs. Montagu." For the rest of her life, Helena would shun rather than court the yellow-eyed media that had slipped from her control, clawing great rents in her privacy and in her marriage, exposing only the sordid and profane.

When reporters from the *Cincinnati Enquirer* came to the Auburn Avenue house, on January 8, Helena refused to see them and sent word that she was ill. When her father's will was read, she was relieved to learn that Kim got nothing, while the income from the $10 million estate was hers for life, then passed to her children. No doubt with Kim in mind, her father had added a clause to the effect that "under no circumstances are the trustees to pay to my daughter any sum to satisfy the claims of any creditor." Her father had named Helena as one of the estate's executors, but since in marrying a Briton she was no longer an American citizen, she could not serve. Once the estate was settled, Helena sought seclusion at Battle Creek, Michigan, in a local sanatorium, arriving on February 1, for a period of rest and recuperation. She was "suffering from severe nervous strain," and reached Battle Creek extremely worn, retiring at once to her rooms.

She sailed back to Ireland on the *St. Louis* on August 7, perhaps reflecting, as she leaned on the rail looking at endless gray seas, that she was returning alone and grieving on the very same ship that had carried her as newlywed fifteen years before, in happy expectation, in an opposite direction.

The headlines still screamed her husband's sins to the world. "Manchester Owes $1,000,000, Has $1,000"..."Manchester a Bankrupt"..."Name Duke of Manchester in London Action, Charging Illegal Sale of War Munitions"..."Duke Not Yet in Movies. Manchester Has Offer, But Nothing Decided." That headline came on October 5, 1921. Agents for some American film company were — so the Duke said — wooing him for a "leading part." Kim was ever hopeful of stardom, regarding stage and screen as his mother had viewed Society: as a magic mirror, reflecting an ideal self. "Duke's Gold Claims Are Canceled"..."Duke Runs Movie House" was the headline for the *New York Times* Sunday supplement on December 10, 1925. A photo of fifty-year-old Kim, described as a "genial fat man," shows flabby jowls, bulbous nose, dangling cigarette, flashy hatband. He looks more like an Al Capone–style gangster than a peer. It seems Kim had become manager of the Gaiety cinema in Manchester, and that one of the first films he would show there was, most appropriately, Charlie Chaplin's *Gold Rush*. "Since it is a film depicting ice and snow," Kim asked reporters, "why confine the illusion of the frozen North to the screen?" Kim had come up with the smashing idea of freezing the audience in their seats as well.

"Manchester Seeks to Divorce Duchess" appeared in the Sunday papers on July 26, 1925. Kim had filed for divorce at Nice, on grounds of "desertion and incompatibility," but Helena still couldn't face the publicity of a divorce and avoided it by paying Kim off with an out-of-court settlement of £9,923 ($49,615).

On October 27, 1928, Kim was hauled into Bankruptcy Court owing, among other bills, "£918 in respect of a separate establishment at Gloucester Gate, £976 for tennis balls and rackets, £197 to a doctor and £1,200 for ladies' dresses." In February 1929, Kim announced to the press that he planned to live part-time in Cuba, and toward that end had purchased a $40,000 building site at Havana's Biltmore Beach, planning to erect a $500,000 home immediately.

Whereas Helena had permanently turned her back on the press, Kim was making ever more outrageous statements to keep their attention. One suspects that for Kim there came a point when his life in print acquired more substance and solidity than his actual existence. The media image he'd so painstakingly created over the years determined his behavior, and not vice versa. Helena saved herself by opting out just in time.

In spite of his frantic efforts to stay in print, Kim's star was fading fast. By the 1920s, Dukes and Earls were déclassé. They yielded pride of place in yellow journals to the escapades of film stars and baseball players, who had succeeded nobles in the popular imagination. In Britain, its nobility groaned under the weight of crippling income taxes and death duties, and their huge stately country houses became homes for the aged, the sick, or — most fitting of all — the insane. Other houses turned into schools or convents. Kimbolton Castle would end as a boys' private school, and Kylemore, with one of fate's delicious ironies, would become a Benedictine nunnery. Helena sold it to the grateful nuns and escaped British taxes by moving in February 1931 to Paris, taking a large apartment on the Quai d'Orsay, with a superb view of the Seine.

In the same month, she served Kim with a divorce suit on the grounds of misconduct. It was undefended and a decree nisi was granted on May 11. Kim told the London papers on November 19 that he would "take his own measures for dissolution of the marriage" and obtain a decree absolute on grounds of desertion in Cuba, where he was currently headed. When it was pointed out to His Grace that a Cuban divorce would not be recognized in

Britain, he replied that "he intended to return to England in April, when he expected to be arrested for bigamy" — a sure way to grab headlines. Nothing more was heard of this, and Helena obtained her absolute decree on December 7. By that time Kim was aboard the *Berengaria* bound for New York, traveling with pretty thirty-four-year-old Kathleen Dawes, a London actress, daughter of William Henry Dawes, a West End theater manager.

Kathleen and Kim turned up at New York's City Hall at four o'clock on December 11, intending to get married. Photographers set up their cameras in Mayor Walker's reception room; guests arrived; a sound movie apparatus stood ready. Then Kathleen got her first inkling of what her future life with the Duke would be like. He had neglected to bring a certified copy of his divorce papers, so that no wedding could take place that day. He married his actress without major mishap on December 17, in Greenwich, Connecticut.

Apart from finding a new wife, Kim had been very busy writing his memoirs, which appeared in England in the spring of 1932. Helena must have been vastly relieved to note that they contained very little mention of "my wife" and that not until page 179, three-quarters of the way through, does Kim even deign to name her. Nor is their much mention of his remarkable mother, Consuelo, who by choice played a minor role in her son's life. Kim struts through the pages as swashbuckling hero, adept at all sports, winning all gambling games, popular on two continents. *My Candid Recollections* — like so much of Kim's public persona — is anything but candid.

On March 6, 1933, the Chancery Court in London ordered the Duke to pay off his debts at the rate of £50 a week. Smoking thick Turkish cigarettes in his suite at the Savoy, Kim explained that his new wife had made him much more "responsible."

Responsible? Two weeks later, Kim was charged in Police Court with pawning jewels that belonged not to him but to the trustees of his mother's estate. He'd wheedled them from the clutches of the trustees with the lie that Kathleen wanted to wear them at Christmas. Kathleen never saw the jewels. Kim took them straight to Thomas Sutton's pawnship in Victoria Street, signed a form declaring that the jewels were his very own property and walked out with a fistful of cash. The Duke's trial lasted two days, and at the end of it William Angus Drogo Montagu, 9th Duke of Manchester, residing at Orchard Court, Portman Square, was found guilty of fraud. "With a bow," he left the dock and was taken to Wormwood Scrubs Prison for a nine-month sentence. "My trouble," Kim explained to reporters that night in his cell, "is that I have been a mug — I am not quite sure I am glad I was born a Duke."

(If Kim was the first exalted peer to find himself behind bars, he was not the last. The Duke of Marlborough's heir, the rebellious Jamie, Marquess of Blandford, was jailed for thirty-seven days in 1991 for driving offenses. In an Oxford jail ten miles from splendid Blenheim Palace, Jamie shared a ten-foot by six-foot cell with a convicted burglar and earned £4.50 a week cleaning toilets. When he was released, Jamie let it be known that he was willing to tell his story to a newspaper, and when asked if he wanted money for it, replied, "I am not doing it for nothing." London's *Daily Mail*, reporting this on November 16, 1991, noted that Jamie was deeply in debt and was currently being taken to court for an alleged £2,000 owing on a piano he'd purchased from an Oxford music shop.)

Kim, Duke of Manchester, was luckier than Jamie in that he served only twenty-five days of his nine-month sentence before it was quashed by the Court of Appeal. On June 5, 1935, he was released and his son Mandy, not Kathleen, came to collect him at the prison gate. Kim's third and last bankruptcy followed on August 6 that year, when the court listed his assets at £5 and his liabilities at more than £9,000 ($45,000).

In 1937, on November 23, Helena quietly and "secretly," to avoid publicity, married, in Edinburgh, that kinsman of Kim's who'd comforted her in time of shipwreck, Lord Arthur George Keith-Falconer, now 10th Earl of Kintore. London's *Daily Mail* and the

New York Times ran the briefest possible four-line wedding announcements. The fifty-eight-year-old Earl had fought valiantly for his country as Captain in the Scots Guards not once but twice, first in the Boer War from 1900 to 1902, and then in World War I from 1914 to 1918.

At the Earl's ancestral seat, Keith Hall, at Inverurie in Aberdeenshire, Scotland, Helena relaxed into the uneventful life of a country gentlewoman, golfing, salmon fishing, enjoying the pastoral views and the companionship of Lord Arthur George, who had many virtues, the chief one being that he never did anything silly or sensational enough to get into the papers. Helena lived at Keith Hall for the next thirty-four years, in blessed privacy and oblivion. A search of newspaper indexes both British and American for that period yields not a single item on Helena, Countess of Kintore.

Kim died at Seaford, Sussex, aged sixty-nine, on February 9, 1947, after an illness lasting some weeks, leaving an estate of £257 ($1,285). Newspaper obituaries were extremely brief for this best-forgotten Duke, the London *Times* commenting tersely that His Grace was "curiously lacking in judgment."

Lord Kintore died at Keith Hall in 1966, and Helena lived on for another five years, outlasting all her children except Mandy, the 10th Duke of Manchester. She died at Keith Hall on December 15, 1971, at the age of ninety-three.

The London *Times* printed the briefest possible obituary, but the *New York Times* seized the opportunity to look back nostalgically to an age that, never having read the headlines of Pearl Harbor, Hiroshima, Auschwitz, Vietnam and the assassination of a hopeful young President, could keep itself amused by the song and dance, the light fantastic, of a British Duke and his American bride. On December 16, the *New York Times* obituary of Helena Zimmerman ran through, for the very last time, the whole amazing story, beginning with the costume ball in Dinard, Brittany, when a pretty young heiress from Cincinnati made the mistake of dressing up as actress Edna May and walking down the stairs straight into a tabloid serial than ran for thirty years.

Helena Zimmerman's ambition was to take her place in the Royal Enclosure at Ascot and in the Sunday rotogravure. But for that she married the wrong man. A Duke who was every inch a self-conscious, thoroughly English Duke, polished and proper right down to his patent-leather pumps — someone like Sunny Marlborough, say — would have suited Helena's purpose admirably. What she got instead was a man whose life was all smoke and mirrors, a bumbling, bumptious cartoon character, a Yellow Kid if ever there was one, punch-drunk and reeling from his own notoriety, yet always coming back for more. What she got was a caricature of a Duke, with no dignity at all.

Perhaps the final irony is that in spite of her hunger for fame, no full-color treatment of Helena Zimmerman's story can ever crown her life. As we search through dusty newspaper files, almost a hundred years later, eager to give Helena her own dignified, distinct place in history, it is the funny little fat man who comes alive, who puffs and prances, who turns his somersaults and gets the laughs. But it is Helena, supplying the props and picking up the pieces, who merits the applause.

V

MAY GOELET

46   May Goelet, 8th Duchess of Roxburghe
(portrait by Edward Hughes)

To every lovely lady bright,
What can I wish but faithful knight?
To every faithful lover too,
What can I wish but lady true?

—SIR WALTER SCOTT,
Marmion, Canto VI

I F HELENA ZIMMERMAN'S MARRIAGE to a Duke was made — and unmade — in headlines, May Goelet's was truly, miraculously, against all precedent and probability, made in heaven. May's was a success story, the union contradicting all the norms. She stands apart from the other four brides and their disastrous, or merely disappointing, alliances. May was different in class, in values, in personality, motive, sentiment and role. She turned the tables, showed the flip side and found the silver lining. If they were living today, Duchess Helena's story might find its way into *People* magazine, and May Goelet's into a Harlequin romance — with a moral, and a twist.

One fine morning in 1897, eighteen-year-old May sat down at a highly polished desk, drew some sheets of thick, creamy notepaper headed "Wimborne House, Arlington Street" toward her, dipped her pen into an antique inkwell and wrote "Tuesday, June 1st" in her flamboyant, self-assured scrawl. Then she paused, and looked out the nearest window of the London mansion that her parents had rented for the summer. She was in such a whirl of excitement, plunging into her first London Season, that it was hard for her to order her thoughts. Like the notepaper, like May's understated morning gown, with none of the showy trims Helena Zimmerman would have favored, like absolutely everything in May's milieu, Wimborne House was the finest money could command, and its Georgian windows looked out on Green Park, where blackbirds sang sweetly from lace canopies of leaves. May could hear staccato hooves on Piccadilly bringing carriages to and from the Ritz Hotel, which stood on the corner, and the heavier, slower clip-clop of dray horses making deliveries. May loved the fact that a well turned out London dray horse in summer sported a posy-trimmed straw bonnet. Everything about London pleased May, but then she was easily pleased, for she had a great talent for being happy. Her joie de vivre, which would last all her life, drawing people to her, recalls Consuelo Yznaga's, except that Consuelo needed an audience to be happy; May needed only her own inner resources.

Her mobile mouth was perpetually smiling, lighting up a pale face too long for beauty, but memorable for its animation. She had dark, moth-wing eyebrows above brilliant black eyes, a petite figure and an extremely beautiful bustline — what the French novels she read called *une belle poitrine*. May loved to read and did so in several languages. She had been educated in Europe, with plenty of tutors and governesses, and was quite as "finished" as her friend Consuelo Vanderbilt Marlborough, who summed up May as "bright, amusing and quick, the three natural attributes of an American girl." Like Gwen Van Osburgh in Wharton's *House of Mirth*, May also had "all the guileless confidence of a young girl who has always been told that there is no one richer than her father."

She bent her small head, its curls piled high in classic rather than faddish mode, to her letter. "Dearest Tante," she scrawled, addressing Aunt Belle, her mother's younger sister, whom May had called "Tante" ever since the days when she wrote to her, for practice, in French. Aunt Belle matched her name, with honey-blond hair and a delicious voice. She was May's favorite aunt, friend and confidante, her ideal of womanhood and wifehood.

May began to write, her hand forming artistic, curlicued letters so large that she needed a fresh sheet for almost every sentence. She wrote as she talked: all in a rush, with no time for any punctuation except long dashes:

> On Sunday the Prince dined with us, and I'm happy to say it all went off most successfully — you have no idea of what a struggle it was though — Everyone we could think of to ask was going out of town, either to Waddesdon [country home of Baron Ferdinand de Rothschild] or some other Rothschild's. It was really quite dreadful.... Lord Brougham gave out *Sunday morning* and we had to send — tearing right and left to find of course every soul out of town. After dinner we had Melba to sing and the Prince was simply delighted. I have rarely seen him in such good spirits. He let everyone go at a *quarter to one* and he stayed till 1:15. He told Mamma it had all been *most beautifully done* and I don't think he could have been bored otherwise he would never have stayed so late.... We are altogether rather pleased with our entertainment.

As well they might have been! An American heiress's family in their first assault on London Society didn't usually begin at the apex by entertaining Britain's future King. The Goelets had been on familiar terms with Prince Edward for eleven years, but then the Goelets weren't New Rich like most American families who came to Europe to buy themselves some class. Goelets had that already; unlike the families of Lily Hammersley, Consuelo Vanderbilt and Helena Zimmerman, May Goelet's was Old Money, and as such could be accepted at once by British aristocrats. America's aristocracy or "patriciate," as Nelson Aldrich prefers to call it in *Old Money: The Mythology of America's Upper Class* (1988), has always endorsed the same ideals and manners as its British counterparts, feeling duty bound to support the arts and the underprivileged, and to treat gardeners as graciously as Dukes. New Money opts for selfish luxury and show, barks at gardeners and grovels to Dukes.

May scribbled prodigally across several more sheets, sprinkled with exclamation marks looking like fringe in a strong updraft:

> I've been to two dances so far. The first was at Mrs. James Arthur James and was the greatest fun in the world. I'd been rather seedy with a most dreadful cold and *something* else as well, so spent Sunday and Monday in bed and only got up to go to Mrs. James'. Mamma didn't want to take me at all, said it was such a foolish thing for me to do, but I wouldn't give in, and I'm glad I was firm or obstinate because I danced every single dance, 22. We got there at a quarter to twelve and only left at 3:30.... On Friday last we dined at Mrs. Bentinck's. A very large dinner, 42 and cotillion afterwards...at two all the electric lights went out — and they didn't come on again! So for three-quarters of an hour we danced with two miserable candles at each end of the room. It was quite dreadful, you couldn't see anyone and it was most depressing. It was such a pity!!!! On Thursday, we went to Mr. Alfred Rothschild's — music, considered a very smart party. Tonight Lady Sarah Wilson's dance [Sunny Marlborough's aunt]. Beatrice [Lord Pembroke's daughter] sniffed, said she was a very fast woman — until she got an invitation (which she only did last night) and now she is crazy to go — as she knows Lady Sarah has secured all the men!!! She is such a little snob that girl!

May looked out the window again. Ladies in floating, sweet-pea-colored gowns with parasols to match strolled along Queen's Walk, leaning on the strong arms of their menfolk, sending laughter toward her. May had already begun her own collection of parasols, fine arsenal of femininity, and had two with handles designed by Carl Fabergé, Queen Alexandra's favorite.

"What has been exciting the minds of everyone," May told Aunt Belle, revealing her own excitement, "is whether they would be asked to Devonshire House for the Fancy Dress Ball!!" (Had she known its import, two exclamation marks would never have sufficed.) "Beatrice received her *invite* on Saturday night and ours came yesterday (Monday) afternoon. Of course we didn't know if we should be asked or not. B. said only 16 girls were invited! I must tear round to tell her our invitations have come!!"

May hardly ever walked anywhere; she was far more likely to "tear round." She finished the last of seven four-sided sheets, sent her "best love" to Aunt Belle and her husband, ending, "Ever yours, May," with a gay little arabesque flying from the tail of the *y*.

Her Aunt Belle Herbert, before marriage, had been the middle Wilson girl, ten years younger than May's mother, Mary Reta,* born in 1855, and five years older than Grace, born in 1870. They were the three daughters of Richard Thornton Wilson, a handsome man six and a half feet tall, said to be Margaret Mitchell's inspiration for Rhett Butler in *Gone with the Wind.* Born in Gainesville, Georgia, in 1829, son of a Scots tanner, Dick Wilson became a traveling salesman. When he turned up one day with his box of trinkets at Ebenezer Johnson's farm, Dick sweet-talked Ebenezer into giving him his eldest daughter, Melissa Clementine, as wife, and enough money to open a general store in Loudon, a hamlet in western Tennessee. When the Civil War came, Dick joined the Confederate commissary department as Major; in 1864 he and Melissa, with their two sons and daughters, Mary Reta and Belle, rode a flatcar camouflaged with branches as far as Wilmington, North Carolina, ran the blockade and sailed for England. There Dick sold Confederate cotton and other goods for the commissary, lining his own pockets as he did so.

After the war, he returned to America with $500,000, bought a mansion at 511 Fifth Avenue, opened an office at 33 Wall Street,

---

*May's mother was usually called May, but to avoid confusion with her daughter, we shall stick to Mary Reta, her christened name.

established a banking firm, bought up Southern railroads and Northern street railways. He had an asset most other robber barons lacked: his Rhett Butler charm and perfect manners. He didn't, like John Jacob Astor, wipe his fingers on the nearest woman's sleeve at a dinner party, or, like Commodore Vanderbilt, let fly a string of oaths. Southern charm oiled the hinges, opened many doors, as Dick and Melissa Wilson told their daughters, realizing, as the Yznagas had, that the one weapon that could completely conquer the North was the Southern belle. But whereas Consuelo Yznaga's Southern softness was coupled with a wanton, rebellious streak, the Wilson girls, Mary Reta, Belle and Grace, were utterly conventional, quite content to swish their way through life focusing on ruffled gowns, unruffled composure, no matter what, and the well-being of their menfolk, passing on their Southern savvy to the next generation.

May's mother, Mary Reta, had married first. The Wilsons were holidaying in the summer of 1876 at the Pequot House, in New London, Connecticut, extravagantly entertaining in a private parlor. One of Mary's beaux was pale, serious Ogden Goelet, who, in addition to chronic asthma, had a puny physique, "emphatically diminutive and therefore not physically attractive," as one gossip sheet put it. He was considered no great matrimonial catch, but Mary Reta fell in love with shy little Ogden and encouraged his suit. "I never liked you so well, or wished more to be with you," she told him in a note, "than last night and yet you left me — heedless of my entreaties, left me with a man too prone to say sweet nothings.... I shall really be awfully disappointed if I do not see you tomorrow, and prefer of course seeing you in the evening. It was very sweet of you to come to the ball, I know it must have been a great bore to you, I appreciate your martyrdom."

All this soft soap did its work, and when twenty-two-year-old Mary Reta and thirty-one-year-old Ogden married in 1877, her father gave them $75,000 in bonds, for Ogden himself wasn't rich at the time, having only his Knickerbocker lineage to recommend him, but that was certainly impressive enough.

47 *May's mother Mrs. Ogden Goelet,*
    the former Mary Reta Wilson

In New York terms, the Goelets (pronounced Guh-*lett*, with
no Gallic pretension), were the very finest Old Money. Early
Goelets fled France for the Netherlands at the time of the
Huguenot persecution; in 1676 Francis and ten-year-old son

Jacobus pushed on to America. Jacobus (1665–1731) had ten children, including John (1694–1753), whose son Peter (1727–1811) sold hardware, musical instruments and pewter spoons in Hanover Square, with a famous Golden Key hung above the door. Like those other early families, the ship-chandler Schermerhorns, sugar-refining Rhinelanders and fur-trading Astors, Goelets had the good sense to buy up city land in all the right places — they once bought eighty lots between Fifth and Sixth avenues, Forty-second and Forty-third streets, for $600 a lot — and to hang on to it, so that 150 years before there were Trumps, Zeckendorfs and Helmsleys there were Goelets casting long shadows across Manhattan. Goelets still own a good deal of it, including the land under the Mobil Building at Forty-second Street and Lexington Avenue, worth $100 million. The Goelets went on prospering and proliferating, filling the family tree with Peters and Roberts and Ogdens, founding New York's Chemical Bank in 1824, now one of the most powerful in the world, with a Goelet still sitting on its board. When Moses Yale Beach, owner of the New York *Sun*, published *The Wealth and Biography of the Wealthy Citizens of the City of New York* in 1844, he listed among the ten families with fortunes over $1 million the Goelets, with $2 million.

After Ogden married Mary Reta, she met his eccentric uncle Peter (1800–1879), who was even more parsimonious than most Goelets, mending his own coat, writing letters on the backs of envelopes, consulting a ten-thousand-volume law library in his brownstone at Broadway and Nineteenth Street to save on legal fees and milking his own cow in the back garden, where peacocks and golden pheasants, his one luxury, paraded about.

May, Mary Reta and Ogden's only daughter, was born on October 6, 1878. She was christened Mary, but always called May, a name that suited her better, with its connotations of springtime when, as Scots poet Robert Burns puts it, "The flowers sprang wanton to be prest / The birds sang love on every spray." May's good luck began almost at once, for when she was just a year old Uncle Peter Goelet died, leaving her father $25 million, with another $25 million hot on its heels when Grandfather Goelet,

Ogden's father, Robert, succumbed to a sudden attack of dysentery a few months later. As she took her first baby steps, May already had what it takes to find and keep the world's most desirable European noble: the right kind of money (inherited, not earned) and the right kind of gentility and noblesse oblige.

Her parents moved into a red-brick mansion at 608 Fifth Avenue, at the southwest corner of Forty-ninth Street, where her mother began a collection of fine paintings, buying with real knowledge and taste, not just blindly by price, and became a highly discriminating hostess, with what one friend called "severely aristocratic" manners. Ogden joined the American Museum of Natural History and the Fine Arts Society, bought shares in the Metropolitan Opera, supported all the right charities and did his best to keep the Goelet name out of the papers. Old Money doesn't make history if it can help it, but history, nevertheless, is its god. Precedence is all: in choice of Christian names or schools; in playing Old Money's favorite parlor game: "Who was she before she married?"; in doing things as they have always been done. Like May's father, present-day Goelets are still chained to tradition, still refusing all interviews, still keeping a finger on history's pulse. One is a past-President of the New York Historical Society, the New York Zoological Society, the American Museum of Natural History and the French Institute.

May's only brother, Robert (Bobby), was born when she was three, in 1881, and three years later her uncle Orme Wilson, her mother's brother, married Carrie Astor, daughter of Caroline, Society's queen and owner of the legendary four-hundred-person ballroom. Ex-President Ulysses S. Grant was a guest of honor at the wedding, and got so drunk that he placed the lighted end of his cigar in his mouth and burned himself badly. In spite of this inauspicious omen, the love match of Carrie and Orme proved a happy marriage, one of many such coming into young May Goelet's view.

In the following year, scholarly Ogden decided that New York Society was rapidly deteriorating into one where you were what you spent rather than what you inherited. At one vulgar party, each guest received a cigarette rolled not in white paper but in a $100 bill engraved in gold with the host's initials; at another, each guest found a large black pearl in one of his oysters. With seven-year-old May, five-year-old Bobby, governess and tutor, the Goelets went in search of a more cultured civilization, renting a yacht called *The White Ladye* from Lily Langtry and cruising about western Europe.

Next year, May's Aunt Belle Wilson joined the Goelets to troll for a husband from a yacht called *The Norseman*, of such perfect beauty and taste that when it tied up at Cowes, Isle of Wight, for the August regatta, Edward, Prince of Wales, invited himself on board for inspection and stayed to tea, prompting Belle to observe that he had "the best manners and more tact than any man I have ever met." He came aboard twice more that week, once for a luncheon for twelve, and again for tea, when he ate, with all his usual relish, hot batter cakes, "entirely a Southern dish," as May's mother explained. This early exposure to Royals would serve May well.

On September 2, Belle told her parents in a letter that Baby May — the family affectionately called her that until she married — was very "brown and well," enjoying her pony, Gold-dust, and getting "the undoubted polish foreign association gives a girl." On the 14th Earl of Pembroke's yacht, Belle met his younger brother, Michael Herbert, always called Mungo, fell in love, and got engaged two years later, which prompted May, aged nine, to send off an enthusiastic letter in French to Tante, saying that she was "*bien ravie*" at the news, felt sure Tante would be "*bien contente*" and could she please be maid of honor. May ended her letter with her characteristic warmth: "*Je t'embrasse bien tendrement ma chère petite tante Belle ainsi que toute la famille et je me rejouis de ton retour.*" (I hug you very tenderly my dear little Aunt Belle, as well as all the family and I rejoice in your return.) Like all our heroines except Lily Hammersley, May was educated abroad in one temporary domicile or another, but she was luckier than they because she moved about inside a warm, supportive family group that usually included Aunt Belle or Aunt Grace in addition to two doting parents.

Belle married Mungo Herbert in November 1888. He had neither wealth nor health, but belonged to one of England's first families, highly cultured and distinguished. There had been Herberts at historic Wilton House, near Salisbury, Wiltshire, for four hundred years, one of them friend and patron of Shakespeare. Wilton House had a Holbein clock tower, England's most beautiful room, the double-cube room built for its Van Dycks, green lawns spreading to the Avon River, peacocks making splendor in the grass. After her aunt's marriage, May would sometimes visit, wrapping Wilton's calm and continuity about her. Wilton would also be the scene of her deepest anguish.

The Herberts welcomed Belle warmly into the family. Mungo's sister Gladys de Grey, Consuelo Manchester's close friend, wrote to Belle: "Now that Mungo has got the wish of his heart, I have nothing left to wish for, and my gratitude towards the person who has brought us such happiness is beyond expression." Mungo's brother Sidney, Earl of Pembroke, told Belle five months later, "It's very nice to hear of you and Mungo being so happy — so much happier than I think people generally are in the first year of matrimony — which is a profession in which there is a great deal to be learnt." Aunt Belle's supremely happy marriage, as she supported her diplomat husband with great love and devotion in his postings to Paris, Constantinople and Washington, would be May's inspiration and ideal.

If in her growing-up years, Goelet ideals gave May culture and polish, Wilson ones reinforced an old-fashioned, True Woman, full-flower femininity. "The quality of tact is all a woman ever needs to be a success. Never forget that," Grandfather Wilson often told her, while Grandmother Wilson would add in her sweet voice, "You can attract more flies with honey than with vinegar." Aunt Grace called this approach "pussy-purring," and young May, by example, soon acquired the knack of it.

Beginning in 1889, the year after Belle married, and finishing two years later, May's parents built Ochre Court at Newport, a transplanted French château of light gray Indiana granite with sheet copper roof, eighteen bedrooms and plenty of Gothic

48   Ochre Court, the Goelet mansion at Newport

extravagances. The house faced east, almost at the northern end of the cliffs, with a view of Seaconnet Point and endless blue ocean. Like Newport's other mansions, Ochre Court was a house without a proper setting, placed on a tiny lot, crowded up against other bastard palaces that faced the Atlantic as if trying to locate their forebears on its far side.

May's mother soon tired of Ochre Court: "Such a lot of trouble and endless domestic worries running that big establishment," she complained to Belle, "with just a housekeeper for the 27 servants, 9 coachmen and grooms, and 12 gardeners." But May loved her summer months at Newport, each new day delicious, with her breakfast tray coming in gleaming with silver, while beyond open casements where muslin-and-lace curtains billowed gently, the watering cart threw its silver semiluna onto the grass and grateful robins hopped and caroled.

May lounged about the garden with its clipped parterres, reading novels full of shining knights and ladies, and when dusk came and sea-cove lights along the coast gleamed like border gems on a purple mantle, she dreamed of her future. Her father was

49   Newport belles and beaux on a picnic:
Consuelo Vanderbilt, center, in a hat with spiky flowers and
May Goelet, to the left, in a hat with scalloped brim

increasingly unwell, walking very slowly on the arm of a nurse down the drive to Ochre Court's immense iron gates and slowly back again, living on a diet of hothouse grapes, unable to digest anything else. Summer stays in Newport grew shorter since her father's asthma and dyspepsia improved in Europe, away from the social whirl, cruising quietly on his yacht.

The Goelets rented *The White Ladye* again for the winter of 1895–6, with pretty, blond, green-eyed Grace on board for the second season. Shy young Neily Vanderbilt, son of Cornelius II and Alice, brother of sculptor Gertrude, soon joined them. His engagement to Grace hit the New York headlines on June 11, 1896, the same day as Gertrude's to Harry Payne Whitney. For some reason — perhaps Dick Wilson's war-profiteering past or Grace's essential frivolity — Cornelius II violently opposed his son's marriage. Neily refused to give Grace up, whereupon Cornelius suffered a near-fatal stroke, and never spoke to Neily again, who bravely married Grace on August 3, 1896. The American public, following every detail of true love's triumph in the newspapers, sent the newlyweds thousands of sympathetic letters, and May Goelet had yet another marriage fueled by love to observe at close range. (When Cornelius II died, he left Neily a mere $1 million, but brother Alfred generously added $6 million more so that Neily and Grace could live in the luxury that, more and more, she required.)

From Europe, where Neily and Grace were honeymooning in September, she told her parents that her sisters and niece May "were in good health and spirits and it was great fun all being together again. All three of us married and only Baby May to look after now."

"We saw a great deal of the Prince, always the same kind friend to us," May's mother told Grace smugly from Geneva in April 1897, "and Beatrice Herbert here with May made all the difference in the world to May's pleasure. Beatrice was mad keen about everything and they had great fun together. I can't say I enjoy chaperoning girls of 18 and Beatrice is a host in herself. We banqueted nearly every night with HRH."

By June 1, the Goelets were ensconced in London's Wimborne House, with May dashing off her euphoric letter to Aunt Belle before "tearing round" to tell Beatrice Herbert that she was indeed invited to the Duchess of Devonshire's costume ball to be held one month hence, on July 2.

When the magical night came, eighteen-year-old May went in a costume that not only revealed her high-busted, shapely little figure, but much of her personality as well. Her Worth golden-gauze gown was embroidered in precious stones and sashed three

*50   May Goelet lounging in her Scheherazade costume
chosen for the Devonshire ball, 1897*

times, in pink, blue and mauve. On her head was a seductive sort
of helmet, with a red rose on one side, a white lotus on the other
and a white plume shooting straight up between like an exuberant
jet d'eau. This tender, teasing drapery turned May Goelet into
Scheherazade, the *Arabian Nights* heroine who could keep a man
in thrall indefinitely with a sparkling flow of words.

No one knows where or when the *Arabian Nights* tales
originated, but Egyptian scholars began recording them about
1400, and the English adventurer Richard Burton published his
rather naughty but popular collection in sixteen volumes in
1885–88. Thus guests at the ball would have known the details of
Scheherazade's story whereby she'd kept her husband, a wicked,
murdering Sultan, enthralled and kindly disposed by telling him a
different tale for a thousand and one nights, after which they lived

271

happily ever after. Donning a Scheherazade costume was as close to advertising as a husband-hunting American heiress could get.

May was in a fever of excitement, there in the crush of real knights and ladies parading their history, many in costumes copied from portraits of their ancestors. As usual — for she had plenty of what was then called "come hither" — May was besieged with dance partners, one being bachelor Kim, Duke of Manchester, who followed her about and whispered compliments into her lotus-decked ear. Was he courting her, that little buffoon of a Duke? Not her type at all, far too brash and boastful.

It was at the Devonshires' 1897 ball that four heroines of this story came together in one room; only Helena Zimmerman, not yet introduced or married to her Duke, was missing.

Kim's mother, Consuelo Manchester, tripping through her paces in her natural milieu, had come to terms with life, lost her illusions, buried her no-good Duke — and daughter Mary, taken from her so suddenly in Rome. But Consuelo still had her Prince, her lovers, her social eminence. She was Society's star turn and that was quite enough.

Lily Beresford had come up to London from the domestic bliss of Deepdene where, at last, with five-month-old son and husband Bill, she had a real home, something she'd never had at bleak Blenheim, where Vera Campbell had filled its corridors, tall as a man and twice as bold.

Consuelo Marlborough, pregnant and unhappy, sat out every dance, hating the pomp, the hierarchy and Sunny's self-satisfied smirk above his gems and spangles, all of it rubbing her democratic spirit raw.

If May Goelet had asked each of these three American Duchesses in turn whether she should follow their example and marry a Duke, all three would probably have answered an emphatic *no!* It was fortunate that May never thought to ask, particularly in light of the fact that Britain's most eligible Duke was only inches away, one of eight young men dressed as Yeomen of the Guard, holding aloft a white-and-gold canopy over Lady

Tweedmouth, dressed as Queen Elizabeth I. The large Elizabethan group, including the Duke's mother, was the first procession to parade past Prince Edward and Princess Alexandra's improvised throne.

Nothing much happened that night between May Goelet and the 8th Duke of Roxburghe. He didn't sweep her off her feet, or swear eternal devotion or flaunt her lotus on his sleeve. We're not even sure that they were introduced. We only know that he saw Scheherazade and she saw a Yeoman of the Guard, and everything else followed very slowly and calmly and naturally, in its own good time, from that initial sighting.

A scarlet-and-gold tunic above scarlet breeches and hose emphasized the Duke of Roxburghe's six-foot frame and broad shoulders, and his facial features above a white pleated ruff — high cheekbones, straight nose, fine mouth and chin — were sculpted by several hundred years of good breeding. He had dark brown hair just visible beneath his black hat, and a nicely trimmed dark mustache. He looked, every splendid scarlet-coated inch of him, a Duke, a Duke divine, exactly the image thousands of maidens conjured up in their heads whenever they thought the word "Duke."

Sir Henry John Innes-Ker, 8th Duke of Roxburghe; Marquess of Bowmont and Cessford; Earl of Roxburghe; Earl of Kelso; Viscount Broxmouth; Baron Roxburghe; Baron Ker of Cessford and Cavertoun — all these titles in Scotland's Peerage, as well as Earl Innes in the United Kingdom's — was born on July 25, 1876, eldest of seven, son of the 7th Duke, Sir James Henry Robert Innes-Ker, and Lady Anne Emily (née Spencer-Churchill), daughter of the 7th Duke of Marlborough, aunt to naughty Blandford and great-aunt to sad little Sunny. The 8th Duke of Roxburghe, always called "Kelso" by his family and "Bumble" by his many friends, went off to Eton in 1890, and succeeded to the dukedom two years later, when he was sixteen. He left Eton in 1894 and began his soldiering career as Lieutenant in the Militia battalion of the Argyll and Sutherland Highlanders. His two

51   The handsome 8th Duke of Roxburghe

principal Scottish Border estates were Floors Castle (pronounced with a French accent as it was once spelled: *Fleurs*) and Broxmouth Park, Dunbar.

The noun "noble," first used to denote a peer, eventually got into the dictionary as an adjective meaning "splendid, admirable, morally elevated" because most peers, in the beginning, were exactly that. By 1897, however, as we well know, less complimentary terms best described them — all except Kelso, 8th Duke of Roxburghe, who really *was* noble, never, ever indulging in conduct that didn't become an officer and a peer. Consuelo Marlborough pronounced him "a fine man and a great gentleman." Like well-named Knightley in Jane Austen's *Emma*, Kelso was a man of "true gentility," considerate of others' feelings, courteous to all classes, ever mindful of his responsibilities to his tenants, his county and his country.

It is important to note that he was not, like gentlemanly little Sunny Marlborough, an Englishman, born in a manicured land of pocket-handkerchief, posy-strewn meadows. Kelso was a Scot, born in rugged Border country that was lonely, windswept, with vast moors and stunted trees and the cold North Sea forever crashing against one's psyche. "There is a country accent," says La Rochefoucauld, "not in speech only, but in thought, conduct, character, and manner of existing which never forsakes a man." Scotland bred men of action who were strong limbed, stout-hearted, practical, doers not dreamers, extroverts not introverts, courageous and daring on the battlefield or in the hunt. Of just such a breed was Kelso, 8th Duke of Roxburghe.

The very best thing about this wondrous Duke, quite enough in himself to turn every republican back again to monarchist, was his domain of 60,418 acres, bringing him an annual rent-roll income of £50,917, which, in that day's reckoning, was $254,585, none of which he squandered or gambled away. When we recall that Consuelo and Sunny Marlborough lived in great luxury and pomp on $200,000 a year, we can see that Kelso had no need of a rich wife. He was free to marry where his heart listed, and for all the right reasons.

It was just seven days after the Duchess of Devonshire's ball that twenty-one-year-old Kim, Duke of Manchester, with creditors as always in hot pursuit, had the gall, the conceit, the presumption to announce to London's *Daily Telegraph* that he was about to marry rich Miss Goelet. One English newspaper declared that the couple's two mothers had arranged the match. This may or may not have been true, but Consuelo Manchester, dedicated, hardworking matchmaker that she was, may well have seen May Goelet, with her fine Old Money background, as Kim's salvation both financially and morally. "England's Poorest Duke After Our Richest Heiress!" screamed the American headlines in alarm. Next day, July 11, the *New York Times* printed Kim's denial of any engagement, which Ogden Goelet had insisted he make. When an English reporter went to Wimborne House, Mr. Goelet declined to see him, and "sent word that so far as he could control the matter, he would not permit any reference being made to his affairs in the newspapers." May and her father shuddered at the very idea, quite the opposite of Kim himself, his future bride, Helena Zimmerman, and her father, Eugene.

Did the Duke of Roxburghe read all about it? He was busy at the end of the month celebrating at his coming-of-age ceremony, receiving a silver bowl and illuminated address from his tenants, giving them a banquet, answering the toast proposed to him by saying, "The ownership of landed property was not the brightest and easiest of inheritances in these days, when agriculture and all that depended on it have such a hard fight to make against falling prices and world-wide competition" but that he was prepared to shoulder his responsibilities and to do his best "to keep the property in the most productive and useful state." And he would be as good as his word.

Several days later, the Goelets left Wimborne House, and May's father took delivery of his magnificent new yacht, the twin-screw 321-foot, 1,800-ton steel *Mayflower*, built at Glasgow to designs by George Lennox Watson, who had built the Prince of Wales's racing yacht *Britannia*, 122 feet long, 221 tons. It worried May to see her father increasingly unwell. A visit to his physician, Dr. Dawson, revealed that his liver was greatly enlarged, and the doctor confided to May's mother that Ogden couldn't live another year. The *Mayflower* anchored at Cowes for the annual August regatta, and the Prince of Wales sent his personal physician, Sir William Broadbent, aboard to examine Ogden, who was growing steadily weaker. May's aunt Belle and uncle Mungo Herbert arrived to help and comfort, and Mungo recounted Ogden's final days to the Wilsons: "On Monday and Tuesday Ogden rallied wonderfully and Mary's hopes were raised again. On Wednesday however, the day we came, he got worse again and from that time he gradually sank from hour to hour. His liver failed to work altogether. He clung to life and did not want to die." May, her mother and brother Bobby were with her father at the end.

"It was a frightful ordeal for the poor children," wrote Mungo, "they were all very brave but they are visibly cut up. Poor little fellow it seems so hard that he should die before he had time to enjoy this splendid boat with all its luxury and comfort. It is wonderful how loved he was over here. He seems to have been really understood and appreciated by so many people." Mungo concludes, "He was the most loveable, honourable man I ever came across, his only failing being, as Lord Brougham said of him last year, that he had too much sense of honour for the end of the nineteenth century." Her father had given May a fine example of what a man should be.

The *Mayflower* bore its owner's body across the Atlantic to Newport, with May and her brother and mother traveling home by steamer. Only the immediate family were present on board the Goelet yacht for the funeral service at Newport on September 16, and as the chill end-of-summer wind ruffled her black mourning veil, May felt the first break in her close-knit family circle.

When the will was read, she discovered that her father had left $10 million to her mother, and $20 million each to brother Bobby and to her, the money to be held in trust to accumulate for six years, until she reached twenty-five, when the whole sum would be hers.

"How I should hate to be May Goelet, all those odious little Frenchmen, and dozens of others crowding round her millions," confided Daisy, Princess of Pless, to her diary in Paris, but May didn't hate it at all. She was "out" in Society for six seasons, moving in a delicious crush of suitors, quite in her element, before she made her mature, judicious choice. May never felt sorry for herself, condemned to the heiress's fate, as Consuelo and Gertrude Vanderbilt had. May's ebullient temperament turned being an heiress into something positive and pleasant and great fun. She described her May-to-July 1902 London Season, for which she and her mother had rented splendid Spencer House, in a letter to Aunt Grace, written from Prince Edward's favorite spa, Bad Homburg, where they'd all gone in the autumn to recuperate:

> I can't begin to tell you what fun I had in London. It simply was glorious. You know how fond I am of dancing, and all my old partners were so kind to me, and I made several new ones.
>
> To go back, though. I must give an account of my proposals. Well, first Lord Shaftsbury popped almost as soon as he returned to London. He came one afternoon. Mamma happened to leave the room for a few minutes and off he went — like a pistol. I told him it was quite ridiculous as he had only known me three weeks and he couldn't possibly know his own mind — and besides I knew nothing of him nor his past beyond the fact that when he was 21 he had been devoted to Lady N——— which he said was true but that was all over long ago — and he was certain he knew his own mind. I like him very much only I have no intention of marrying him or anyone else at present.

May was twenty-four when she wrote this, but she refused to be hurried or pressured. She would dance on, sure-footed, skillful, standing far enough from her partners to see them clearly, relishing the humor of it all, tactful, coquettish, relaxed, laughing, in that frantic marriage market where even King Edward more than once observed in peremptory tone, "Miss Goelet must marry." But May kept on waltzing, wanting to make sure that when the dance ended, she found herself with the right partner for the rest of her life.

The next paragraph in her letter to Aunt Grace is a most revealing one: "Mamma is terribly afraid I will accept Lord Shaftsbury, though! The Duke of Roxburghe is the man that everyone says I am engaged to. I didn't see him at all at first as he never goes to balls, but at a dinner at Mrs. James' he came and talked to me and the following night we met at Lady Curzon's where we were dining. Such a nice dinner."

May found the Duke, as his contemporaries did, "very well read, rather reticent and quiet and very modest" with perfectly charming manners. Since the Duchess of Devonshire's ball, Kelso had been zealously doing his duty. In 1898 he had received his Lieutenant's commission in the Royal Horse Guards, and served in the South African War from 1899 to 1900. It was Kelso's first war, but not his last. In one engagement against the rebellious Boers, Kelso had scooped up the bleeding body of a wounded trooper from the dust, mounted him on his own horse under heavy fire, carried him to safety, and he was duly rewarded with a medal.

King Edward himself pinned it onto Kelso's broad chest on March 18, 1901, at Portsmouth, where Kelso was about to embark on the *Ophir* as aide-de-camp to King Edward's second son, George (later King George V), and his wife, Mary, former Princess of Teck, on a seven-month tour of the colonies. They visited Australia, New Zealand, Cape Colony (South Africa) and Canada, and Kelso had plenty of time to observe the happy marriage of his future monarch. Prince George was the antithesis of his party-loving, pretty-lady-loving father. Throughout his life, George would remain a stay-at-home by choice, devoted to wife, children and his stamp collection specializing in stamps bearing his own image. When the *Ophir* returned to London on November 1, Prince George penned a note to Mary affirming that he loved her "with my whole heart and soul and thank God every day" for a consort "who is such a great help and support." For the rest of his life, Kelso would be not only a loyal subject but close friend and occasional host of the staid royal couple.

As May and Kelso chatted at Mrs. James's dinner party, May must have been aware of the newspaper rumors that had been circulating for several years saying that he was courting American heiress Pauline Astor, daughter of William Waldorf Astor, but May probably discounted them, realizing that the Duke, the world's most desirable peer, moved in the same buzz of wild speculation as she did as the world's most desirable heiress.

They came together briefly, but for the rest of that London Season of 1902, May went on being wooed but not won by her thousand and one suitors, as the next paragraphs in her letter from Bad Homburg to Aunt Grace reveal:

> Mrs. Benson is crazy to make a match between Captain Holford and myself! And Lord Grey who married Captain Holford's other sister is very anxious to arrange it too. The Prince said to Lord Grey, "It's quite time George (Captain H.) was getting married. I know just the right person for him — a charming girl, Miss Goelet. It really must be arranged."…
>
> Well, the next offer was from George Cornwallis-West, Princess Pless' brother [and Jennie Churchill's future husband]. Such a dear, attractive, good-looking boy, and quite the best dancer in London. Anyway he fancies himself very much in love with me. So foolish of him. I am so sorry about it — but what can one do? I like him ever so much as a friend — but why they always have to wish for something more, I can't imagine.

Other young men courting May included Viscount Crichton, heir to the Earl of Erne, and tall Captain Oswald Ames of the Horse Guards.

As May describes her keen suitors in her breathless, bubbling way, we begin to see the special attraction for her of the Duke of Roxburghe, the still, calm, unmoved center of this feverish male whirl around the heiress with the mostest. Daisy, Princess of Pless, in that same diary entry where she commented on all the young men crowding round May's millions, puts her finger on a Duke's appeal: "An English Duke doesn't crowd around — he merely accepts a millionairess." May felt the challenge of Kelso's cool composure, his proud refusal to compete, his six-year-long resistance to her legendary charms — and rose to it.

During the next year, the courting of May Goelet by the Duke of Roxburghe, or vice versa, as the case may have been, continued in growing intimacy and privacy, away from rude reporters' stares, as an ideal courtship should. Then in July 1903, May's mother returned to New York without her, while May and Aunt Grace booked into London's Claridge's Hotel, with the Duke of Roxburghe in a room just down the corridor. He and May announced their engagement to their immediate families at that time, and to the press two months later. On September 1, Kelso's mother, Duchess Anne, from the secondary ducal seat in Scotland, Broxmouth Park, Dunbar, where she resided, informed the Provost of Dunbar by letter — doing the whole thing with all due custom and ceremony — of her son's engagement to Miss May Goelet. The next day, from Ochre Court, Newport, Mrs. Goelet confirmed the betrothal to the American press.

The happy couple, chaperoned by Aunt Grace, sailed for America on the *Campania,* reaching New York on August 15 and moving on to Newport two weeks later. They set the wedding date for November 10.

Kelso was twenty-seven; May would turn twenty-five on October 6. Consuelos Yznaga and Vanderbilt had both been eighteen when they married their Dukes, and Helena Zimmerman only twenty-one. In contrast, May Goelet was mature enough, and experienced enough, to know what she wanted in a mate, as did Kelso. Their marriage would be securely based on long acquaintance, mutual esteem and deep, lasting affection. Cynics, of course, whispered under Newport's awnings that the Duke had clearly fixed the wedding date to coincide with May's coming into full possession, on her twenty-fifth birthday, of her $20 million plus accrued interest.

In the midst of May's happiness, while she and Kelso strolled the cliff walk arm in arm, one dark cloud appeared. Aunt Belle's adored husband, Mungo Herbert, died in Davos, Switzerland, on September 30, of the tuberculosis he'd been fighting for years. He'd been made British Ambassador to the United States in October 1902, but had to give it up and enter the Davos sanitarium less than a year later. His distraught widow, only thirty-eight, with two sons, aged thirteen and ten, to raise, wrote from Davos to May and her mother just after Mungo died: "He was so uncomfortable in his little cramped bed. But I hardly left him for an hour during those 10 days and I sat by his bed holding his dear hand all day long and most of the night. But could I have done more? This will drive me mad, the thought." "I don't suppose anyone ever did so much for any man in his home and career," one English friend wrote to Belle. "A sense of having been in contact with a happiness so fine and exquisite," Edith Wharton told Belle in her sympathy letter, "made of such rare and beautiful elements, was almost a new experience to me." On the eve of her own marriage, May had the inspiring example of Aunt Belle's complete devotion to her husband brought poignantly into view.

By October Mrs. Goelet and May were in residence at 608 Fifth Avenue, "getting ready for dear little May's wedding," as Grandmother Wilson put it, commenting that May "seems to be very happy."

Kelso's mother, Duchess Anne, and his sister Isabel, who would be one of eight pink-gowned bridesmaids, landed in New York on the *Campania* two days before the wedding. Kelso was there at the pier to meet and embrace them. In this, as in so many other ways, May's wedding differed from the previous four, for the bridegroom's mother hadn't graced any of them with her presence. "I have never met Miss Goelet," the Duchess of Roxburghe told a *New York Evening Journal* reporter as she disembarked, wearing a large purple hat heavily veiled over her gray hair, "but I know that she is a charming girl, and furthermore I believe the union will be the happiest international match ever known. Everybody who knows Miss Goelet says nice things about her, and when no one has harsh things to say about a girl she's bound to be just as charming as her best friends think she is." The Duchess had brought the famous Roxburghe emeralds, valued at $300,000, passed down for two centuries, to be given, as tradition decreed, to the new Duchess, and Lady Isabel brought a jeweled miniature of Kelso to give to May. One hopes that May considered the latter the greater treasure.

The Duke himself told reporters next day, as he left the Savoy Hotel at noon to attend the first of two wedding rehearsals, "I never felt better in my life." But when an *Evening Journal* reporter had earlier requested a formal interview, the Duke, who in this as in so many ways was the antithesis of Kim Manchester, sent a tactful refusal: "More than anything else I have been impressed with the energy of American newspaper men," wrote the Duke. "I assure you I have no antipathy to the press, and if it were in my power I should grant you an interview. Under the circumstances, however, I shall have to deny myself the privilege owing to the multiplicity of duties. I will say that I am feeling excellently. Roxburghe."

November 10 dawned with a touch of Scotch mist but the sun soon dispersed it. At two-thirty, at St. Thomas's Episcopal Church, where Consuelo Vanderbilt's ill-fated marriage had taken place eight years before with May serving as bridesmaid, Miss May Goelet married her Duke, all very quietly and discreetly, with none of the New Rich splash of Consuelo's wedding. Decor and decorum were as English as possible. There were only two hundred guests in the church, part of which had been hedged around with palms to create the intimacy of an English chapel. Baskets of growing primroses hung from the tops of stone columns around which English ivy twined. May wore a gown of antique English point lace patterned with mayflowers, with the white satin beneath covered with chiffon, lest it appear too shiny. She carried a spray of heather in her white orchid bouquet, and her only jewel was an emerald-and-diamond pendant, gift of the groom.

At 608 Fifth Avenue, an awning from vestibule to curb proved an effectual bar to sightseers, as only fifty guests gathered for a simple English-style tea, with sandwiches and small cakes and a wedding cake topped with an English maypole and the Roxburghe crest. (The crest neatly captured the essence of Scotland, combining as it did the sentimental with the savage: a delicate unicorn poised above two wild men with clubs, wearing only laurel leaves strategically placed.) The Duke and Duchess left for Newport's Ochre Court with May in pale gray dress and coat discreetly embroidered in gold.

They stayed at Ochre Court for a week, enjoying the silence, the space, the bared shapes of trees. With most of its mansions

shut for the winter, Newport had shed its barbaric gold-leaf gloss
and returned to its rugged, primitive self, with no loud parties
and dance orchestras to drown out the sound of waves crashing
against the cliffs.

After steaming across the ocean, May and Kelso headed for
Broxmouth Park, Dunbar, to spend Christmas with his mother.
When they arrived by train the evening of December 22 at
Dunbar, an east-coast seaside resort with stone cottages and sandy
coves, thousands of people gathered there to cheer their beloved
Duke and new bride, and to send up fireworks, which looked like
great golden thistles against black velvet sky.

As soon as May and Kelso stepped into their waiting carriage,
its horses were unhitched, and the carriage drawn toward Broxmouth, two miles away, by coast guardsmen, preceded by kilted
pipers and two hundred torch bearers. As bagpipes sounded their
haunting, ancient tunes, and torches lit up the way she had chosen, May at that moment took her place proudly in Scottish
history and tradition. She was no longer May Goelet, independent
heiress and American girl. She was the wife of Scotland's premier
noble, caught by filaments of custom and ceremony five hundred
years old. Because she herself belonged to an Old Money family
that had put down roots in America more than two hundred years
before, and because she was schooled to Kelso's kind of reverence
for the historic past, May settled with perfect contentment and
accord into her new role and context.

For May, beginning her marriage, there would be no unre-
solved conflicts, no difficult adjustments. She had made her
mature choice; she was ready and willing; she'd been in training for
just such a chatelaine's role all her life.

The newlyweds stayed two weeks at Broxmouth. The house
itself was modern, but Kelso showed May, in the beautiful grounds
sloping down to the sea, the cedar that Queen Victoria had
planted — his mother had been her Mistress of the Robes — and

the tree under which Oliver Cromwell had stood in 1650 while his Roundheads defeated the Scots army, loyal to Charles II, and gave Cromwell the dictatorship of England.

Early in the New Year, May and her Duke made the journey south across wild Border country to her permanent home, Floors Castle. At Kelso, where the Tweed River embraced the Teviot, townspeople cheered and the Courthouse tower chimes pealed as Kelso's lord and lovely lady at last came home. The poet and novelist Sir Walter Scott rightly described Kelso as "the most beautiful, if not the most romantic, village in Scotland." He himself had attended its Grammar School, and read books of ancient ballads at Rosebank, the house his uncle left him, while the young Scott sat on an elm bough overhanging the river. Kelso's cobbled market square was as wide as a French one, with color-washed buildings ranged around and John Rennie's hundred-year-old stone bridge arching five times across the Tweed, one of Scotland's great salmon rivers, noble in its volume, rich in its clear, brown color.

May and Kelso clattered in their carriage along Roxburghe Street, through the gates in the stout stone wall that enclosed Floors park, past the stone lodge and bowing porter — and there was Floors!

It looked exactly like every castle sketched from time immemorial on the linen page of a fairy tale. It was immense, with two pavilions right-angled to a central core. The core had been built by John, 1st Duke of Roxburghe, between 1721 and 1726, to the plain Georgian design of William Adam, father of more famous Robert, but it was when the twenty-one-year-old 6th Duke, just after his marriage, called in William Playfair in 1841 that Floors acquired its spreading pavilions and lyrical, larking, storybook roofscape of castellated parapets, pepper-pot turrets, molded corbeling, ornamented water spouts. Floors was joyous, exuberant, exaggerated; it was May's joie de vivre worked in golden stone.

The rooms of Scotland's largest inhabited house were big and well proportioned and full of light, with main-floor reception

52   Aerial view of Floors Castle

rooms ranged along the south front, with a breathtaking view westward toward Kelso: in the foreground, green fields where sheep and cows grazed; in the middle ground, the silver-ribbon Tweed with the ruins of Roxburghe Castle on its opposite bank; in the background, the blue-tinged spire of Kelso church.

But the furnishings at Floors were frightful: dusty Victorian with far too much buttoned plush and too many gimcracks. May eagerly made plans in her head, but would proceed slowly, tactfully, to carry them out.

First, in those early weeks, she took time to make the acquaintance of Kelso's forebears. She read the illuminated parchment charters and deeds signed by one sovereign or another, giving land and titles to male Roxburghes, beginning: "Our right, trusty and entirely beloved Cousin," or "Most High, Potent and Noble Prince." All Dukes, Kelso explained, were considered "cousins" and "Princes" of the King in formal parlance.

During cozy, fire-lit evenings in the library, May, having inherited some of her father's scholarly zeal, dipped into books of Scottish history, their soft old leather bindings embossed with golden thistles and lyres. She learned that the first Scandinavian Kers had come to Britain with William the Conqueror and acquired land in Scotland in the eleventh century, receiving the Barony of Auld Roxburghe in 1452, and the site of Floors in 1545, during the Reformation upheaval.

May gazed hard at family portraits on the walls, looking for resemblances to Kelso. Her favorite was the 3rd Duke, with farseeing brown eyes below well-shaped black eyebrows, painted by Hoppner in blue coat and yellow gold trousers. John, 3rd Duke, had been an arch-romantic. While making the Grand Tour of Europe in his youth, he had fallen in love with the eldest daughter of the reigning Duke of Mecklenburg-Strelitz, and she with him. They were about to marry when King George III of England came courting her younger sister Charlotte, and made her his wife. Court etiquette decreed that an elder sister couldn't be subject of a younger, so the Duke of Roxburghe and his betrothed couldn't marry. They both died celibate and still besotted; she remained at the German court, refusing all suitors, playing Scottish love songs on her spinet; he turned to literature and collected a valuable library, dying in 1804. The ducal succession skipped to a distant cousin, Lord Bellenden, who also died without issue.

The dukedom then was hotly contested by various claimants before the House of Lords' Committee of Privileges, who decided in favor of Sir James Innes as 5th Duke of Roxburghe, who changed the family name to Innes-Ker from plain Ker. Over the library mantelpiece hung Sir Henry Raeburn's portrait of this red-cheeked, robust old man, sitting on a russet chair, wearing a plain brown coat. He'd taken a young wife, and fathered a son and heir at age eighty-one. He "footed it with the youngest of them" at the celebrations that followed, "and snapped his fingers to the dancing of the Highland fling." His son became 6th Duke at age seven. His adult portrait showed a handsome man with wavy hair and the same well-shaped mouth as Kelso. He was a favorite with Queen Victoria, and it was this Duke who had called in the Edinburgh architect William Playfair to enlarge and embellish Floors in 1841.

In the early spring of 1904, May warmly welcomed to Floors her widowed aunt Belle, who sent off her impressions to her parents: "I liked Kelso very *very* much," Belle told them. "He is really rather *old* for his age, or perhaps serious is more the word. He doesn't seem to have any of the *wildness* of youth and has very good and *respectable* ideas so I do hope he will make little May a good husband.... Little May seems perfectly happy and contented and he seems to love to be with her. He is quiet and undemonstrative like many Englishmen, but is fond of her I am sure."

Letters that May and Kelso wrote to each other when they were separated reveal their physical closeness, and his tendency to cloak his deepest feelings in peasant dialect. He called her "Tigy"; she called him "Boysie." A letter written that year from Kelso at Floors to May in London tells her, as always, all the details of his fishing and shooting exploits and ends: "I does miss you so hope you will come back Friday so as to love I. Lots of love and kisses. I hate being very cold and lonely in that big bed all by myself but promise to be good."

On the Atlantic's far side, on June 14, 1904, May's brother, Bobby, a sallow-faced young man with a wry sense of humor who, according to Alice Roosevelt, "did not enjoy parting with his money," married tall, dark-haired Elsie Whelen, daughter of Henry Whelen, Jr., of Philadelphia's smart set. Whereas May was blessed in her marriage, Bobby would try it three times, be divorced twice and finally declare that "marriage is hell."

Although May and Kelso kept a London residence, Chesterfield House in South Audley Street, and sometimes went to house parties at various country seats both in Scotland and England, it was at Floors that May's life found its center, and its special crusade. While the other four American Duchesses wandered from one temporary perch to another, May put down lasting roots in her chosen home and country.

Floors's interior cried out to her to be made beautiful, worthy of its Roxburghe heritage, consonant with its glorious heyday. She discussed her plans with Kelso, who was enthusiastic, but told her firmly that Queen Victoria's bedroom must not be touched, not even a pincushion. It must stay as Her Majesty had left it after her three days' visit in August 1867, en route to Balmoral Castle in the Highlands.

With great passion and purpose, loving every minute of it, May became the castle's fairy godmother. Waving over Floors's rooms her checkbook and her tape measure, she set to work to turn them back in time, back 150 years, to the mid-eighteenth century, the age of finest artistry and craftsmanship, when Floors was lived in by its builder, John, 1st Duke of Roxburghe, a cultured, traveled man "improved by much reading and learning." May secured the foremost Parisian decorator, Boulanger, to help her work her magic.

May was everywhere at once, ordering workmen about, holding up swatches of silk, ransacking Floors's attics for clues to its beguiling, elegant eighteenth-century guise. Ballroom and drawing room walls were hung with silk brocades specially woven to the exact patterns of the original coverings; other rooms were wallpapered in authentic period designs.

Accompanied by Kelso, or with her mother, who was often in France, May made frequent forays abroad, returning with exactly the right object for a certain wall space or window embrasure. With taste and knowledge and none of Alva Vanderbilt's or William Randolph Hearst's indiscriminate accumulating, May chose exquisite examples of eighteenth-century French and English furniture, Oriental porcelains, *objets de vertu* and, her greatest love, antique tapestries, which stitched fable and myth into forms larger than life and much more lasting. Over the years she would assemble collections of Bilston enameled snuff boxes, Postimpressionist paintings, Meissen and Dresden china. The Duke, for his part, contributed a forebear's collection of stuffed birds.

When the rest of Floors had been transformed and Kelso had beamed his approval, May made herself a private bower, in Louis XVI style, choosing a tiny room in the southeast tower. She covered its walls in damask the exact color of an American beauty rose.

May performed her duties on the estate as zealously as Kelso did his. She entertained royalty and Border gentry; organized and supported charities; attended local functions while Kelso made graceful speeches; visited sick tenants. Old-timers on the Roxburghe estate still speak of her fondly.

When weather permitted, in her own auto, or sometimes with Kelso in his, May explored the Border country, which had seen so much warfare and bloodshed, changing back and forth between English and Scottish rule, with its own eighteen clans between times stealing one anothers' horses, murdering and plundering. It was peaceful enough now, with a great cloak of purple heather flung across its hills in August, and the blue Cheviot hills on the horizon.

May and Kelso fished for salmon in companionable silence in the River Tweed, where the fish leaped silver in the sun. On summer days when the air quivered with heat, there were picnics on the moors, elegant picnics from well-stocked wicker hampers, where only the hoarse cries of grouse broke the silence.

May made a pilgrimage to Abbotsford, Sir Walter Scott's wildly Gothic home at Galashiels, on the bank of the Tweed, wanting to pay homage to the man who more than any other had given Scotland back its self-respect and its romantic past. When Scott was born in 1771, no British monarch had thought Scotland worth a visit for 120 years, and the general English attitude was well expressed by the writer and lexicographer Samuel Johnson:

"The noblest prospect which a Scotsman ever sees is the high road that leads him to England." With the publication of Scott's many verse and prose romances, Scotland's past sprang vividly to life. Ten years before Scott died, in 1822, George IV came to see his northern kingdom for himself, wearing a kilt and asking tactfully for Glenlivet whisky. His niece, Queen Victoria, settled happily into Balmoral Castle in the summers and filled every room with tartan. The next four monarchs, King Edward VII, King George V, his sons Edward VIII (later Duke of Windsor) and George VI, May herself would entertain as houseguests at Floors Castle. (In our own time, Queen Elizabeth II's son Prince Andrew would become engaged to Lady Sarah Ferguson at Floors.)

Sir Walter Scott had his own liking for Floors, of which he once wrote enthusiastically: "The modern mansion of Floors with its terrace, its woods and its extensive lawns, forms altogether a Kingdom for Oberon or Titania to dwell in."

Abbotsford was a modest farmhouse that Scott, with an obsessive love and much money, had transformed into a magnificent mansion, much as May, with far better taste, had worked on Floors. May walked through a square-walled garden planted with yews, entered the five rooms open to the public by a side door, saw the desk where Sir Walter wrote, his funny white beaver top hat, his homely square-toed black boots.

Romantic May helped to promote the match between Kelso's younger brother, Lord Alastair, and her American heiress friend Anna Breese, "highly cultivated and classically beautiful," whose wedding took place in September 1907. Lord Alastair, charming, elegant and amusing, had previously been enamored of Consuelo Manchester's friend, the red-haired novelist Elinor Glyn, who once categorized lovers by nationality in her commonplace book, noting that American ones were "fatherly and uncouth" while British ones were "casual and adorable."

Lord Alastair was heir to the Dukedom, for it pained May deeply that in spite of her idyllic union, she hadn't yet been able to give Kelso an heir. From May 27 to July 2, 1906, May had been at Ems, a German spa whose hot baths were guaranteed to induce fertility. While she was away, Kelso stayed in London and wrote her a short letter every two or three days, giving details of his evening's lonely dinners and bridge games at his club. His letters are boyish and ingenuous, revealing his psychological dependence on May. A letter of June 10 is typical: "Today I play polo but am rather low about it for the long-tailed pony which was playing so well will be laid up for three weeks or more.... I heard from Bond [employee at Floors] this morning that grouse prospects have in no way improved but he reports fairly cheerily of the partridges.... Well my darling I am sadly lonely and miss you awfully but cheer up and the time will soon pass. With lots of love from your own Boysie." On June 30 he wrote: "I was so excited to get your wire last night and conclude that you are feeling your affairs coming on and will leave Monday night [July 2nd] and arrive Paris Tuesday morning. I shall leave here for Paris some time on Monday and will meet you at the station. I am so looking forward and excited at the idea of being with you again and hope you are not feeling very pulled down. We will make further plans when we meet."

The trip to Ems didn't result in the longed-for pregnancy. Later May consulted a gynecologist in Vienna to whom Kelso paid £1,000, with the promise of another £1,000 if the Duchess bore a male child. The physician thought less sweetness was called for, and eliminated sugar from May's diet.

There were other, smaller clouds in May's life, in addition to her empty nursery. Her affectionate family circle contracted; Grandmother Wilson died in June 1908 and Grandfather Wilson, lost without his helpmate, died two years later. May clung to her aunts and mother, seeing them frequently. They gave her the warm, spontaneous, easily expressed affection that Kelso found so hard to communicate. On November 22, 1909, while hunting, Kelso was thrown from his horse and sustained a simple fracture of the leg and collarbone, which, for a time, prohibited the active sports that were such a large part of his life.

It was during this period when May was trying so hard to conceive that the British press launched its most vitriolic attack against American heiresses poaching on its peers, accusing them of being vulgar, superficial and selfish, lacking in *noblesse oblige* and culture. This may have been true of the majority of heiresses, who were New Rich, but didn't apply to May, who came from a higher stratum. But in two articles in *The Nineteenth Century and After* (November 1903 and September 1904), H. B. Marriott-Watson launched a barb that hit home. He accused American heiresses of ignoring motherhood, and an anonymous author in the *Contemporary Review* (June 1905) cited statistics to prove their infertility, noting that in seventy-four marriages of American women to British peers, thirty were childless and fourteen had only one child.

On the American side of the Atlantic, where the tide had also decisively turned against the transatlantic marriage, it was, of course, the foreign husbands, not the American wives, who were the main focus of disapproval, the press sounding shriller in their old complaint: European nobles went through women and hard-earned American money with equal abandon. In 1909 the *New York American* listed "How American Incomes Are Being Spent in England," attesting that Consuelo, Duchess of Marlborough had used up $15 million for charities, Helena, Duchess of Manchester $8 million for "feeding the peasantry" and May, Duchess of Roxburghe, $20 million for country-house parties.

On October 24, 1909, the *New York American* ran a two-page spread headed "How Titled Foreigners Catch American Heiresses" with a subhead in Hearst's usual sensational style: "Astonishing New Revelations of the Sordid Bargains, Heartless Schemes and Shameless Conspiracies Foreign Noblemen Have Employed to Win American Girls' Fortunes." The text described forty marriages that had turned out badly, with no mention of May's, seemingly the one exception. Leering at the reader from the very bottom of the page, like a row of wicked Humpty Dumptys, were drawings of ugly male heads, each one in a different coronet. The article commended the newly released novel by the socialite Emily Post, called *The Title Market*, in which an American girl, Nina

Randolph, is wise enough to reject a dissolute Italian nobleman and marry an innocent, hardworking young American instead. The press also ran savage cartoons in which the new chattel slave who had succeeded Uncle Tom in the popular imagination was the pathetic heiress, sold by her ambitious family into lifelong servitude to some Count or Duke.

The times were a-changing. The great American stampede toward European titles was almost over and World War I would finish it off. It was Society in the Gilded Age that could be singled out as villain and prime mover, for Society fired the ambition of all those New Rich daughters to get in, stay in and reach the top, using a handy noble to give them a boost. After World War I, Society would be replaced by café society, a very different group where what mattered was talent and wit rather than an inherited title; public adulation focused not on real Dukes and Counts, but on celebrities like Duke Ellington and Count Basie.

If the British press accused the American heiress of sterility and the American press criticized her spendthrift ways, William Armstrong, in his September 1912 article on "The Three Duchesses" for *Woman's Home Companion*, was more complimentary, particularly to May. He speaks of her marriage as "a union very happy in its outcome" and notes that "stored in the Duchess is a vitality and energy equal to the undertakings she masters," along with "pronounced executive ability" that "makes her a dominant figure in the control of both people and affairs." He goes on to tell the story of a certain Scotsman who tramped to Floors Castle to see the master. "There is a maister in this hoose" was the reply of a footman, "but he is not the Duke. You should see the Duchess."

May, however, was quite content to confine her managerial skills to the traditional domestic domain. From her own perspective as a committed New Woman working for a wider sphere of influence, Consuelo Marlborough, when she sat down to write *The Glitter and the Gold*, spoke slightingly of her friend May, as a

"Scottish chatelaine" whose "chief interests were needlework, salmon fishing and bridge. To these diversions she devoted a good brain which might perhaps have been used to better purpose."

Was Consuelo perhaps envious of May's successful marriage? Suppose Consuelo had married Kelso, the very model of a modern Duke. It would probably have been disastrous, for her American democratic ideals of equality and independence would have created friction from the beginning.

May Goelet was not only different, but wiser, too. Like her aunt Belle Herbert, she made her vow to live for and through her British husband, to focus on his career, his concerns, his country. This choice on May's part may make modern feminists shudder but there is no denying that for that time and that place, like one other heiress, Lily Hammersley, May found the only way to make a marriage with a European noble work, and so achieved great happiness and fulfillment. We can dispute her choice of role, but not her evident success.

Christmas 1912 had a very special sparkle for May; earlier that month, she had learned, to her great joy, that at the age of thirty-four she was pregnant. On September 7, 1913, at London's Chester-field House, with her mother at her side, May gave birth to a son, ten years after her marriage, and that night on the Floors estate bonfires were lit, bells pealed and everyone made merry. May's mother accompanied her home to Floors, and wrote to her sister Grace Vanderbilt: "May is improving and little Lord Bowmont (as the nurse likes to call him) is sleeping and eating and growing splendidly. The King has written a charming letter beginning 'Dear Bumble' and saying he and the Queen wish to be godparents to the son and heir. It is very unusual for both King and Queen to be godparents. Isn't it wonderfully kind and nice of them?" King George V and Queen Mary had stayed at Floors in the previous autumn, when the King had been a most informal, if dull, guest, happy to be released from London duties for grouse shooting, insisting on being treated as one of the family.

May and Kelso's son was christened George Victor Robert John in the Chapel Royal of London's St. James's Palace on October 16, with water for the baptism brought from Scotland's River Bowmont and the christening robe an Innes-Ker heirloom. The baby's formal title was Marquess of Bowmont and Cessford; when he learned his first words, he called himself "Bobo," which is what family and friends would call him for the rest of his life.

Nineteen fourteen began badly, with May's brother's wife suing him for divorce. In June Kelso went as usual to Norway for salmon fishing. In August Archduke Francis Ferdinand was murdered in Bosnia's capital, Sarajevo, and Britain plunged into World War I, after which life would never be the same. Thirty-eight-year-old Kelso at once rejoined his old regiment, the Scots Guards, as Lieutenant, and eagerly, courageously, like so many Border Scots before him, marched into the carnage. May tried to keep busy with Bobo and various kinds of war work.

Aunt Belle always visited Floors in the autumn so that May could cheer and distract her as the anniversary of Uncle Mungo's death came round, but that year it was Belle who had to comfort May. On October 22, Kelso was grievously wounded at the front and, after a brief consultation with physicians in London, was borne home to Floors for a long, slow, painful and only partial recovery. He had been hit in the back of the thigh, severing his sciatic nerve. Kelso would never be able to ride again, which was hard for an active man who'd been a first-rate polo player and superb hunter, riding to hounds every winter. Henceforth his sporting activities would be limited to fishing and to shooting grouse and partridge. He needed May's wit and cheerfulness more than ever.

At least before others, May put on a happy face. "Dearest Tante," she wrote on January 3, 1918, as she'd been doing for more than twenty years, but now her letters were typed. "Your cheque for the butter will last several years! And it will take me days to work out just how many pounds you are entitled to for that goodly sum." May glanced out the window to where sheep safely grazed on green slopes, but far away the war dragged on, and Aunt Belle's two sons, Michael and Sidney, were still at the front. "We went on New Year's Day," May continued brightly, "to the annual feast at the Poorhouse. Those poor relicts of humanity were allowed to eat their fill and over." May then recounted the tale of a bomb that had landed in a friend's London house, and added, with her usual courtesy: "I dare say you have heard all these details, if so forgive me!" Her euphoria is always tempered now to a single exclamation mark. "Lovely frosty weather here," she concluded, "and I have at last got rid of my cold, but I was very generous about it, and gave it to Kelso and Bobo. Your loving May."

With the war finally over, May and Kelso sailed to America for the summer of 1919, and strolled the Newport cliffs still arm in arm but with slower, heavier tread. Used to Britain's recent wartime deprivations and rooted traditions, May found the Newport scene incredibly luxe and vulgar and pointless. Aunt Grace had anointed herself Society's new queen, after Mrs. Astor had gone mad in a singularly appropriate fashion, parading through her empty reception rooms, elaborately gowned and jeweled, talking to imaginary guests, before dying in 1908. Newport and New York Societies were, in 1919, already singing their swan song, but Grace never seemed to notice, carrying both entertaining and conspicuous consumption to the point of burlesque. She gave dinners by alphabet, the A's in her address book invited one night, the B's the next. She owned five hundred pairs of shoes, a diamond rose as big as a plate, and hundreds of gem-encrusted gowns, all laid on twelve-foot shelves and wrapped in blue tissue. "Grace Vanderbilt sees herself in a kind of perpetual fairy-tale," Teddy Roosevelt once observed, but it wasn't May's kind, far too all-American and all-material.

After Newport, May and Kelso stayed with her mother at 608 Fifth Avenue. Here, too, much had changed, for the avenue was turning from a residential to a shopping street. B. Altman's department store rose twelve stories in French stone and covered an entire block at Thirty-fourth Street; Gorham's sold silverware, and Gunther's furs, at Thirty-sixth Street; Tiffany's displayed its jewels at Thirty-seventh, and farther downtown, Henry James thought the new skyscrapers looked like "extravagant pins in a cushion already overplanted, stuck in anywhere and anyhow."

Back home where antiquity counted, the Duke gave the ruins of Kelso Abbey to the nation, on December 23, as a kind of Christmas gift, to be preserved under the Ancient Monuments Act. The Norman Abbey had been built by Scotland's King David I in 1128, for a group of French Benedictine monks, and in 1460 James III had been crowned there, after his father had been killed at Roxburghe Castle by an exploding cannon. When an English army with Reformation zeal led by the Earl of Hertford arrived in 1545, they killed the monks, destroyed much of the Abbey, its land eventually given to Robert "Habbie" Ker, a "wise and valiant" man,

53   *The ruins of Kelso Abbey*
(steel engraving from Sir Walter Scott's Border Antiquities, 1814)

made 1st Earl of Roxburghe in 1616. His portrait at Floors showed a big nose and long face with pointed reddish beard above a white ruff. He accompanied his Scottish King south to England to be crowned James I of England in 1603, when the two kingdoms were made one.

When, on June 20, 1923, Kelso's mother, Dowager Duchess Anne died, she was buried where Roxburghes had rested ever since Habbie's day, in the family burial ground in the Abbey cloisters.

May and Kelso moved from Chesterfield House to London's 2 Carlton House Terrace, giving her another spurt of decorating, and she continued her entertaining both there and at Floors, where Edward, Prince of Wales, came for a visit in July 1926, ten years before he would give up the throne to marry American Wallis Simpson.

The *New York Times* noted that the Duchess of Roxburghe "has the reputation of being one of the most exclusive and inaccessible of all British noblewomen." No dinners by alphabet for May. "It is said," continued the *Times*, "that it is easier to be welcomed at Buckingham Palace than at her castle or her town house. No photograph of her only child, the Marquess of Bowmont, now 13 years old, has ever been published in the papers, and no account of her entertainments ever appears in print."

May and Kelso celebrated their twenty-fifth wedding anniversary in 1928, an achievement none of the other American Duchesses even came close to. Consuelo Manchester separated after a dozen years from her no-good Duke; Lily Hammersley had only four years with Blandford, and had to share them with his mistress; Consuelo Vanderbilt separated after eleven years of marriage, and finally divorced; Helena Zimmerman opted out after fourteen years, and also divorced. The Duke and Duchess of Roxburghe were presented with a silver tea and coffee service by the Kelso townspeople, to reflect their shining achievement.

In the year following May and Kelso's silver anniversary, her mother died of pneumonia in her suite at New York's Savoy-Plaza Hotel, at 1:30 p.m. on February 23. A private funeral was held at her huge Fifth Avenue mansion, which had been closed for three years while Mrs. Goelet lived more cozily in hotels. As her coffin, covered with orchids and violets, was carried out the door en route to Woodlawn Cemetery, hurrying shoppers stopped to gawk as one more Gilded Age Hostess went to her well-deserved rest. The Goelet house at 608 was one of only a few private residences left between Fourteenth and Fifty-ninth streets; it would be demolished a few years later to make way for a commercial building.

May left Scotland for New York on February 27, and when the will was read there in March, found that her mother's millions were equally divided between herself and brother Bobby, by then married to wife number three. May was left all her mother's clothes, jewels, books and an outstanding collection of paintings; Bobby got Ochre Court, which he would donate, in 1947, to the Archdiocese of Rhode Island to be turned into a girls' school, Salve Regina College. May was amazed to find that her mother had never given her old clothes to charities or servants; with Old Money's reverence for the past, she'd hung on to every dress and hat, every pair of gloves and shoes. There were more than a thousand gowns. May disposed of them all to Eaves, New York's theatrical costumer, so that for years to come, actresses in summer stock companies trailed across dusty stages in the limp seafoam green gown, gently shedding pearls, that Mary Reta Goelet had once worn so proudly to see her daughter wed a Duke.

May was in London supervising changes to 2 Carlton House Terrace when Kelso, at Floors, celebrated his fifty-sixth birthday on July 25, 1932. She sent him an affectionate letter: "Darling, this is written on your birthday instead of reaching you on that day. But I drank your health at dinner and am thinking of you.... I send love to you. Your own Tigy."

Later that year, on September 8, Kelso soberly and dutifully presided over the annual meeting of the River Tweed commission, of which he was chairman. He reported that the river had been running so low in the previous autumn that salmon fishing had been quite hopeless. The spring season of 1932 had opened with splendid prospects, but a spell of dry weather had driven all the salmon to congregate in certain pools, so that one pool might yield a considerable number but the next pool would have none at all. And although the fungus disease that had previously depleted the salmon was a thing of the past, there had been two outbreaks in Selkirk of furunculosis.... The Duke shifted painfully in his chair; he had grown stout over the years, and his voice sounded tired.

Later in the month he accompanied May to Wilton House, the Earl of Pembroke's lovely home in Wiltshire, for the funeral of Aunt Belle's son, Michael, who, like his father, had died of tuberculosis. Kelso was suddenly stricken at the funeral; doctors were summoned but told May they could do nothing. On September 29, 1932, her faithful knight died.

The 8th Duke of Roxburghe's funeral was held in Kelso Old Parish Church, packed tight with mourners, on Saturday, October 3, at twelve-fifteen. May thanked the Duke of Atholl for representing the King and, leaning on the correctly held arm of her nineteen-year-old son, tried to take comfort from the ancient ritual and custom as Kelso's body was borne to his final rest next to his ancestors in the cloisters of the eight-hundred-year-old Abbey.

The London *Times* obituary recognized the Duke's worth: "As a great territorial noble, owning about 60,500 acres, he was an admirable landlord, and he fulfilled all the responsibilities of his position, to which he succeeded while still at school, with the same sense of duty which made him so good a soldier." The *Times* also printed a letter from one of the Duke's friends: "The country has lost one of the truest type of a British gentleman," the letter began, and ended: "Much as he loved shooting and fishing, he was ever ready to give up a day to attend to his duties as chairman of the county council or any other duty where his county or his country called him. England and Scotland, but more especially the Border country that he loved so well, are indeed the poorer for his loss."

May drove to St. Giles's Cathedral in Edinburgh on December 4, walked slowly, heels echoing in all that hallowed, hollow space, to its southeast corner, entered the Chapel of the Most Ancient and Most Noble Order of the Thistle, with its elaborately carved stalls and stained-glass heraldic windows. Since 1902 Kelso had been a Knight of the Thistle, the premier order of chivalry for Scotland, and its Chancellor since 1926. A commemoration service was held for him, with the Knights processing solemnly in their dark green velvet robes.

It was a fitting way for May to take final leave of her liege-lord, who, in various kilts and ermine robes and scarlet tunics and golden epaulettes and silver thistles as Lord-Lieutenant of Rox-burghshire, as one of the Royal Company of Archers, guarding the monarch when he came to Scotland, as Knight of the Thistle, as ducal helper in two coronations, as Scots Guardsman, had marched through life shoulders back, head high, mouth unsmil-ing. Life for Kelso, 8th Duke of Roxburghe, was an earnest, formal pageant, from first to last. Given May Goelet's sprightly tempera-ment, perhaps marriage to a Duke-by-rote wasn't quite perfect after all. Did she, perhaps, amid all that panoply and must, some-times long for something suddenly, wildly spontaneous, or something brand-new, state of the art, shiny all-American?

Perhaps. After Kelso's death, May learned to fly. Thanking the Wright brothers' American technological know-how, she soared and dipped over Floors's cloud-capped towers, got a novel bird's-eye view and smiled to see it all so small.

Bobo, now 9th Duke of Roxburghe, grew into a handsome young man very like his father, and celebrated his coming of age at Floors on September 7, 1934. On April 27, 1935, having chosen an English, not American, bride, he married Lady Mary Crew-Milnes, daughter of the Marquess of Crewe, in Westminster Abbey, with all due pomp, including Queen Mary in gray-fox-trimmed gown and matching toque, and fourteen bridesmaids in flame-red velvet.

May built a new cloister in memory of her husband in 1936, next to Kelso Abbey, just as a devoted Dowager Duchess should. She often walked there in the long twilights while her memories of Kelso kept a measured pace beside her.

May Goelet, 8th Duchess of Roxburghe, died at her London residence at Carlton House Terrace, on Monday, April 26, 1937. She was only 58, two years older than Kelso when he died. She had survived him less than five years. She was buried next to him in the burial ground adjoining the Abbey, with the service held first in Kelso Old Parish Church, as tradition demanded. When in the following month, King George VI and Queen Elizabeth were crowned, Bobo's wife Mary, the new Duchess of Roxburghe, held one corner of the canopy, and history marched on....

So there it is: a true tale of a transatlantic marriage which actually worked, and lasted, in defiance of all norms and precedents. One true-gold nugget in all that hopeful gilding.

That strange reverse migration from New World to Old that began in the 1870s, grew to a mad rush in the 1890s and ended with World War I caught five remarkable heiresses in its swell. Consuelo Yznaga played a long run on British Society's stage; threw down its rigid social forms; raised up a sprite at play. Lily Hammersley, yearning for domestic bliss, had to confront a mistress on the hearth, yet won the day with sheer benevolence. Consuelo Vanderbilt flew free of hierarchy's escutcheoned dragons and found fulfillment in feminist causes. Helena Zimmerman rushed eagerly into the media's yellow glare, became reduced to Duchess stereotype and wisely retreated to a private shell. May Goelet wrapped herself willingly in history's colorful plaid and beat the British at their own game by her graceful accommodation to the peremptory voice of the past.

In choosing British peers, all five faced heavy odds against successful marriage. As "American girls," they were handicapped by too much talk of independence, petted and lauded by a country that turned them into national symbols. As New Rich girls, all but May Goelet were hampered by an emphasis on external show rather than on the *noblesse oblige* ethics that British aristocrats endorsed. As *very* rich girls, they were hindered by the fact that they, not their husbands, had all the money. Few men have the psychological strength to live happily off their wives and to be reminded every day that they are doing so. It doesn't sit well with a man's inborn sense of being the superior sex, and it certainly didn't sit well with arrogant Dukes. And lastly, as products of still-Puritan, still-sentimental America, these brides were conditioned by sexual mores and romantic expectations not shared by bed-hopping, cynical British husbands.

The lives of these women clearly show that it wasn't a strange cage of British conventions that held them fast and caused their problems, but rather one that was long-familiar, American-made, whose bars were independence, materialism, wealth, sentiment and chastity, all of which turned into distinct liabilities on the ocean's far side.

If, in their marriages, the peeresses failed on a practical level, they nevertheless succeeded on an imaginative level, both in their own gratification and that of the American public. Their version of the national dream began in the imagination with a great incandescent glow, with a vision of somehow recapturing everything that America had thrown into Boston harbor in 1773 along with the tea. These women had the same desire to marry themselves to Old World roots, the same "extraordinary gift for hope" and "romantic readiness" as Scott Fitzgerald's New Rich hero in his novel *The Great Gatsby* (1925). If Jay Gatsby had been female, he would probably have married a Duke. What Fitzgerald wants us to admire in Gatsby is the "colossal vitality of his illusion," its creative fire and freshness, as he and other Americans like him "beat on, boats against the current, borne back ceaselessly into the past." America's five Duchesses, who prefigure Fitzgerald's fictional hero by half a century, deserve our wholehearted approval: we can admire the white heat of their imagination, the single-minded devotion of their quest, and the tenacity with which, in spite of all evidence and examples to the contrary, they clung to it.

If the brides dreamed, so did the rest of America. In an era when everyone was bent on material gain, deserting the countryside for hustling cities which never slept, the nation had need of dreams. Five fairy tales of Duchesses' coronets landing on American heads added a fine patina and hush to all that rush and rawness. It was during the Gilded Age that America's collective unconscious was first able to satisfy its fixation, latent since the Revolution rejected monarchy, on Britain's blue-bloods. In today's popular culture, it is Diana, Princess of Wales, who holds the central spotlight, but a hundred years before Diana came two Consuelos, Lily, Helena and May. They were America's very first glamor goddesses and female icons of success. Their life stories, like Diana's, tap into such age-old female archetypes as Cinderella, Rapunzel and patient Griselda.

By their marriages these five American cult figures also gave their homeland a new spiritual wholeness, by reuniting New World to Old, substance to soul, riches to ritual. To a nationalism built on strictly material, gold-brick foundations, they added lions and unicorns, ancient roots and mist-shrouded towers.

But Their Graces' contribution didn't end there, in the past. Today one feels their charm perhaps more in the context of history than myth. The tales told here of titled brides illuminate a homeland that still had its innocence, its optimism and its quaint faith in marriage as women's manifest destiny and main moral commitment. Today a sadder, wiser adult America can look back over its shoulder and smile indulgently at its idealistic, adolescent self.

ACKNOWLEDGMENTS

I am indebted, first of all, to Marilyn Warnick, then senior editor at Penguin Books, U.K., who suggested to me in the fall of 1987 that a book on the dollars-for-dukedoms theme would be an interesting project.

My research was carried on mainly at the Robarts Library, University of Toronto, and the Metropolitan Toronto Reference Library, whose staffs were extremely helpful and efficient. Other librarians who helped me in my research include: P. C. Saunders and Lesley James, County Record Office, Huntingdon, Cambridgeshire; Patricia Cahill and Bernard Crystal, Rare Books and Manuscripts Division, Butler Library, Columbia University; J. Conway, Executive Officer, Manuscripts Division, The British Library; Elliot S. Meadows, New York Historical Society; Petta Khouw, Genealogy Section, State Library of Ohio; Robert Tonnies, Volunteer Researcher, Cincinnati Historical Society; Brenda M. Finn, Redwood Library and Athenaeum, Newport; Bertram Lippincott III, Newport Historical Society; Winston Atkins, Humanities Research Center, University of Texas; James H. Hutson, Library of Congress; Pamela Arceneaux, The Historic New Orleans Collection; Louisiana Division, New Orleans Public Library.

I spent a delightful week in the spring of 1992 at England's historic Wilton House, near Salisbury, Wiltshire, reading the Herbert family papers, and am grateful to the Earl of Pembroke, Veronica Quarm, Hazel Macarthur and R. W. Stedman for making my visit there so pleasant and rewarding.

I am also grateful for their help in various ways to R. E. Jackson, Assistant Factor, Roxburghe Estates Office; Sir John

Lister-Kaye; Robert G. Goelet; Thomas A. Goldwasser; John M. Stratford, Curator of Kimbolton Castle at Kimbolton School; Dr. Donald J. Lyle.

I would like to thank those persons and institutions who granted me permission to quote from unpublished manuscript material. These include the Earl of Pembroke; Elizabeth, Duchess of Manchester; the Duke of Roxburghe; Rare Book and Manuscript Division of the Butler Library, Columbia University; Ohio State University Libraries.

Friends and relatives who helped me in various ways include Wendy Campbell, John Creelman, Gretchen Eggleston, Sue Girvan, Adele Hurley, Katherine and Christopher Matthews, Joan and Michael Pierson and Mary Scott. My son, Tim, as with all my books, contributed his very perceptive criticism and amazing general knowledge, while my mother gave approval and some welcome financial assistance. I also received a grant from the Ontario Arts Council.

My editor at Random House, Catherine Yolles, worked her usual magic on the book, improving it wonderfully and offering many useful insights and suggestions. Copy editor Alison Reid was eagle-eyed and efficient. Louise Dennys at Alfred A. Knopf Canada took time to read the manuscript in an early stage and to offer advice and encouragement. I am also grateful for their help and support to my agents, Lucinda Vardey and Carolyn Brunton.

M.F.
Kilmara, Lisle, Ontario

BIBLIOGRAPHY

I. MANUSCRIPT SOURCES:

JAMES CREELMAN PAPERS, Rare Book and Manuscript Division, Ohio State University Libraries.

HARPER & ROW PAPERS, Rare Book and Manuscript Library, Columbia University.

HERBERT PAPERS, Wilton House, Wiltshire.

DONALD J. LYLE, M.D. "Distinguished Citizens," typescript in archives of Cincinnati Historical Society, Cincinnati.

MONTAGU PAPERS, County Record Office, Huntingdon, Cambridgeshire.

ROXBURGHE PAPERS, Floors Castle, Kelso, Roxburghshire.

II. MAGAZINES AND NEWSPAPERS:

U.S. SOURCES:

Cincinnati Enquirer
Harper's Bazaar
New Orleans Times-Democrat
New York American
New York Evening Journal
New York Times
North American Review
Woman's Home Companion

U.K. SOURCES:

Contemporary Review
Country Life
Illustrated London News
Nineteenth Century
Nineteenth Century and After
Queen
Times
Vanity Fair

III. BOOKS. FICTION:

ATHERTON, GERTRUDE. *American Wives and English Husbands.* New York: International Association of Newspapers and Authors, 1901.

———. *The Aristocrats.* Ridgewood: Gregg Press, 1968.

———. *His Fortunate Grace.* New York: D. Appleton and Company, 1897.

———. *Tower of Ivory.* New York: The Macmillan Company, 1910.

BURNETT, FRANCES HODGSON. *The Making of a Marchioness.* New York: Frederick A. Stokes, 1901.

———. *The Shuttle.* New York: Frederick A. Stokes, 1907.

DUNCAN, SARA JEANNETTE. *An American Girl in London.* New York: D. Appleton and Company, 1891.

FITZGERALD, F. SCOTT. *The Great Gatsby.* New York: Charles Scribner's Sons, 1925.

JAMES, HENRY. *Daisy Miller and Other Stories.* New York: Airmont, 1969.

———. *The Golden Bowl.* London: Oxford University Press, 1983.

———. *The Great Short Novels of Henry James.* New York: Carroll & Graf, 1944.

———. *Pandora, The Patagonia and Other Tales.* New York: Charles Scribner's Sons, n.d.

———. *The Portrait of a Lady.* New York: Airmont, 1966.

———. *The Reverberator.* London: Rupert Hart-Davis, 1949.

———. *The Wings of the Dove.* London: The Bodley Head, 1969.

MOORE, GEORGE. *A Drama in Muslin.* London: Vizetelly & Co., 1886.

POST, EMILY. *The Title Market.* Toronto: William Briggs, 1909.

RAE, WILLIAM FRASER. *An American Duchess.* London: R. Bentley & Son, 1891.

SACKVILLE-WEST, VITA. *The Edwardians.* London: The Hogarth Press, 1978.

[SHERWOOD, MARY E.] *A Transplanted Rose.* New York: Harper & Bros., 1882.

WHARTON, EDITH. *The Age of Innocence.* New York: D. Appleton and Company, 1920.

———. *The Buccaneers.* New York: D. Appleton and Company, 1938.

———. *The Custom of the Country.* London: Penguin Books, 1987.

———. *The House of Mirth.* New York: International Collections Library, n.d.

IV. BOOKS. NON-FICTION:

ALDRICH, NELSON W., JR. *Old Money: The Mythology of America's Upper Class.* New York: Alfred A. Knopf, 1988.

ALLEN, ELIZABETH. *A Woman's Place in the Novels of Henry James.* New York: St. Martin's Press, 1984.

AMORY, CLEVELAND. *The Last Resorts.* New York: Harper & Brothers, 1948.

———. *Who Killed Society?* New York: Harper & Brothers, 1960.

ANDREWS, WAYNE. *The Vanderbilt Legend: The Story of the Vanderbilt Family 1794–1940.* New York: Harcourt, Brace and Company, 1941.

ATHERTON, GERTRUDE. *Adventures of a Novelist.* London: Jonathan Cape, 1932.

AUCHINCLOSS, LOUIS. *The Vanderbilt Era.* New York: Charles Scribner's Sons, 1989.

BALSAN, CONSUELO VANDERBILT. *The Glitter and the Gold.* New York: Harper & Brothers, 1952.

BALTZELL, E. DIGBY. *An American Business Aristocracy.* New York: Collier Books, 1962.

————. *The Protestant Establishment.* New York: Random House, 1964.

BANKS, F. R. *Scottish Border Country.* London: B. T. Batsford, 1951.

BARRETT, RICHMOND. *Good Old Summer Days.* Boston: Houghton Mifflin, 1952.

BARROW, ANDREW. *Gossip: A History of High Society from 1920 to 1970.* New York: Coward, McCann & Geoghegan, 1979.

BATTISCOMBE, GEORGINA. *Queen Alexandra.* London: Constable, 1969.

BEARD, MARY R. *Woman as a Force in History.* New York: The Macmillan Company, 1946.

BEATON, CECIL. *The Glass of Fashion.* London: Cassell, 1989.

BEEBE, LUCIUS. *The Big Spenders.* New York: Doubleday, 1966.

BEERBOHM, MAX. *Letters to Reggie Turner.* London: Rupert Hart-Davis, 1964.

BENSON, ARTHUR CHRISTOPHER. *The Diary of Arthur Christopher Benson.* London: Hutchinson & Co., 1926.

BENSON, E. F. *As We Were.* London: Longmans, Green and Co., 1930.

BERESFORD, CHARLES WILLIAM. *The Memoirs of Admiral Lord Charles Beresford.* London: Methuen, 1914.

BERLIN, ELLIN MACKAY. *Silver Platter.* New York: Doubleday, 1957.

BLUNDEN, M. *The Countess of Warwick: A Biography.* London: Cassell, 1967.

BOLD, ALAN. *Scotland: A Literary Guide.* London: Routledge, 1989.

BOTT, ALAN, ed. *Our Mothers: A Cavalcade in Pictures, Quotation and Description of Late Victorian Women 1870–1900.* London: Victor Gollancz, 1932.

BRADFORD, SARAH. *Disraeli.* London: Weidenfeld & Nicolson, 1982.

BRADLEY, HUGH. *Such Was Saratoga.* New York: Arno Press, 1975.

BRANDON, RUTH. *The Dollar Princesses: The American Invasion of the European Aristocracy, 1870–1914.* London: Weidenfeld & Nicolson, 1980.

BRITTAIN, VERA. *Lady into Woman: A History of Women from Victoria to Elizabeth II.* London: Andrew Dakers, 1953.

BROUGH, JAMES. *Consuelo: Portrait of an American Heiress.* New York: Coward, McCann & Geoghegan, 1979.

BROWNE, JUNIUS HENRI. *The Great Metropolis.* New York: Arno Press, 1975.

BULLOUGH, VERN. *The Subordinate Sex: A History of Attitudes Towards Women.* Chicago: University of Illinois Press, 1973.

BURCHELL, S. C. *Upstart Empire: Paris During the Brilliant Years of Louis Napoleon.* London: Macdonald, 1971.

CAFFREY, KATE. *The 1900s Lady.* London: Gordon & Cremonesi, 1976.

CAMPBELL, CHARLES S., JR. *Anglo-American Understanding 1898–1903.* Baltimore: Johns Hopkins Press, 1957.

CAMPLIN, JAMIE. *The Rise of the Plutocrats: Wealth and Power in Edwardian England.* London: Constable, 1978.

CARLIER, AUGUSTE. *Marriage in the United States.* Boston: Devries, Ibarra & Co., 1867.

CARLSON, OLIVER AND ERNEST SUTHERLAND BATES. *Hearst, Lord of San Simeon.* Westport: Greenwood Press, 1970.

CARNARVON, HENRY, 6TH EARL OF. *No Regrets.* London: Weidenfeld & Nicolson, 1976.

CASTELLANE, BONI DE. *Confessions of the Marquis de Castellane.* London: Thornton Butterworth, 1924.

CAVENDISH, LADY. *The Diary of Lady Frederick Cavendish.* London: John Murray, 1927.

CHURCHILL, ALLEN. *The Upper Crust. An Informal History of New York's Highest Society.* New Jersey: Prentice-Hall, 1970.

CHURCHILL, PEREGRINE AND JULIAN MITCHELL. *Jennie. Lady Randolph Churchill.* London: Collins, 1974.

CHURCHILL, RANDOLPH S. *Lord Derby: "King of Lancashire."* London: Heinemann, 1959.

CHURCHILL, WINSTON S., THE RT. HON. *My Early Life. A Roving Commission.* London: Odhams Press, 1930.

CLEMENT, WILLIAM EDWARDS. *Plantation Life on the Mississippi.* New Orleans: Pelican Publishing Company, 1952.

CLEWS, HENRY. *Fifty Years in Wall Street.* New York: Irving Publishing Company, 1908.

COLLIER, PRICE. *England and the English From an American Point of View.* New York: Charles Scribner's Sons, 1914.

COMPTON, PIERS. *Victorian Vortex: Pleasures and Peccadilloes of an Age.* London: Robert Hale, 1977.

CORELLI, MARIE. *Free Opinions Freely Expressed on Certain Phases of Modern Social Life & Conduct.* London: Arnold Constable, 1905.

CORNWALLIS-WEST, G. *Edwardian Hey-Days.* London: Putnam's, 1930.

CORNWALLIS-WEST, MRS. G. *The Reminiscences of Lady Randolph Churchill.* London: Edward Arnold, 1908.

CORTISSOZ, ROYAL. *The Life of Whitelaw Reid.* London: Thornton Butterworth, 1921.

COWLES, VIRGINIA. *Edward VII and His Circle.* London: Hamish Hamilton, 1956.

CRANE, STEPHEN. *The Correspondence of Stephen Crane.* Ed. by Stanley Wertheim and Paul Sorrentino. New York: Columbia University Press, 1988.

CROW, DUNCAN. *The Edwardian Woman.* London: George Allen & Unwin, 1978.

CROWL, PHILIP A. *The Intelligent Traveller's Guide to Historic Scotland.* London: Sidgwick & Jackson, 1986.

CURZON, MARCHIONESS OF [GRACE]. *Reminiscences.* London: Hutchinson, 1955.

CUST, LIONEL HENRY, SIR. *King Edward VII and His Court: Some Reminiscences.* London: John Murray, 1930.

DAVIDOFF, LEONORE. *The Best Circles: Society, Etiquette and The Season.* London: Croom Helm, 1973.

DAVIES, MARION. *The Times We Had: Life with William Randolph Hearst.* New York: The Bobbs-Merrill Company, 1975.

DAVIS, EDWIN ADAMS. *Louisiana: A Narrative History.* Baton Rouge: Claitor's Publishing Division, 1961.

Debrett's Peerage and Baronetage. London: Debrett's Peerage Ltd., 1980.

DECKARD, BARBARA SINCLAIR. *The Women's Movement: Political, Socio-economic and Psychological Issues.* New York: Harper & Row, 1979.

DE GRAMONT, E. *Pomp and Circumstance.* London: Jonathan Cape, 1929.

DELAMONT, SARA, AND LORNA DUFFIN, eds. *The Nineteenth-Century Woman: Her Cultural and Physical World.* London: Croom Helm, 1978.

DEPEW, CHAUNCEY M. *My Memories of Eighty Years.* New York: Charles Scribner's Sons, 1924.

DIETRICHSON, JAN W. *The Image of Money in the American Novel of the Gilded Age.* New York: Humanities Press, 1969.

DISRAELI, BENJAMIN. *The Letters of Disraeli to Lady Bradford and Lady Chesterfield.* London: Ernest Benn, 1929.

EDISON, THOMAS. *The Diary and Sundry Observations of Thomas Alva Edison.* Ed. by Dagobert Runes. New York: Philosophical Library, 1948.

EISLER, PAUL E. *The Metropolitan Opera. The First Twenty-Five Years.* Croton-on-Hudson: North River Press, 1984.

ELIOT, ELIZABETH [pseud. for Lady Elizabeth Kinnaird]. *Heiresses & Coronets.* New York: McDowell, Obolensky, 1959.

ELLIOTT, MAUD HOWE. *This Was My Newport.* Cambridge: The Mythology Company, 1944.

ESCOTT, THOMAS HAY SWEET. *King Edward and His Court*. London: T. Fisher Unwin, 1903.

———. *Society in the Country House*. London: T. Fisher Unwin, 1907.

———. *Society in London*. By a Foreign Resident. London: Chatto and Windus, 1885.

FIELDING, DAPHNE. *The Face on the Sphinx: A Portrait of Gladys Deacon, Duchess of Marlborough*. London: Hamish Hamilton, 1978.

FISKE, STEPHEN. *Off-Hand Portraits of Prominent New Yorkers*. New York: George R. Lockwood & Son, 1884.

FLEXNER, ELEANOR. *Century of Struggle: The Woman's Rights Movement in the United States*. Cambridge: Harvard University Press, 1959.

FOWLER, MARIAN. *Blenheim: Biography of a Palace*. London: Viking, 1989.

FRIEDMAN, B. H. *Gertrude Vanderbilt Whitney*. Garden City: Doubleday & Company, 1978.

GEORGE, CAROL V. R., ed. *"Remember the Ladies": New Perspectives on Women in American History*. Syracuse: Syracuse University Press, 1975.

GLYN, ANTHONY. *Elinor Glyn: A Biography*. London: Hutchinson, 1968.

GLYN, ELINOR. *Romantic Adventure*. London: Ivor Nicholson and Watson, 1936.

GORE, JOHN. *King George V: A Personal Memoir*. London: John Murray, 1941.

HARRISON, MRS. BURTON. *Recollections Grave and Gay*. New York: Charles Scribner's Sons, 1912.

HARTMAN, MARY S., AND LOIS BANNER, eds. *Clio's Consciousness Raised: New Perspectives on the History of Women*. New York: Harper & Row, 1974.

HEARST, WILLIAM RANDOLPH. *William Randolph Hearst. A Portrait in His Own Words*. New York: Simon and Schuster, 1952.

HELLERSTEIN, ERNA OLAFSON, LESLIE PARK HUME AND KAREN M. OFFEN, eds. *Victorian Women*. Stanford: Stanford University Press, 1981.

HIBBERT, CHRISTOPHER. *Edward VII: A Portrait*. London: Allen Lane, 1976.

HICHENS, ROBERT SMYTHE. *Yesterday*. London: Cassell & Company, 1947.

HOLBROOK, STEWART H. *The Age of the Moguls*. New York: Doubleday & Company, 1953.

HOLLAND, BERNARD. *The Life of Spencer Compton, Eighth Duke of Devonshire*. London: Longmans, Green, 1911.

HOYT, EDWIN P. *The Vanderbilts and Their Fortunes*. New York: Doubleday & Company, 1962.

HUGHES, THOMAS. *Thomas Edison: Professional Inventor*. London: Her Majesty's Stationery Office, 1976.

JAHER, F. COPLE. *The Urban Establishment: Upper Strata in Boston, New York, Charleston, Chicago and Los Angeles*. Urbana: University of Illinois Press, 1982.

JAMES, HENRY. *The American Scene.* New York: Harper & Brothers, 1907.

————. *The Selected Letters of Henry James.* ed. by Leon Edel. New York: Anchor Books, 1960.

JAMES, ROBERT RHODES. *Lord Randolph Churchill.* London: Weidenfeld & Nicolson, 1959.

JOSEPHSON, MATTHEW. *The Robber Barons: The Great American Capitalists 1861–1901.* New York: Harcourt Brace, 1934.

JUERGENS, GEORGE. *Joseph Pulitzer and the New York World.* Princeton: Princeton University Press, 1966.

JULLIAN, PHILIPPE. *Edward and the Edwardians.* Translated from the French by Peter Dawnay. New York: Viking, 1967.

KANE, HARNETT T. *Natchez on the Mississippi.* New York: William Morrow, 1947.

KENIN, RICHARD. *Return to Albion: Americans in England 1760–1940.* New York: Holt, Rinehart & Winston, 1979.

KING, ROBERT B., AND CHARLES O. MCLEAN. *The Vanderbilt Homes.* New York: Rizzoli, 1989.

KLEIN, VIOLA. *The Feminine Character: History of an Ideology.* London: Routledge and Kegan Paul, 1946.

KRAUS, RENÉ. *Young Lady Randolph: The Life and Times of Jennie Jerome.* New York: G. P. Putnam's Sons, 1943.

LANGNER, LAWRENCE. *The Importance of Wearing Clothes.* New York: Hastings House, 1959.

LANGTRY, LILY. *The Days I Knew.* New York: George H. Doran, 1925.

LAVER, JAMES. *The Age of Optimism.* London: Weidenfeld & Nicolson, 1966.

————. *Costume and Fashion: A Concise History.* London: Thames and Hudson, 1982.

————. *Edwardian Promenade.* London: Edward Hulton, 1958.

LEE, SIDNEY. *Queen Victoria: A Biography.* London: Smith, Elder & Co., 1902.

LEHR, ELIZABETH DREXEL. *"King Lehr" and the Gilded Age.* New York: Arno Press, 1975.

LESLIE, ANITA. *The Gilt and the Gingerbread.* London: Hutchinson, 1981.

————. *Jennie: The Life of Lady Randolph Churchill.* London: Hutchinson, 1969.

————. *Mr. Frewen of England: A Victorian Adventurer.* London: Hutchinson, 1966.

————. *The Remarkable Mr. Jerome.* New York: Henry Holt and Company, 1954.

LEWIS, R. W. B. *Edith Wharton: A Biography.* New York: Harper & Row, 1975.

LEWIS, R. W. B., AND NANCY LEWIS, eds. *The Letters of Edith Wharton.* New York: Charles Scribner's Sons, 1988.

LONGWORTH, ALICE ROOSEVELT. *Crowded Hours.* New York: Charles Scribner's Sons, n.d.

MCALLISTER, WARD. *Society as I Have Found It.* New York: Cassell, 1890.

MACCOLL, GAIL, AND CAROL MCD. WALLACE. *To Marry an English Lord. The Victorian and Edwardian Experience.* London: Sidgwick & Jackson, 1989.

MAGNUS, PHILIP. *King Edward the Seventh.* London: John Murray, 1964.

MARTIN, FREDERIC T. *Things I Remember.* London: Eveleigh Nash, 1913.

MARTIN, RALPH G. *Jennie: The Life of Lady Randolph Churchill.* Vol. I. *The Romantic Years.* Vol. II. *The Dramatic Years.* Englewood: Prentice-Hall, 1969 and 1971.

MASSIE, ROBERT K. *Dreadnought: Britain, Germany and the Coming of the Great War.* New York: Random House, 1991.

MAURICE, ARTHUR BARTLETT. *Fifth Avenue.* New York: Arno Press, 1975.

MAUROIS, ANDRÉ. *The Edwardian Era.* New York: D. Appleton Century Company, 1933.

MENZIES, MRS. STUART [AMY CHARLOTTE]. *Lord William Beresford, V.C.* London: Herbert Jenkins, n.d.

MONTAGU, WILLIAM ANGUS DROGO, 9TH DUKE OF MANCHESTER. *My Candid Recollections.* London: Grayson & Grayson, 1932.

MONTGOMERY, MAUREEN. *"Gilded Prostitution": Status, Money and Transatlantic Marriages, 1870–1914.* London: Routledge, 1989.

MOORE, GEORGE. *Letters to Lady Cunard 1895–1933.* London: Rupert Hart-Davis, 1957.

MORRIS, LLOYD R. *Incredible New York.* New York: Random House, 1951.

MURPHY, SOPHIA. *The Duchess of Devonshire's Ball.* London: Sidgwick & Jackson, 1984.

MYERS, GUSTAVUS. *The History of the Great American Fortunes.* 3 vols. Chicago: Charles H. Kerr, 1911.

NEVILL, LADY DOROTHY. *My Own Times.* London: Methuen, 1912.

NEVILL, RALPH, ed. *Leaves from the Note-Books of Lady Dorothy Nevill.* London: Macmillan and Company, 1907.

O'NEILL, WILLIAM L. *The Woman Movement: Feminism in the United States and England.* New York: Barnes and Noble, 1969.

PAPASHVILY, HELEN WAITE. *All the Happy Endings.* New York: Harper & Brothers, 1956.

PAYNE, GEORGE HENRY. *History of Journalism in the United States.* New York: D. Appleton and Company, 1920.

PEACOCK, VIRGINIA TATNALL. *Famous American Belles of the Nineteenth Century.* London: J.B. Lippincott, 1901.

PEACOCKE, MARGUERITE D. *Queen Mary: Her Life & Times.* London: Odhams Press, n.d.

PEARSON, JOHN. *Edward the Rake.* London: Weidenfeld & Nicolson, 1975.

PLESS, DAISY, PRINCESS OF. *Daisy, Princess of Pless: By Herself.* New York: E. P. Dutton, 1929.

———. *From My Private Diary.* London: John Murray, 1931.

———. *What I Left Unsaid.* London: Cassell and Company, 1936.

PONSONBY, ARTHUR. *Henry Ponsonby: Queen Victoria's Private Secretary: His Life from his Letters.* London: Macmillan and Company, 1942.

PONSONBY, SIR FREDERICK. *Recollections of Three Reigns.* London: Eyre & Spottiswoode, 1951.

POPE-HENNESSY, JAMES. *Queen Mary.* London: George Allen & Unwin, 1959.

PORTLAND, DUKE OF. *Men, Women and Things.* London: Faber, 1937.

PUTNAM, EMILY JAMES. *The Lady: Studies of Certain Significant Phases of her History.* New York: Sturgis and Walton, 1910.

RANDALL, RONA. *The Model Wife, Nineteenth Century Style.* London: The Herbert Press, 1989.

RATNER, SIDNEY. *New Light on the Great American Fortunes: American Millionaires of 1892 and 1902.* New York: Augustus M. Kelley, 1953.

ROSS, ISHBEL. *The Expatriates.* New York: Thomas Y. Crowell, 1970.

———. *Ladies of the Press.* New York: Harper & Brothers, 1936.

———. *Silhouette in Diamonds: The Life of Mrs. Potter Palmer.* New York: Harper & Brothers, 1960.

ROSSMORE, LORD. *Things I Can Tell.* London: G. Bell, 1912 .

ROWSE, A. L. *The Later Churchills.* London: Macmillan and Company, 1958.

RUBINSTEIN, W. D., ed. *Wealth and the Wealthy in the Modern World.* London: Croom Helm, 1980.

RUDORFF, RAYMOND. *The Belle Epoque: Paris in the Nineties.* London: Hamish Hamilton, 1972.

RYAN, MARY P. *Womanhood in America: From Colonial Times to the Present.* New York: Franklin Watts, 1975.

ST. HELIER, LADY [MARY JEUNE]. *Memories of Fifty Years.* London: Edward Arnold, 1909.

SAUNDERS, EDITH. *The Age of Worth.* London: Longmans, Green, 1954.

SCOTT, ANNE FIROR. *The Southern Lady: From Pedestal to Politics 1830–1930.* Chicago: University of Chicago Press, 1970.

SCOTT, SIR WALTER. *The Border Antiquities of England & Scotland.* London: John Murray, 1814.

———. *Caledonia.* Edinburgh: William P. Nimmo, 1878.

———. *Lady of the Lake and Other Poems.* New York: Airmont, 1967.

SEWELL, J. P. C., ed. *Personal Letters of King Edward VII.* London: Hutchinson, 1931.

SINCLAIR, ANDREW. *The Emancipation of the American Woman.* New York: Harper and Row, 1965.

SLOANE, FLORENCE ADELE. *Maverick in Mauve: The Diary of a Romantic Age.* New York: Doubleday & Company, 1983.

SMALLEY, GEORGE W. *Anglo-American Memories.* London: Duckworth & Co., 1910.

———. *London Letters and Some Others.* 2 vols. New York: Harper & Brothers, 1891.

STADIEM, WILLIAM. *A Class by Themselves: The Untold Story of the Great Southern Families.* New York: Crown Publishers, 1980.

STENTON, DORIS MARY. *The English Woman in History.* London: George Allen & Unwin, 1957.

STODDARD, S. R. *Saratoga, Lake George and Lake Champlain.* Glens Falls: published by the author, 1903.

STRANGE, MICHAEL [pseud. for Blanche Oelrichs]. *Who Tells Me True.* New York: Charles Scribner's Sons, 1940.

SWANBERG, W. A. *Citizen Hearst: A Biography of William Randolph Hearst.* New York: Charles Scribner's Sons, 1961.

———. *Pulitzer.* New York: Charles Scribner's Sons, 1967.

———. *Whitney Father, Whitney Heiress.* New York: Charles Scribner's Sons, 1980.

TEBBEL, JOHN WILLIAM. *The Life and Good Times of William Randolph Hearst.* New York: E. P. Dutton, 1952.

TUCHMAN, BARBARA. *The Proud Tower: A Portrait of the World before the War: 1890–1914.* New York: Macmillan Company, 1962 .

TWAIN, MARK. *The Autobiography of Mark Twain.* New York: Harper & Brothers, 1959.

VANDERBILT, BYRON M. *Thomas Edison, Chemist.* Washington: American Chemical Society, 1971.

VANDERBILT, CORNELIUS. *Queen of the Golden Age: The Fabulous Story of Grace Wilson Vanderbilt.* New York: McGraw-Hill, 1956.

VAN RENSSELAER, MRS. JOHN KING. *The Social Ladder.* London: Eveleigh Nash & Grayson, 1925.

VEBLEN, THORSTEIN. *The Theory of the Leisure Class.* New York: The Modern Library, 1934.

VICINUS, MARTHA, ed. *Suffer and Be Still: Women in the Victorian Age.* Bloomington: Indiana University Press, 1972.

———. *A Widening Sphere: Changing Roles of Victorian Women.* Bloomington: Indiana University Press, 1977.

VICKERS, HUGO. *Gladys, Duchess of Marlborough.* London: Hamish Hamilton, 1987.

WARRENDER, LADY MAUD. *My First Sixty Years.* London: Cassell & Company, 1933.

WARWICK, FRANCES, COUNTESS OF. *Afterthoughts.* London: Cassell & Company, 1931.

WARWICK AND BROOKE, FRANCIS RICHARD, 5TH EARL OF. *Memories of Sixty Years.* London: Cassell and Company, 1917.

WASSERSTROM, WILLIAM. *Heiress of all the Ages.* Minneapolis: University of Minnesota Press, 1959.

WAUGH, NORAH. *Corsets and Crinolines.* London: B. T. Batsford, 1954.

WECTER, DIXON. *The Saga of American Society.* New York: Charles Scribner's Sons, 1937.

WELLS, H. G. *Social Forces in England and America.* New York: Harper & Brothers, 1914.

WELTER, BARBARA. *Dimity Convictions: The American Woman in the Nineteenth Century.* Athens: Ohio University Press, 1976.

WEST, REBECCA. *1900.* New York: Viking Press, 1982.

WESTMINSTER, LOELIA PONSONBY GROSVENOR, DUCHESS OF. *Grace and Favour.* London: Weidenfeld & Nicolson, 1961.

WHARTON, EDITH. *A Backward Glance.* New York: D. Appleton-Century Company, 1934.

WILSON, MARGARET GIBBONS. *The American Woman in Transition. The Urban Influence, 1870–1920.* Westport: Greenswood Press, 1979.

WINKLER, JOHN KENNEDY. *W.R. Hearst. An American Phenomenon.* New York: Simon and Schuster, 1928.

WORTH, JEAN PHILIPPE. *A Century of Fashion.* Boston: Little, Brown and Company, 1928.

PHOTO CREDITS

1 and 41, County Record Office, Huntingdon, Cambridgeshire;
2, 3, 37, 38, 42, 43 reproduced by Robarts Library, University of
Toronto; 10 and 25, BBC Hulton Picture Library; 20, Christopher
Sykes; 14, *Country Life* magazine; 24 and 26, Preservation Society
of Newport County; 35 and 36, Cincinnati Historical Society; 28,
29 and 50, Trustees of Chatsworth Settlement; 48 and 49, Newport
Historical Society; 4, 11, 13, 15, 18 and 51, *Illustrated London News*;
52, the Duke of Roxburghe; 5, 6, 7, 8, 9, 12, 16, 17, 19, 21, 22, 23,
27, 30, 31, 32, 33, 34, 39, 40, 44, 45, 46, 47 and 53 reproduced by
Metropolitan Toronto Reference Library.